YOUTH
AND
MEDIA

ANDY RUDDOCK

YOUTH AND MEDIA

Los Angeles | London | New Delhi
Singapore | Washington DC

Los Angeles | London | New Delhi
Singapore | Washington DC

SAGE Publications Ltd
1 Oliver's Yard
55 City Road
London EC1Y 1SP

SAGE Publications Inc.
2455 Teller Road
Thousand Oaks, California 91320

SAGE Publications India Pvt Ltd
B 1/I 1 Mohan Cooperative Industrial Area
Mathura Road
New Delhi 110 044

SAGE Publications Asia-Pacific Pte Ltd
3 Church Street
#10-04 Samsung Hub
Singapore 049483

© Andy Ruddock, 2013

First published 2013

Editor: Mila Steele
Editorial assistant: James Piper
Production editor: Imogen Roome
Copyeditor: Solveig Gardner Servian
Proofreader: Neil Dowden
Marketing manager: Michael Ainsley
Cover design: Francis Kenny
Typeset by: C&M Digitals (P) Ltd, Chennai, India
Printed and bound by CPI Group (UK) Ltd,
Croydon, CR0 4YY

Library of Congress Control Number: 2012946400

British Library Cataloguing in Publication data

A catalogue record for this book is available from the British Library

MIX
Paper from
responsible sources
FSC® C013604

ISBN 978-1-84860-091-1
ISBN 978-1-84860-092-8 (pbk)

Dedicated with much love to Jian Shi and
our daughter Zhenni Shi Ruddock, born on 20 February 2011

CONTENTS

ACKNOWLEDGEMENTS

I'd like to thank my many co-authors and editors who have, in the course of working with me on different projects, given vital help in articulating the ideas behind *Youth and Media*. The chance to collaborate with Brett Hutchins and David Rowe has been especially appreciated, and I owe a huge debt of thanks to James Nicholls for our advice on alcohol research. Virginia Nightingale, Jim Shanahan, Michael Morgan, Nancy Signorelli, Helena Bilandzic, Geoffroy Patriarche, Paul Traudt, Johanna Sumiala, Glenn Muschert and Lemi Baruh have all given invaluable guidance on my writing. Your time has been much appreciated.

I've also been very lucky to have expert eyes cast over drafts, and thanks go to Nick Couldry, Jukka Jouhki, Graham Meikle, James Stanyer, Andrys Onsman and Philip Flavin for their help. Special thanks to James for giving me early access to his excellent book.

Writing this was hard, but it was much easier than having a c-section, or spending your first two weeks of life in an incubator with a tube up your nose. Love and admiration to the redoubtable Jian Shi and our little Zhenni. Gratitude and love to Zhang Chen Xiang, Shi Qin Qun and Christine Ruddock for being around when we needed them.

As ever, this is written in the memory of David Ruddock, who served crown and country for 39 of his 57 years, and without whom nothing would have been written.

1

WHY YOUTH MEDIA?

WHY MEDIA, WHY YOUTH, WHY RESEARCH?

In 2012, the organisation Invisible Children tried to raise global awareness about child abuse in Africa by releasing the documentary *Kony 2012* on YouTube. The video was named after Joseph Kony, leader of a rebel Ugandan-based paramilitary group called the Lord's Resistance Army (LRA). Since the late 1980s, the LRA has been responsible for numerous human-rights crimes in several African countries. Many of its victims have been children, including tens of thousands forced into military service (BBC News Africa, 2102). Kony was wanted for war crimes by the International Criminal Court, but until *Kony 2012* few people knew about him. Within four days of its YouTube release, 50 million people had seen the documentary, numerous celebrities enthusiastically urged their fans to check it out, and the Obama administration was praising the thousands of Americans who had helped to raise awareness about the warlord and his crimes (Molloy, 2012). The video had been targeted at high-school students (Curtis, 2012), and was most watched by 13–17-year-olds (Shaughnessy, 2012). Young social media users appeared to be on the cusp of making the world a better place.

Kony 2012, it seemed, showed media at their best: depicting the world as it is, making young people care about injustices and encouraging them to do things to ensure that such horrors are never repeated. But many critics urged caution. *Kony 2012* was pilloried for oversimplifying the complexities of African history, Invisible Children's motives were questioned, and young social media users were ridiculed for thinking that sharing and liking online materials could change the world.

Whatever its merits, *Kony 2012* provoked an interesting discussion about media influence. What do we want media to do in the world? What are some of the practical problems in making media a force for good? What kinds of effects do media have? Where and when should we look for them? For example, should anyone have expected *Kony 2012* to change the world, directly? What if today's young 'slactivists' have at least started to think about their peers in other parts of the world? What outcomes might this sensitivity produce in the future? All of this boils down to three important questions: Why do media matter? Why do young people feature so prominently in contemplations on this issue? What are the different ways that scholars have conceived and researched media influence, as it is experienced among young people? These are the concerns of this book.

MEDIA, YOUTH AND SOCIETY

So, this book is really about conceiving and researching the social influence of media, with a particular focus on how young people experience the world *as* young people. When one speaks of 'media influence', it's tempting to focus on various ways that media are said to damage our social fabric. The idea that media harm society, and that young audiences are especially vulnerable in this regard, is a familiar refrain. Media are frequently blamed for making young people think and act anti-socially. When South Africa's murder rate increased by 130 per cent in the decade after the introduction of broadcast television in 1976, critics blamed the nation's first television generation (Beresin, 1999). In the US, former army psychologist David Grossman apocalyptically warned the lurid capacities of films and video games had become so adept at short-circuiting the natural human aversion to violence in the minds of young audiences that the situation warranted its own science – 'killology'. In *Stop Teaching Our Kids to Kill: A call to action against TV, movie and video game violence* (1999), Grossman and Degaetano argued that video games don't just glamorise violence; they teach teens how to be good at it. Their thesis was inspired by Michael Carneal, a 14-year-old Kentucky high-school student who stole a gun and hit eight peers with eight shots despite, he claimed, having only practised his marksmanship on video games.

The issue of media effects is far more complicated than these studies imagine. This is not to say that media do not affect how young people think about and live in their social worlds. Quite the reverse: a broader understanding of media influence leads to the conclusion that media are far more important than the positions offered by people like Grossman and Degaetano allow. The limitations of their position on effects is explored in Chapter 2, but for now this book proposes an alternative approach to media influence, framing that influence as political, historical and ordinary. The case for a political understanding of media influence, with a youth focus, is introduced through making four points:

- Studying how youth is represented in the media tells us a great deal about the public sentiments and concerns that defined particular historical moments. This is the basis for designating media influence as being political.

- A political take on media influence is supported by the international debate on media literacy, which defines the ability to understand and use media as a precondition for participatory democracy.

- The way that young people use media in everyday settings is an important measure for the depth of social inclusion.

- Studies of youth subcultures (groups of young people who used fashion and music to find their place in the world) have established that ordinary young people have used media resources to communicate political views and identities for a long time.

These studies also show that media influence can only be understood in the context of cultural history. Critiques of these studies have raised important methodological and conceptual questions about how youth and media are studied. Decisions about who to study, how to gather evidence, and how to interpret and present that evidence mean that media studies doesn't just examine the politics of representation, but also involves the politics of representation. The politics of research is an important practical consideration in research design.

MEDIA, ORDINARY YOUTH AND SOCIAL HISTORY

Good or bad, the way that young people use media, or the way that young people are represented in the media, are both interesting topics to study because they show how media structure the ideas we use to make sense of the world. As an identity, youth is no longer wasted on the young; it is a role that many people play, with the media's help. British Prime Minister David Cameron, for example, began to build his political persona as a potential national leader by defining himself as a 'youthful' politician at the age of 40. We will reflect more on this case study later. For now, the idea is that media influence society when they create and share ideas about what youth is, because people use these ideas when they think about themselves and the societies they live in.

The task is to show how this happens in routine ways that have considerable – and recognisable – political outcomes. This chapter does this by presenting the tale of Ryan Florence, an English teenager who became infamous in 2007 when he was filmed pretending to assassinate Cameron. Florence's prank became a mediated political event because it was *made* to encapsulate politicised arguments about youth, as Cameron sought to redefine the public image of the Conservative Party that he led by presenting himself as a person who understood young people. The fact that an unintentional media event, perpetrated by a young man who didn't mean to make a political statement, became a bellwether for life in Britain in 2007 begins to explain why representations of young people in media tell us a lot about how media bring social reality to life. Exploring this question connects media studies with longer traditions in social history.

THE FLORENCE/CAMERON INCIDENT

A winter's afternoon in January 2007 found David Cameron strolling through a Manchester housing estate discussing the topic of gun crime with local community leaders. The tyro leader was so engrossed in his conversations that he barely noticed the small group of male teenagers who passed him. Why would he? All were dressed in familiar teen style: training shoes, track pants and, of course, the 'hoody' that had become the de facto uniform of British teens. Naturally, then, neither Cameron nor his entourage noticed as one of the boys,

Ryan Florence, turned, fashioned his right hand into the shape of a pistol, and, smirking, fired an imaginary round into the unsuspecting politician. Images of the faux assassination were beamed around the world, as clear proof that – as Cameron repeatedly argued – Britain was a 'broken society', fractured by ingrained incivility.

For Cameron, the incident was serendipitous. In his 2005 campaign for election as leader of the Conservative Party, Cameron promised that his youth would help reverse a decade of electoral humiliation:

> In an age where economic stability and prosperity are increasingly taken for granted, younger generations care just as much about quality of life concerns – the environment, urban space, culture and leisure – as the traditional policy boxes in which we've conducted our debates. I know this is how young people feel because this is how I feel. (Cameron, quoted in Sparrow, 2005)

Cameron engineered a series of media events that showed him empathising with young people, for example vignettes that sold his brand of 'compassionate Conservatism'. Even if it started in happenstance, the Florence incident became one in a series of youth stories, where Cameron variously urged listeners to a London R&B station to 'keep it real' (BBC News, 2005), recruited the 19-year-old Olympic silver boxing medallist Amir Khan in his campaign to introduce youth community service (Pascoe-Watson, 2007) and had snot smeared on his back by a teenage prankster (Peterkin, 2008). If these stunts did not always stay on message,[1] Cameron's run-in with Florence was at least spun in the politician's favour. Against the charge that the teenager had made a fool of Cameron, or underlined the insincerity of one who could be so engrossed in explaining his commitment to youth that he walked right past a group of the very people he wanted to serve, a Conservative spokesperson said 'this picture illustrates precisely the sort of problems of anti-social behaviour and the need for positive role models that David was talking about' (Hoodie pic 'proves Cameron point', 2007). Citizens were assured that Cameron understood that social problems were matters for collective action, since they could see him being ridiculed and threatened by young people in pursuit of his beliefs. For a time, an obscure teenager from Manchester became a symbol of everything that was wrong with Britain.

FLORENCE, CAMERON AND SOCIAL HISTORY

There are good reasons why this book should begin with an obscure teenage prank that just happened to be caught on camera. Social historians have made a persuasive case for focusing social commentary on the ordinary people that history normally ignores. Vic Gatrell's *The Hanging Tree* (1994), for example, starts to explain why English public opinion quickly turned against public executions in the mid-nineteenth century (representing a remarkable change in attitudes toward justice and civilisation) by discussing the 1832 hanging of

14-year-old John Amy Bird Bell. Gatrell argued that Bird's execution was an unremarkable event that ended up catalysing an astonishing change in attitudes to capital punishment. Provocatively, Gatrell noted that much as the public despatching of a child is repugnant to today's sensibilities, our 'obvious' empathetic response to such a prospect would have been quite alien to the public mind of the early nineteenth century. Today's natural disgust at the image of a dead teen swinging from the gibbet would have seemed unusual in 1832. Repulsion and pity were impossible emotions until they were enabled by politicians who used newspapers to change the public's view of how the world was.

The most shocking thing about Bell's execution is that in the England of 1832 neither his crime nor his punishment was regarded as shocking; at least, not at first. As England's bloody Capital Laws scythed their way through the peasantry and working classes in the early-modern period, it was simply assumed that poor people would commit crime. So the idea that one child would deliberately stab another to death over a small amount of cash was not especially confronting. It did not violate assumptions about the innocence of youth, because no such assumptions existed (Gatrell, 1994). Despatching poor people like Bell seemed nothing but a sensible means of maintaining social order. Barbaric as it looks today, there was nothing about the life and death of John Amy Bird Bell that contemporaneously demanded that he should become a historical figure. He only became one because *writers* turned him into an icon of an attitude to justice that had seen its day. So, Gatrell's treatment of this execution teaches how ordinary events are infused with significance by scholarly work. In doing so, he established a blueprint for selecting case studies that we would do well to follow.

Bell was not the first teenager or child to be hanged in England; indeed, the practice had been relatively common in the eighteenth century (Gatrell, 1994). But his was the first case where an ordinary death stirred impassioned pleas against public executions that, eventually, helped produce a major constitutional change. The politician Edward Gibbon Wakefield wrote a heart-rending account of the boy's final moments, describing how the child-like Bird had even broken the hangman's heart as the noose was placed over the condemned's neck. Wakefield's account signalled the emergence of melodramatic, popular politics, where stories about the suffering of ordinary people infused political arguments with new emotional registers. Gatrell credited Wakefield with being one of the first politicians to grasp how 'vividly visualised narrative engagement . . . especially of an obscure boy's killing, would intensify and communicate emotion' (1994: 2) with an eye on promoting popular outrage that would lead to change.

Gatrell's point was that 'fleeting' historical incidents show how power becomes power when it happens in ordinary places. In this sense, we can say that Florence was to Cameron as John Amy Bird Bell was to Edward Gibbon Wakefield, the poor young soul who proved how uncivilised life had become. Like Bird, Florence was an unremarkable youth who was pushed into the political limelight by forces beyond his control. Yet things have changed, and media have something to do with that. Unlike Bird, Florence had a sense of the bigger picture he was being painted into, and responded in a way that showed how media literacy is lived by young people who know they are being watched.

So, as a starting point, we can say that societies have long dramatised their fears and aspirations by dealing in images of youth, and these are now processes that many 'resource-poor' young people can participate in, should fate allow. For these reasons, the matter of how young people are represented in and use media is integral to the social history of democracy. This is why media influence is political. Florence's story allows us to define why this is so in three ways. Most obviously, the way he was used, and the way he responded to his infamy, displayed why representations of young people in media are ideological. Less obviously, the fact that he could respond placed the matter of media literacy – what young people know about media, and what they do with this knowledge – on display, where this notion of 'literacy' is a key concept that articulates media with democracy. Less obviously still, his story is an opportunity to reflect on the politics of media studies as a discipline. The study of media influence and young people is political in so far as it involves choices about studying certain people and events using certain methods that affect the kinds of young people and the kinds of media experiences that become public through scholarly accounts. That is, when studying young people and the media, it is important to consider how media research has its own effects, because it shapes what societies know about young people and therefore what they do about and for them.

YOUTH AND DEMOCRACY

The Florence story was about how young people cope with situations that confront them with the full force of the media – understanding this can happen far more easily than one might imagine. Random as it was, the Florence incident raised issues that have been the subject of an extended international academic and political debate for the last quarter of a century on how young people manage media-saturated worlds. In these worlds, the matter of how young people understand media, and how they understand themselves as citizens with rights and responsibilities, are closely connected. The presence of this debate shows that the question of how media influence young people is often about the nature of democracy.

Florence was far from the first person to find his idea of fun being subjected to public scrutiny, and the things that young people do with media often place other youths in a similar spotlight. Young gamers, for example, have found themselves at the centre of highly charged constitutional battles. The matter of minor access to violent and sexually explicit games in the US has moved into a legal fight over how First Amendment rights to free speech square with a changing media age (Collier et al., 2008). Media practices like gaming affect social relationships by making people think about what youth is, what it deserves, and how it should be managed by governments and parents (Coleman and Dyer-Witheford, 2007).

When parents and their children bargain over games, they are also figuring out how their relationship should work (Nikken et al., 2007). In this sense, gaming is an activity that creates the reality of youth.

Another way to look at this is to say that youth media habits are places where significant ideas about political rights are micro-managed. For Henry Giroux, the matter of how youth use media, and how they are permitted to do so, is the very stuff of democracy:

> In many respects, youth not only registered symbolically the impor-
> tance of modernity's claim to progress, they also affirmed the importance
> of the liberal, democratic tradition of the social contract in which adult
> responsibility was mediated through a willingness to fight for the
> rights of children, to enact reforms that invested in their future, and to
> provide the educational conditions necessary for them to make use of
> the freedoms they have while learning how to be critical citizens.
> (2003: 141)

YOUTH AND MEDIA LITERACY

UNESCO agrees. In 1982, the organisation's International Symposium on Media Education issued the Grünwald Declaration. The Declaration identified media education as a lynchpin in the project of universal political enfranchise-ment, given the global reality that most of us live in media-saturated worlds. 'Rather than condemn or endorse the undoubted power of the media', the text read, 'we need to accept their significant ... penetration throughout the world as an established fact.' Media had to be conceived as 'instruments for ... citi-zens' active participation in society'. Media education was crucial. Simply, it had become impossible to exercise one's right as a citizen without under-standing media.

When the 25th anniversary of Grünwald was marked by Carlsson et al.'s *Empowerment through Media Education* (2008), the enquiry into how well global literacy initiatives had faired since 1982 was explored with particular reference to the young and differing views on media influence. The book clearly showed the conflict between those who felt the pressing critical question was how to deal with the power of media industries, versus others who maintained the value of looking at how youth positively engaged with media resources. On one hand, the argument that media education can only work by closing the chasm between young people's media tastes and their formal schooling (Buckingham, 2006) was accepted by Abdul Waheed Khan (2008), UNESCO's Assistant Director-General for communication and Information, as the basis for future action. On the other hand, the book's editors and Davinia Frau-Meigs (2008) all argued that the reason why media education has never been so important was because media industries have never been so powerful, and national governments have never been less enthusiastic about regulating them. For Frau-Meigs, any sober analysis of global media industries shows a trend towards self-regulation that has been abused to peddle 'violent and other harmful content' (2008: 170) onto youthful audiences who, Carlsson et al. argued, have been mostly left to fend for themselves. For Carlsson et al., the key issue was what *adults* need to guide youth in their choices, helped by media industries willing to 'assume its share of responsibilities vis-à-vis young people' (2008: 21).

Sanjay Asthana countered that youth cannot be politically engaged when viewed as 'problems' or 'people in making' (2008: 146) whose media habits need to be controlled. Cary Bazalgette (2008) warned that something is lost in starting from a position of hostility to the things that young people enjoy. Media studies inevitably replicates deficit models by looking at what young people don't know, rather than looking at the literacies and knowledge they develop in their own media practices. As Asthana and Bazalgette showed, the closer researchers get to young media users, the more sanguine they become about mediated democracy, and that media help young people in many respects.

The apparent disagreement between Frau-Meigs and Carlsson et al., on the one hand, and Asthana and Bazalgette, on the other, illustrates an important truth about media studies as something that is, in and of itself, a representational form: that is, the way that media scholars set about conceiving and studying young media users exerts its own influence on how young people attain a social voice, and on how they are represented to society. Seen this way, questions of theory and method are about much more than simply how to go about collecting valid and/or reliable data about what media do. To an extent, academics create the objects they set out to analyse, and it is remiss to discuss the topic of youth media without seeing research and teaching on the topic as cultural activities in their own right. The challenges of teaching media and cultural politics to young students who grappled with issues of race, class, gender and sexuality both inside and outside the seminar room have been recognised (e.g. Cooks, 2003). Bell hooks applauded the radical potential that studies of popular culture held as a means of uniting teacher and student in a common project of social criticism, but warned that this potential was often stunted by academics engaging in the 'voyeuristic cannibalisation' of popular culture for 'opportunistic' reasons (1994: 4). hooks felt media studies failed when academics were not genuinely committed to understanding the world from their students' point of view. What she meant was that it was impossible to address media and social power without considering the politics of research.

Let's think about John Amy Bird Bell again. The poor boy was exhumed twice. Once by Edward Gibbon Wakefield, and once again by Gatrell. Or, more kindly, Gatrell's social history was itself a representation: an expression that gave a particular meaning to Bell's story that, as Gatrell himself pointed out, differed significantly from how that reality was experienced at the time. In some ways, the question is less about what Bell was really like, and more about what the purpose of remembering him is. The same can be said of Florence, and in considering why we are also required to reflect on the purpose of media studies' engagement with young people. UNESCO's position on media literacy has tried to understand and enable the media conditions that give young people a public voice, but media studies does not simply observe this; it has itself become a force that articulates those voices by researching them in particular ways, using particular methods that have accessed particular voices. It is imperative to ask how the ideas and methods scholars select to research questions about youth and media affects their conclusions. In this regard, Florence's story is also noteworthy because of the insights it gives to a particular debate in youth media studies: the legacy of subcultural studies, which was, in the 1970s, a powerful force in directing media scholarship away from the question of effects.

RESEARCHING ORDINARY YOUTHS: SUBCULTURE AND THE POLITICS OF METHOD

Gatrell's opus on execution tells us there is nothing especially new about societies using youth in media to comment on the state of society – and his observation is internationally true. In the Netherlands during the 1650s, the Dutch press interpreted war and pestilence as divine retribution against drunken, sex-crazed teens who ignored the Sabbath (Roberts and Groenendijk, 2005). By some estimates, the English public have worried about working-class youth since the 1850s (Yeo, 2004). Between the turn of the twentieth century and the Great War, Danes fretted about young people gripped by alcohol, tobacco, pulp fiction and the movies (Coninck-Smith, 1999). In South Carolina during the 1920s, newspapers warned that a gang of young female arsonists represented an entire generation of deviant youth, created by the shift from rural to urban living (Cahn, 1998). These histories tended to treat young people as the targets of media and political campaigns over which they exercised little influence. The contribution of media studies to this topic has been to explore how the young *engage* with these framing processes, either as audiences who make sense of media messages according to what they know from their own social experience, or as 'actors' who use media resources to build meaningful lives. That is, when Ryan Florence seized the opportunity to disrupt a choreographed media event, he was following in a long tradition of young people using media to shape the meaning of the places where they live.

This was a major theme in British subcultural studies. In his influential book *Subculture: The meaning of style*, Hebdige defined subculture as 'the expressive forms and rituals of those subordinate groups ... who are alternatively dismissed, denounced and canonized' (1979: 2). Hebdige was talking about the various youth movements that had proliferated around the post-war British music scene, and he and other sociologists saw studying these groups as a means of putting the voices of ordinary youth back into the history of momentous post-war shifts in British culture. They were interested in what young people did with media amidst a world of meaningful objects (including clothes, social space, readings of history, drugs). The rationale for looking at youth groups with distinctive tastes in music and clothes was that post-World

War II social changes, like improvements to the public education system, rising industrial wages and immigration, made classed, raced and gendered identities feel suddenly fluid and contingent. When young people adopted styles and tastes associated with musical genres, their habits reflected more-or-less conscious, quasi-political efforts to make sense of what it meant to be young and British (Hall and Jefferson, 1978; Hebdige, 1979). Hebdige wrote that when the Mods of the 1960s donned suits, bought motor scooters, listened to Jamaican ska music and took amphetamines, they embraced the multicultural, class-mobile consumer society that Britain had become. In contrast, Clarke et al. (1978) described 1960s skinheads as 'counter-revolutionaries', determined to recover forms of working-class communities that were threatened by the very forces that Mods embraced.

In either case, subcultures connected the worlds of media and politics in two ways. First, they showed how young people lived cultural change by using media resources. Second, they showed how media industries used images of young people to alarm audiences with frightening tales of social anarchy, stoking the imaginations of people whose social worlds were changing in significant ways. Media turned people like Mods into 'folk devils'. A term coined by sociologist Stanley Cohen in 1972, 'folk devils' were young people who dressed in distinctive styles who the media used as 'visible reminders of what we should not be'. The creation and circulation of 'folk devil' images reflected an amplification of long-running historical trends that have been noted across time and space:

> The behaviour and morality of young people ... has ... prompted regular unease. Here, the media have often been instrumental in orchestrating anxiety. Through a 'negative stereotyping' of youth, the media have constructed a succession of fearful images that have functioned as a symbolic embodiment of wider controversies – the media presenting youth crime, violence, and sexual license as woeful indicators of broader patterns of social decline. (Osgerby, 2004: 71)

This 'orchestrated anxiety' represented an *intensification* of established traditions in public political thought. As societies became more media saturated, so the John Amy Bell Birds of this world multiplied. Images of young people, bearing lessons of what the world was like or should be like, became more common, and began to affect how young people made identities by 'internalising' the images of themselves that they saw reflected in the media (Cohen, 1972).

FROM SUBCULTURE TO MEDIA STUDIES

The subcultural concept of youth informs general media research, because it has taken on a meaning that can be applied to a far broader range of people and practices. To some, 'youth' is such a powerful index of how people use media to make identities that it no longer refers simply to the things that young people do. Andy Bennett notes that many of the punks who appeared in 1970s subcultural studies are still *actively* punk, despite their approaching old age. And so

> the term *youth* is no longer seen as straightforwardly linked with the condition of being young ... contemporary youth is seen to be lacking the perceived tendencies towards subversion and resistance deemed to have characterised the youth of previous generations ... many of the traits one connected with youth are now observed across a far broader age range. (2007: 23)

In this reading, youth is a commitment to ongoing political engagement with society. For Bennett, youth is something you do, not something you have (2007).

So, subcultural studies developed two ideas that explain why we should be interested in what happened when Ryan met David. First, young people use media and the language of style to comment on where they are in history. Second, the language of youth has ubiquitous appeal. The unpremeditated showdown on a nondescript housing estate dramatised both ideas. On one level, Florence was Cameron's John Amy Bell Bird, as the Tory leader grasped the opportunity to generate political capital by playing at youth. But unlike Wakefield's use of Bird, Cameron's strategy gave Ryan Florence a voice. Revisiting evidence on the life and death of John Amy Bell Bird, Gatrell found evidence that Wakefield's account of the wide-eyed innocent was questionable, and warned that there is little evidence to show what the youthful murderer was really like. We have a better sense of Florence's motivations, because he was widely interviewed in the national press. Speaking in the British tabloid newspaper *The Sun*, Florence explained: 'I did it for a laugh and a buzz. I thought it would be fun to showboat for the lads, so I went up behind him and made like I was pulling the trigger' (Patrick, 2007). Even if Florence was unaware that his behaviour was likely to become of public interest, the young hoody quickly embraced the spotlight, confidently associating his actions with David Cameron's political agenda and the socio-cultural state of Mancunian youth. As the BBC was later to report:

> A teenager pictured giving a gun salute to David Cameron claims the Tory leader did not listen during his visit to an estate in Manchester ... Ryan, who claims to be a member of a gang called the Benchill Mad Dogs, said politicians were doing little for the area.
>
> 'What are they doing for us around here? Nothing,' he said ... 'David says he is coming around to stop the crime and that but what is he doing?' (BBC News, 2007b)

Even if we dismiss Florence's actions and argument as inarticulate, insincere and clichéd, they still reveal how media multiply the range of places and people where politics is dramatised through the idea of youth, making that idea a battleground where power is won and lost. Academic work like sub-cultural studies help us conceive how and why this happens, despite the enormous shifts in media cultures that have taken place since that work took hold in the 1970s.

MEDIA PANICS AND EVERYDAY LIFE: LIVING LIKE A FOLK DEVIL

We should also be interested in Florence's tale because stories such as his do matter to other young people living in similar circumstances. Florence's experience showed how mediated 'hoody panics' were realities that ordinary young people regularly had to deal with when going about their business. As a media event, it triangulated with evidence from my own research on youth and anti-social behaviour among people who defined themselves as 'hoodies'. This evidence supported the idea that young people were aware of national media anxieties about them, and that news events like the Florence story did affect their social experiences by generating fear and suspicion among adults in their community. Compare Osgerby's earlier description of moral panics with the following quote, taken from an interview with a 16-year-old from Liverpool, a city some thirty miles from Manchester, in 2006:

> Before, I was what you call one of the hoodies. The trend was to wear all black, and something that wouldn't show your face. People would look at you and think, oh he's just a hoody, and deep inside you're not. You're just a person trying to make friends and get on with people. (Ruddock, 2008: 252)

This quote comes from 'Terry', a young person taking part in a study of how negative media stories influenced the lives of teens taking part in a fire-safety course run by the Merseyside Fire and Rescue Service. The course meant to improve relations between fire fighters and young people in a city where the former are not infrequently attacked by the latter. Fire officers worried about misrepresentations of the course published in the local press. This coverage, in their opinion, drew too enthusiastically upon national media panics about youth gone wild. One story in particular had incorrectly stated that all of the students had been convicted of criminal acts. This hampered the Fire Service's community efforts by offending students, not to mention their parents and teachers who were loath to co-operate with the scheme if it risked seeing their children/pupils being publicly vilified.

Unsurprisingly, then, Terry explained his situation in relation to media. In it, he aligned himself, stylistically, with Ryan Florence. Terry was talking about his wish to be social, and the way that mediated hoody panics made it hard for him to deal with normal teen anxieties about making friends. Terry's 'fun' was certainly a serious business. In an interview with a former student, it became clear that some sorts of fire offending weren't malicious, but were about not having much to do. The student claimed that friction between local youth and fire fighters sometimes occurred around the building of illegal bonfires. This, the young man explained, was something that young people did for fun. Having attended the fire-safety course, he now understood the hazard that bonfires created. But when, in his younger days, fire fighters arrived to dismantle or extinguish a bonfire that he and his friends had taken days to build, the Fire Service had seemed to be just another adult institution bent on extinguishing the little pleasure there was to be had in boring places.

'Fun' was therefore a flashpoint between Merseyside youth and local institutions. It had also been politicised in media in a way that produced students as political subjects. Their criminalisation carried real threats, regardless of how important media were seen to be. Students on the course were rarely willing to discuss this in depth, mostly because they were too busy having fun. Students got to dress up as fire fighters, ride around on fire trucks and learn to use fire equipment. But since they had been represented in the local press as villains who should be punished, certain powerful adults believed that the course rewarded bad kids. When students were seen having fun in the media, moves were made to make that fun disappear. Bad news about them could affect them in tangible ways. Like it or not, the students were in a media game, and their only choice was to play or lose. And so the hoody example shows quite clearly that media representations of people like Ryan Florence create everyday issues for young people, in ways that are good and bad, and that this has political effects for them. This makes the mediated idea of youth a cultural matter that runs through society as a whole.

RESEARCHING ORDINARY YOUTHS: SUBCULTURES AND THE POLITICS OF GENDER

The final thing that makes this analysis of hoody culture relevant to the broader practice of youth media studies are the people who are not it-girls. Their absence lets us talk about the politics of research. Early British subcultural studies were criticised for being stories about boys written by men (McRobbie and Garber, 1978). Starting this book with Ryan Florence hardly solves this problem. Angela McRobbie, a leading critic of the subcultural tradition, conceded that studies of boys in action had established how media power penetrated everyday life – but they had not explored just how commonplace this was, because they ignored women's experiences. Subcultural studies would remain incomplete until this was rectified. There is a wider issue at play here: who makes it into youth media studies and who does not, which becomes increasingly important in the face of diverse student bodies created by the mass, international tertiary education. There is a concern that McRobbie's warning has not been sufficiently heeded, because media, communications and cultural studies has become institutionalised in often racialised and gendered ways (McLaughlin, 1995; Cooks, 2003; Maras, 2007). So, why tell a tale of British hoodies to an international audience? There are two explanations on offer.

First, the hoody is a compelling example of a 'folk devil', different since it represented a wider range of youth internationally, but also gave the young people it targeted some resources they could use. By April 2008, the hoody was being used as a global symbol of everything that was wrong with Britain. Florence's picture was spread around the world. A year later, *Time* magazine's international edition of 7 April featured a photograph of a young man wearing the garment against a backdrop of the Union Jack, bearing the headline 'What's wrong with Britain's youth?' (*Time*, 7 April 2008) Battles around youth were still, then, being symbolically fought through media in the language of style in a manner that scholars like Hall and Cohen would recognise. Yet the 'hoody' theme also invites us to explore how media matter in different ways to different people in different contexts with variable effects. Whether explaining situations to a curious adult or entertaining friends when presented with the sudden chance to grab media attention, media and culture are places where youth take action.

Second, the case study raises questions about how academic work gets done, and what students have a right to expect from their education. Media studies is just as involved in 'making' youth as a meaningful category as are the media (Cooks, 2003), and this has practical implications for the way that research is organised:

> Our first epistemological observation is: that social and symbolic worlds are to be known not through some prescribed, fixed and logical method ... they are ... discovered by attending to many levels of practice through which meaning is generated, within particular social and cultural settings. (Gray, 2003: 22)

Selecting Ryan Florence as a symbol of what youth studies is about is itself an academic 'practice' that generates meaning. Florence didn't represent hoody culture until the media made him one; it's just as true that he doesn't 'represent' a history of thought on media, subculture and politics until we work on him, using theory and evidence. The methodological principle here is really quite simple. The task it is not to prove that Florence was important, but rather using a combination of empirical evidence and theoretical levers to make as persuasive a case for his significance as we can. The process can be mapped. We may notice something in the media that seems worthy of attention, then go through a research framing process where we:

- sensitise ourselves to the themes that our case study might be about through reading academic work;

- determine what evidence we need (and what we can get) to make a case;

- decide what sort of case we can make on the basis of that evidence

- stitch theory and evidence together to persuade the reader that our story is worth his or her attention.

The general process is shown in Figure 1.1.

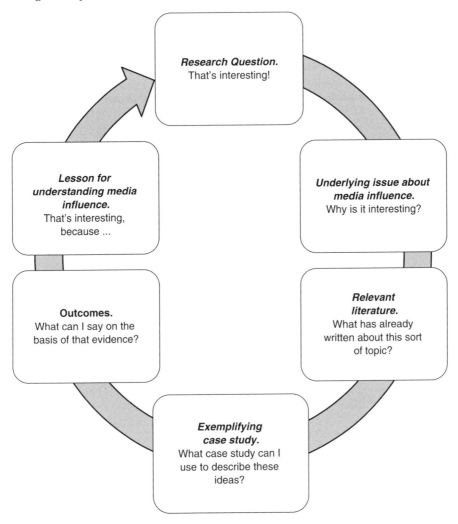

Figure 1.1 Researching and writing about media influence: a six-step model

And with regard to this chapter, the process looks like that shown in Figure 1.2.

We can only understand how media shape the lives of young people by engaging with general principles in how to frame and study media influence. Anyone reading this is putting youth together as a meaningful idea, so at this point you might pause and think: Where would I begin? Who would I talk about? What ideas would I start with? And, of course, why bother? Each chapter of this book sets out to help answer these questions.

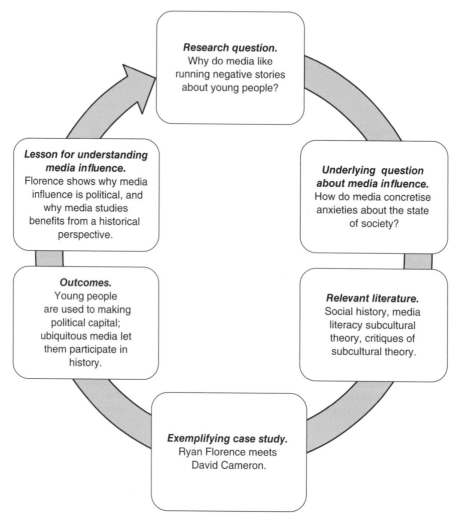

Figure 1.2   Researching moral panics

MOVING FORWARD: OUTLINING THE BOOK

The first section of this book defines significant concepts, approaches to case studies and choices of method when analysing media influence. Generally speaking, this section follows the advice of the seminal cultural-studies scholar Raymond Williams. Williams argued that the most significant effects of culture could be found in the ordinary things that people did to give their everyday lives order and meaning (1961). Studying 'ordinary' stories of culture in action is a founding interest in qualitative approaches to media, because in many ways it is only when people start doing things with media that the 'power' of those media becomes a force in the world. Following in this tradition, the first five chapters consider how studies of ordinary young people doing ordinary things with media enriches understanding the *depth* of media influence. This argument begins in Chapter 2 by reflecting on the importance of 'ordinary' people in social scientific studies of media effects. In media studies, the term 'media effects' conventionally refers to research that uses quantitative data, derived from either experiments or surveys, to examine how exposure to media influences how people think or act. Effects researchers do not assume that media effects are always harmful, or that young people are especially vulnerable to them. Effects researchers explore how media interact with other social forces to foster general tendencies within social groups. These studies are about 'ordinary' audiences, because they look for subtle influences among 'normal' young people who, in many respects, know what media are doing to them and willingly subject themselves to these effects. Research on why soldiers in Iraq (normal people who find themselves living under pressures that are anything but) listen to rap is used to illustrate this point.

Chapter 3 uses debates on social media and public dissent to explain why the effects of social media are 'ordinary', in the sense that they help existing media forms and cultural practices evolve. This idea is illustrated by a story of how social media, local journalists and student protestors produced a change in policing practices in the city of Tallahassee, Florida. It is easy to fall back into 'direct-effects' thinking when faced with evidence that new phenomena, such as social networking, have radically altered the risks that young media users face, or have afforded them unprecedented opportunities to engage with national and international politics. In this chapter, we have seen the tension between arguing that 'older' ideas about how media work are still useful because today's media environment has a history, although the 'present' takes that history in new directions. Chapter 3 continues this theme by examining what is *not* new about digital media, and thinking about how technological change *stabilises and extends* the life of media forms, habits and practices that already exist. The chapter locates the topic of social media and youth activism in historical approaches to studying popular dissent and the history of crowds by using the work of another social historian, E. P. Thompson. Thompson developed a way to conceive the role that ordinary people played in major historical shifts; in his case, the Industrial Revolution. His method can be used to consider the role that young media users play in connecting social, mobile media with political change.

By this stage, the book will have established a social and historical take on the effects of media content and media technologies. Chapter 4 applies this framework to the analysis of international media flows, using audience theory to interpret what Chinese reality television says about trends in global media. Here, the focus on 'ordinary' takes the form of considering how potential conflicts between the Chinese state and international media formats are ameliorated by convergent media platforms that encourage depoliticised media habits among young audiences. These habits are significant, because they explain how the macro politics of international media industries can be connected to the things that young audiences do when they seek entertainment.

Chapter 5 uses the topic of girls and mobile phones to discuss how media affect social space by policing the boundaries between the public and the private; addressing the idea of the ordinary by describing how the things that teenage girls do with mobile phones in their own bedrooms are affected by public policy and cultural traditions. It describes why private moments in non-public spaces are the ultimate testament of the media's political significance. This becomes particularly clear when we consider how media affect the body as a political text, a matter that has been admirably explained in girl studies, which forms the conceptual core of the chapter. Chapter 5 focuses more squarely on notions of performance and identity, elaborating on the contribution of feminist scholars, and empirical studies of 'girls', to the broadening of understandings of citizenship and politics that have been highly influential in broadening the scope of the media/politics nexus.

The second section of the book applies these general principles in connecting the idea of the ordinary to the practice of research by revisiting popular topics in media studies: understanding media violence, advertising, political campaigning and celebrity (through the prism of media sport). The purpose of these chapters is to offer strategies for taking conventional media-studies questions in new directions. In particular, this section considers how relations between young people, the media, business and the state have changed in the digital age. Some suggest that we should stop speaking of audiences and start thinking instead of media users. The danger of this shift is that it underestimates the scale of participation in earlier times (Napoli, 2010), and draws attention away from other sorts of roles that young people play in media cultures: performers, workers, researchers and conscripts. It could be that young media users drive the 'mediatisation' of society. Broadly speaking, 'mediatisation' refers to the process whereby politics, culture and society become increasingly media-dependent (Livingstone, 2009, 2012). From an analytical point of view, this dependence means that young people who appear to be doing all kinds of creative and unpredictable things with media might speak to a more coherent, general process where 'media logic' becomes a defining feature of social thought. The second section of the book considers case studies where this possibility comes into play.

Chapter 6 uses the topic of school shootings to argue that media violence matters because it is a commodity of strategic value to message systems. The question of why young people accept media violence as a normal part of their cultural environment is as important as the matter of how it provokes some people into real violence. Additionally, the democratisation of media production through social media has also made moral questions about what it means to profit from violent images, a question for the public as well as film, television, music and gaming producers. This became clear in the context of the murders at Virginia Tech (where, if anything, Cho Seung-Hui appeared to have been provoked by the news) and Jokela and Kauhajoki, Finland (where news of the shootings broke in social media before the stories could be processed by professional journalists). School shootings reflect the general logic of digital media systems because as they are paradoxical media events, as the means of signification multiply (meaning more people can tell public stories), so the range of stories that are told becomes narrower (where young people often tend to repeat the narratives of mainstream media). So, concerns that one might have about publicly available media content do not necessarily change when that content comes from ordinary media users rather than media industries. That is, 'active' young media users can re-create many of the messages that concerned media scholars in the pre-digital era.

Chapter 7 applies this idea to studies of how the alcohol industry has recruited social media users in promoting drinking as fun. Contemporary alcohol marketing is a case study on the capacity of new media technologies to work in sympathy with existing cultures (as developed in Chapter 3). When it comes to drinking, alcohol manufacturers have always tried to work with audiences by appropriating cultural traditions. The targeting of student drinkers through social networking is simply the latest incarnation of this centuries-old trend. Like school shootings, this is another example where the multiplication and apparent 'democratisation' of signifying practices may simply reproduce familiar, problematic media narratives on a larger scale, giving them a greater common-sense appeal because they seem to come from the public rather than media industries. At the same time, the chapter explores how this also means that students can use their everyday surroundings as a source of rich data on how media power works in media societies by connecting media content, cultural tradition and social space.

Chapter 8 applies notions of message systems and the evolution of cultural forms to the US presidential campaign of 2008. Barack Obama's victory was widely attributed to his capacity to use social media to engage young voters. Scholars have also regarded it as an event that was only possible because of fundamental changes in the nature of political communication, and the way that voters relate to the political realm. In this sense, Obama's victory illustrates the idea that changes in how young people use media reflect important general shifts in media culture. Chapter 8 explores this in relation to the growing importance of 'intimacy' in political communication, as it operates through convergent media cultures (Stanyer, 2012).

Chapter 9 considers why celebrity culture seems to be so attractive to young people, using a case study of a global celebrity who consciously draws on narratives of youth. The celebrity in question is street-skater-turned-*Jackass* star Bam Margera. In many ways, Margera's fame is based on his success in making a career of hanging *out* with his boyhood friends, and hanging *on* to an adolescent lifestyle. MTV series such as *Viva La Bam* and *Bam's Unholy Union* were essentially about Margera's parents' and fiancée's failed attempts to stop him spending all day everyday skateboarding, drinking and concocting elaborate, destructive practical jokes with his teenage peers. Margera's radio show on the Sirius satellite system, broadcast from his home studio, is rarely more than a litany of his group's escapades. However, viewed through Graeme Turner's work on celebrity (2004, 2010), Ellis Cashmore's analysis of David Beckham's celebrity career (1999) and David Rowe's description of 'media sport cultural complex' (2004a), Margera's career testifies to the role of sport in drawing audiences to and across changing media platforms. The opening credits for *Viva La Bam* end with Margera making the claim that he can do 'whatever the fuck I want to'. This may be true, but Margera's autonomy is only possible because of the take-off of skateboarding as a spectacular media sport, the changing production focus of MTV, Sirius' decision to use extreme-sports stars to define its public image and the growing importance of celebrity as a means of dragging audiences between media platforms. As such, he allows us to examine why celebrity is a valuable vehicle for how media might affect the expectations that young people have from life.

Chapter 10 summarises the book by considering what model of media influence is appropriate to global media cultures where 'the creation of shared content takes place in a networked, participatory environment which breaks down the boundaries between producers and consumers and instead enables all participants to be users as well as producers of information and knowledge' (Bruns, 2007). Some scholars fear that this case for popular, widespread creativity (what Axel Bruns calls 'produsage') has been overstated, and that the 'boundaries between producers and consumers' are stronger than ever (e.g. Bird, 2011). This controversy addresses the core thesis that this book makes on media power. This book approaches media as message systems whose power rests in their ability to encourage particular forms of expression, and this matters politically since many of the debates about youth and media influence are really about competing versions of social reality: ideas of what is, and what is to be done. This message systems perspective likens media power to a conversation, where conventional media production practices affect who speaks, what speakers say and, crucially, who hears them. The point that Bruns makes is that the management of this conversation has become more difficult in the face of multiplying forms of media production that increase the number of people who have the opportunity to participate in the framing of reality. Consider the Florence/Cameron incident once more. David Cameron used media and the concept of youth to create the impression that Britain was 'broken', and he was the right person to fix it. However, in the presence of a diversified news industry characterised by multiple outlets and a strong 'tabloid' sphere that prioritised entertaining news, this very serious project was not treated entirely seriously, and nor were his framing efforts unopposed. There is also something curiously dated about this story. Florence was able to speak because of the presence of journalists who wanted to seek him out. Had it happened just a few years later, Florence wouldn't have needed them; one of his friends would have recorded the prank on a mobile phone, and the scene would have been posted on YouTube. This is the crux of the case for popular creativity; although media have always had to create 'open' spaces, where media content and events are open to various forms of interpretation and engagement, in order to be popular, the frequency and impact of these 'unexpected social outcomes' have intensified in the digital age. But how easy is it for young people to use media creatively in ways that make their lives better and, when they do, who profits most from it? How can we argue that new media environments where young people make and share more media content than they ever have before in fact solidify particular forms of media power, and why is this a question that matters? To consider these issues, the conclusion considers how media production connects with social well-being among child soldiers and young victims of violence in Nigeria, Sierra Leone and Colombia: groups of disadvantaged, resource-poor young people who would really benefit from having a public media voice. There experiences, I will argue, encapsulate the central matters at stake in a new era of research on media influence.

CHAPTER SUMMARY

- Studying the topic of youth media means engaging with very basic questions about the social nature of media influence. Generally speaking, this influence takes the forms of a framing of social reality that has political motivations and political outcomes.

- This is not to take a deterministic or negative position. 'Motivations' and 'outcomes' can take many (often contradictory) forms, and can have unpredictable outcomes. Here, the question of how young people use media is a key factor in deciding the exact form that the media's social impact takes.

- When discussing how representations of young people affect how we understand the world that we live in, we have to recognise that academic studies on youth and media are also 'representations'. As with media content, when assessing academic research, we have to ask why studies are written in particular ways, using specific theories, methods and case studies. This is because different choices in each area produce different ideas of how media influence young people.

- At any rate, the literature on youth and media connects with important debates on the history and future of media studies.

NOTE

1   'Keep it real' was also the catch phrase of Sacha Baron Cohen's 'Ali G' character. The joke behind Ali G is that he is a middle-class boy desperately seeking credibility by connecting with hip-hop culture. Some commentators therefore saw a good measure of irony in Cameron's 'Keep it real'.

2

UNDERSTANDING MEDIA CONTENT: SOCIAL AND CULTURAL APPROACHES TO MEDIA EFFECTS

Research question.
Can violent rap make
violent people?

*Underlying question
about media influence.*
What are the differences
between quantitative
and qualitative studies of
media influence, and can
these different approaches
complement one another?

*Lessons for understanding
media influence.*
Effects researchers agree
that media influence is a
social thing that targets
groups of young people.

Relevant literature.
Critical reviews of
effects studies from
effects researchers

Outcomes.
Young people sometimes
knowingly inflict negative
effects upon themselves –
although they don't control
the conditions that lead
them to do so

Exemplifying case study.
Soldiers at war who listen
to rap – even when they
don't like it.

The benefits of applying quantitative methods to the study of media influence, and the relationship of these methods with qualitative techniques of data gathering and analysis, have been the subject of some controversy throughout the history of media research. Public debates on the question of media effects – like, say, the role that rap music might play in encouraging real-world aggression – often draw on quantitative effects studies in selective and unrepresentative ways. As media scholars, it's important to be clear on what quantitative methods claim to be able to do, and how their findings sit in relation to the sorts of research inquiries that typify qualitative studies. This basic methodological competency is the foundation for any meaningful engagement with the conversations on media effects that abound in public culture.

So, when faced with the matter of how rap fits into the world of real violence – a topic which has been studied with statistical methods, like content analysis, surveys of rap fans and experimental studies of what happens when young people are exposed to it – the first thing we need to do is ask how effects can be conceived and 'measured' in different ways, and how quantitative and qualitative approaches might complement one another. This is the underlying question of any debate on media effects. This chapter does this by looking at recent reviews on the history and main findings of effects research. These reviews make humble claims about what effects researchers have discovered, are open to the limitation of quantitative methods, and agree that media influence cannot be understood through experiment and surveys alone. Next, the chapter considers how qualitative methods – interviews with young rap listeners which contextualise the reception of rap in the life histories of the listener – complement effects studies by showing how rap effects 'work' for real people in real situations. Taken together, these quantitative and qualitative studies indicate a general agreement where, no matter their method, media scholars concur that where public debates tend to focus on media content which young people cannot control, the real risk factor for youth are the social conditions that they have to deal with through no fault on their own, and media content only becomes problematic when it aggravates the 'harm' that is already being inflicted on young people by society.

By engaging with this literature and case study, you will be able to critically analyse the disputations on media effects that frequently crop up in the news. These scandals often focus on what research has 'proved' about media effects, but having read this chapter you will know that the first thing we must do when faced with evidence of media effects is to ask how that research defined 'effects', how it gathered its data, and how its findings have to be interpreted in the context of the strengths and weaknesses of different research methods.

YOUNG PEOPLE AND THE ORIGINS OF MEDIA RESEARCH

In March 1931, the punishment block at Samarcand Manor, an institute for female juvenile offenders in the state of North Carolina, USA, was consumed by flames. Sixteen prisoners between the ages of 13 and 19 were accused of arson, and placed on trial for their lives. In a fascinating account of the incident, Cahn (1998) describes how the case inflamed the imagination of a public who were torn between pity and fear: pity for youths who clearly weren't bad, as at that time girls could be imprisoned for crimes that weren't crimes, like contracting sexually transmitted diseases (STDs) or simply being hard to handle, and fear about a new generation of female delinquents who emerged alongside the industrialisation and urbanisation of the southern states. Pity triumphed in the end: the trial revealed horrifying details of the criminally sadistic punishment regularly meted out at Samarcand, the charges were commuted to non-capital ones and the longest sentence given out was five years.

Perhaps another reason why the Samarcand girls found public sympathy was because their case was heard at a time when reformers, legislators and researchers were collaborating to research if mass media could make good kids bad. By World War I, the enormous popularity of the movies among adolescents was a matter of great concern (Pietilä, 2005). In 1928, W. W. Charters, a Professor of Education at Ohio State University, was approached to arrange research on the effects of movies on the attitudes and behaviours of young people. The research was paid for by the Payne Fund, a philanthropic organisation with a history of supporting studies of young people (Charters, 1932; Pietilä, 2005). The Payne Fund studies were a research milestone, since they encapsulated a tension that continues in media studies to this day: the matter of whether qualitative or quantitative methods are best for finding out how media affect society. Charters gathered a team of psychologists and sociologists, who set out to turn suspicions about movie effects into researchable questions and evidence-based answers. The preponderance of psychologists meant the series was dominated by a social-scientific orientation, where the only effects that were worth talking about were those that could be measured. Some researchers used the 'electric galvanometer', a device that could be attached to research subjects as they watched movies, with a needle that moved when the viewer was frightened or excited (Charters, 1932). Peterson and Thurstone (1932) used surveys to discover if exposure to movies could affect attitudes to racial minorities, famously finding that watching D. W. Griffith's *The Birth of a Nation*, a post-American Civil War drama depicting the Ku Klux Klan as an heroic organisation that saved the South from delinquent freed slaves, increased racist attitudes among young white audiences.

Sociologist Herbert Blumer (1933) thought it more useful to explore how movies became important to young people by having them write autobiographical accounts of their encounters with the medium. Rather than exposing them to potentially dangerous content, then measuring how their physiologies or opinions changed, Blumer asked over 1000 college students to tell stories about how and why they started going to the movies; how they had integrated characters and stories from movies in childhood play; the role of movies in daydreaming; the role of movies in shaping approaches to love and romance; and who they preferred to go to the movies with. Blumer believed this sort of evidence, where young people explained their involvement with film in their own words, recalling real experiences, was just as important as more the experimental data collected by colleagues such as Peterson and Thurstone.

Reviewing the Payne Fund studies (PFS), Pietilä (2005) argued the project is wrongly remembered as a failed venture that floundered due to a moral bias against movies and an inability to reconcile irreconcilable differences between qualitative and quantitative researchers. Charters and his team were misrepresented for three reasons. First, they were never given the chance to present their findings in congressional hearings on movies, effects and classifications. Second, people who did want to argue that movies were a corrosive influence on youth selectively presented data from the studies to suggest the researchers had found a case for direct effects, whereas close analysis of the studies shows none of the researchers believed movies alone could cause bad behaviour. Third, qualitative or quantitative, PFS researchers agreed that movies were an important force in the lives of young people, but the impact of this force was modified by social background and social networks (Pietilä, 2005) .

The Payne Fund studies offer a number of lessons, when thinking about contemporary effects research, which continues to focus on young people. When considering if, say, rap music glamorises violence, and reflecting on what effects research says about the question, the lesson from the PFS is that, historically, effects researchers never believed in direct effects, their findings have been substantially misrepresented in public conversations, for political reasons, and the divisions between quantitative and qualitative researchers is less marked than is popularly believed. Moreover, the PFS suggested that experimental and naturalistic approaches could work together to explain the social context of media power. So, returning to the topic of rap and effects, to research this topic we would need to play close attention to what effects researchers truly claim about media power, and find a case study where young people explain how effects work in particular life histories.

MEDIA EFFECTS: A BROADER VIEW

Focusing on how the content of films, television, games and the like might encourage young people to behave anti-socially obscures a range of other ways that media contribute to making the world what it is. To explain why media matter, it is better to consider how their content might shape the perceptions of ordinary groups of young people who are not manipulated by what they see, hear, read or play in obvious or spectacular ways. Where people like David Grossman insist the influence of media is most clearly seen in shocking violence acted out by teenagers such as Michael Carneal (see Chapter 1), most effects researchers are more interested in how exposure to media messages invoke barely perceptible, yet significant general effects across youth populations. These effects are difficult to see because they rarely announce themselves in obvious ways. Most effects researchers believe that any effects that media violence might have can only emerge over a long period of time, because even subtle behavioural changes are the outcome of a complex process of social learning (Bandura, 2009). Effects researchers believe that media have social effects because they are part of the social world: that is, media power is contingent on the context of their use. However, the purpose of making this point is not to reduce media power to a secondary force, but rather to show how the analysis of that power does not depend on the ability to find cases where media are independently responsible for the production of social outcomes. Media effects are *opportunistic*: media affect young people by providing easily accessible ways of responding to social needs and tensions originating elsewhere.

To illustrate the argument, this chapter contrasts Grossman's view on how media violence affects young audiences with Jonathan Pieslak's analysis of why young soldiers listened to rap music when in theatre during the second Iraq war. Pieslak's research (2007, 2009) illustrates how media affect young people in powerful ways even when those young people who know what is being 'done' to them. Pieslak shows that qualitative research methods are particularly good at explaining how effects work in practice with the participation of the effected. This is a point of general disciplinary significance, since it suggests that effects research, which tends to use experiments, survey and quantitative methods, and cultural, qualitative approaches to media cultures, with methods that focus on allowing young people to explain their media use in their own words, on their own terms, share significant ontological assumptions about media influence. This *opportunistic* definition of media influence informs subsequent chapters on how media drive binge drinking, transform school shootings into spectacular cultural events, mobilise the youth vote in political campaigns and encourage young people to participate in celebrity culture. This chapter:

- explains what effects research is, and why all media researchers need to acquire a reading knowledge of its main claims;

- explains why effects is a 'youth' question, given conventional practices in effects research;

- outlines the political and methodological objections that have been raised against effects studies;

- explores a strong tradition in effects research that recognises the social complexity of media influence and rejects the idea that media content can be independently responsible for making young people think and do things, regardless of who or where those young people are;

- highlights Pieslak's study as an instance of media research where close attention to the experience of media cultures as it is seen through the eyes of young people provides compelling evidence of how powerful media industries exploit socially vulnerable young people – even though those young people know this is happening to them.

WHAT IS EFFECTS RESEARCH, AND WHY DO WE NEED TO KNOW ABOUT IT?

This book began by debunking simplistic understandings of media effects. However, it is important to note that very few effects researchers actually subscribe to such views. So, before progressing further, it is important to consider what most effects researchers actually think about the relationship between media and society, and explore the role that studies of young media users have played in developing this thinking.

Again, 'effects research' conventionally refers to experiments and surveys that generate quantitative data to examine how thoughts and actions are affected by exposure to media content (Gunter, 2008; Sundar, 2009). Over the last decade, careful reviews of the evidence have shown that these studies consistently find that exposure to media violence increases aggressive tendencies in audiences, both in the short and the long term (e.g. Brown and Hamilton-Giachristis, 2004; Anderson et al., 2010). Unsurprisingly, then, many youth media topics circulate around 'effects', one way or another. Even studies of how youth use media to do positive things often start by dismantling the idea that insidious media messages are corrupting. As such, effects research is something everyone should know about. Consequently, this chapter surveys contemporary effects research, explains why 'effects' is a 'youth' question, and shows how effects studies and cultural studies complement one another. My essential point is that effects research does not seek to explain why small numbers of young people sometimes mimic screen violence. Instead, effects research analyses what it means to live in societies where media act on general tendencies within social groups. The primary question in this research is: How do media affect 'normal' people in everyday circumstances? The question assumes that effects are social, because they are driven by social circumstances rather than personal psychologies. The outcome of this position is the realisation that it is possible to speak of media effects without assuming that young people who may succumb to this influence are weak or naive.

It's an axiom that social fears about media effects are older than scholarly studies of the same.[1] On the surface, the circularity in writing on the subject implies that little has changed in 40 years – social scientists still run tests apparently proving that video games, horror movies and the like make young people aggressive, where the humanities think the evidence is gerrymandered. This schism threatened to expand in the first decade of the new millennium; effects studies gained new confidence, energised by the challenge of changing technologies, new methods, and the insights of scholars who could respond to criticisms of their work with the benefit of almost a century's worth of data. For years, critical scholars argued that experiments were too contrived to say anything meaningful about media power since the experiments took users out of their natural habitats, showed them things they wouldn't normally watch in the company of large groups of strangers and used unrealistic proxies for real violence.[2]

Nevertheless, effects researchers are interested in the context and experience of media use, meaning that qualitative and quantitative studies share more than we might think; indeed, Pieslak's conclusions are almost entirely compatible with contemporary accounts of effects processes. Young people have been at the hub of these debates because they have been the dominant subjects of effects research, and because their role as *participants* in the *cultures* of effects studies has played a distinct role in shaping what we 'know' about what media do. Young people may be easy to 'capture' in experiments and surveys, simply because they sit in large numbers right in front of the academics who want to study effects. But there is evidence that many conclusions drawn from studies of students are *affected* by the actions of youths who know exactly what is being 'done' to them. There is also evidence that young people knowingly visit effects upon themselves. These insights are important to a more complex model of media influence than is offered by simple stories of 'hypodermic needles', where media are blamed for injecting bad ideas into the minds of otherwise innocent young people. The youthful experience of effects studies therefore bears significant lessons for anyone wishing to develop their critical reading skills in media studies.

Contemporary effects research does not begin from the assumption that media change audiences in ways that those audiences are powerless to resist; once this is acknowledged, we can move towards more complex and interesting models of media power that open a wider range of methodological choices for researchers. In explaining his idea of social learning, eminent social psychologist Albert Bandura argued that young people learn from the media because they want to, and indeed because under many circumstances it is perfectly sensible to do so (2009).[3] Effects research is a dynamic and diverse field that provides models for turning curiosity into properly structured investigations, even for those who do not end up using statistical methods. Anyone interested in researching media has to know about effects research, because the reality of being a media scholar is that one is often asked to comment on public concerns coming from anecdotes and misinterpretations of what experimental studies actually claim to show.[4] Our reading knowledge needs to bear the following points in mind:

- Recent effects research does not reject the social and the cultural, and does not regard research subjects as individuals defined by internal psychological traits.

- It is worth studying effects research as it is a field that clearly shows how pragmatic methodological decisions affect data and conclusions. Even if we do not want to do effects research, understanding the methodology presents important skills in how to structure our own studies.

- Quantitative and qualitative techniques do trade in different sorts of knowledge, but knowing about both builds a better picture of media as a social experience. We can see this by examining how and why young people knowingly inflict negative media effects upon themselves using Pieslak's model research.

But first, why is the effects debate specifically about youth?

WHY ARE EFFECTS ABOUT YOUTH?

Controversies over effects studies are largely about how knowledge is made in institutional settings, and the use of young people in these studies tells us exactly why. Youthful students have been so over-used in effects research that they have probably affected the things that we think we know about what media do. Again, we are left to ponder an apparently parasitic relationship between media studies and its students. More positively, this lets us reflect on fundamental social-science principles. Effects studies have to prove their external validity – the extent to which the things that are measured in experiments mirror other things that happen in the real world. The validity of effects research is compromised by its reliance on student samples. On validity, Barry Gunter remarked that:

> It remains to be convincingly demonstrated that the motives of experimental participants invited to use analogues of aggression in laboratory settings are psychologically equivalent to the motives of, for example, children fighting at school, husbands beating their wives, drunks in alcohol-fueled fights late at night, perpetrators of muggings or armed robberies, or motorists involved road rage incidents. (2008: 1111)

For George Comstock, a leading figure in media-effects studies since his participation in the 1972 US Surgeon General's Scientific Advisory Committee on Television and Social Behavior, this weakness was compounded because student samples know exactly what they are supposed to do to get the 'right' results. Imagine the following scenario: you are an undergraduate in a large communications unit, and your lecturer asks you to take part in an experiment. The class is divided into two groups. You are sent into a cinema, where you see a film where a man hits a woman who has mocked him. Next, you are asked to administer a general knowledge quiz to a fellow undergraduate. Funnily enough, you've met her before – she said something rude to you right before the screening. You are given permission to punish this student every time she gives a wrong answer by administering a mild electrical shock. It's up to you how long that shock is. As a communications student, you recognise this as a conventional frustration/aggression test (Anderson and Murphy, 2003; Kirsh, 2007), and you will also know that you have been exposed to the stimulus that is supposed to produce anger. This is the source of the validity problem: you know what's happening. You might give longer shocks, because you know this is what you are supposed to do. Or you might refuse to give any at all, because you know this is what your lecturer is looking for. Either way, your response is not representative of the general public.

Comstock's explanation of the validity issue shows that effects researchers do understand that their work is social, even as their methods seek to sequester media consumption from society. Here, scholars have to be careful to distinguish between hypothesis and conclusion. Some object that experiments approach people as individual and psychological objects rather than social and cultural beings: subjects are treated as if they are simply bundles of mental traits and impulses that can be isolated, manipulated and triggered by scientific interventions. The criticism is only half right. In their account of early effects studies, Defleur and Ball-Rokeach (1989) explained that the first experimental media academics certainly emphasised psychological traits. And, in today's accounts of why effects research still matters, scholars maintain the benefits of examining effects under conditions where subjects can be taken out of the normal context of their media consumption (Murray, 2008). However, it is more accurate to say that effects researchers appreciate that the social aspects of their work affect the validity of research findings. Comstock cautioned that the cumulative conclusions of effects studies are made from data that comes from university students who probably know exactly how they are being 'manipulated' and who respond accordingly. In a sense, what is being 'measured' is students' socialisation into the discipline.

So, the debate about media effects is a quarrel over how knowledge is made, who makes it, and the unacknowledged role that youth has played in shaping the discipline. To support this argument, consider the following exercise: suppose a Media and Cultural Studies student had been asked, in late 2010, to write an essay on media effects, covering the familiar themes of pornography and violence. Suppose also that said student began with a literature search in the database Communications & Mass Media Complete™, which maintains a record of peer-reviewed articles in the field. Suppose, finally, that search used the terms 'violence and effects' and 'pornography and effects', limiting the search to the years 2000–2010.[5] The student would have found 120 empirical studies. The results of classifying them according to their location, setting and sample are shown in Figures 2.1, 2.2 and 2.3.

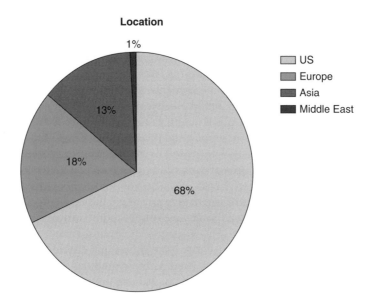

Figure 2.1   Location of studies on media effects

This pilot 'meta-analysis' shows that while public concerns about media effects are typically directed at children and teenagers, when it comes to research, these ideas tend to be tested on young adults. Anyone wanting to know more about studies of media effects in late 2010 was likely to end up reading about how North American university students responded to experimental

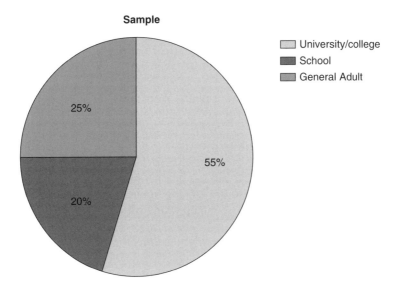

Figure 2.2   Settings for effects studies

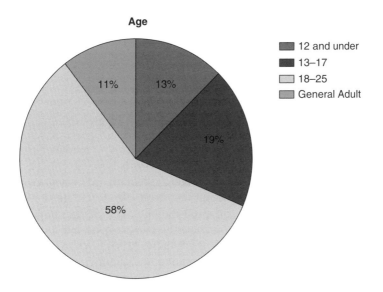

Figure 2.3   Age of samples

stimuli, surveys that tried to map exposure to violence and pornography and real-life aggression, or a combination of both.

Media effects, then, is a youth issue by default. There often are good reasons for studying youth in particular. Although a university undergraduate isn't necessarily a young person, when age was reported in these student studies the medians and means always fell between 19 and 21. Some deliberately targeted a youth sample. In their study on the relationship between exposure to media violence and the possession of aggressive political opinions, Eyal et al. justify their youth focus since 'early adulthood comprise a particularly important period of development in political attitudes' and 'young adults are particularly heavy users of violent media' (2006: 404–405).

Youth, once again, is central to research practice. Within this sample, 75 per cent of studies took place in universities and schools. Assuming that university studies tend to be conducted on young adults (because this is true whenever age is reported), then the 18–25-year-old age bracket (and in effect more likely the 18–21 range) are the people we are talking about. Thus youth is central to effects studies because scholars depend on young students to furnish them with data about how media work.

Having established 'effects' as a youth question, it is now time to turn to the matter of what it is effects researchers actually say about what media do. We need to review the following questions:

What do effects researchers want to know?

How do they understand the knowledge they produce?

What sorts of objections do qualitative researchers direct at these studies?

Why do effects researchers robustly defend their position?

What does experimental and survey research on effects say about society and culture in the early twenty-first century?

EXPERIMENTS AS SOCIAL PRACTICE

There is an inevitable gap between social concerns about media effects and the studies that academics use to address them. This is because empirical studies have to convert complicated concepts like 'aggression' into categories that can be unambiguously defined, coded and measured. However, the size of the gap between the social and the experimental should not be exaggerated.

Consider Erica Scharrer's study of how the 1980s cop drama *Miami Vice* instigated aggressive responses from undergraduates (2001). Scharrer used a classic test group/control group design. She divided her sample into two groups. One watched the show, while another saw a non-violent programme. Both were then given a survey asking how aggressive they were. Scharrer reached a conventional conclusion: after exposing a group of young American undergraduates to media violence, she found those who watched *Miami Vice* were significantly more likely to report being more aggressive than those who did not. However, Scharrer was aware that the significance of this finding was a matter of interpretation. Her study was a good example of how effects scholars try to make social ideas tangible; Scharrer wanted to know how media prompt gendered performances. Her hypothesis was that media violence taught male viewers how to act like men.

Miami Vice was chosen as a research stimulus because Scharrer thought its violence provided identity narratives, and it was this connection, rather than the violence in itself, that led to the hypothesis of why this sort of content might be effective:

> The protagonists themselves are appealing and attractive, thereby allowing for feelings of admiration or identification on the part of audience members. The violence of both the 'good guys' and 'bad guys' is rewarded through rich surroundings, financial success, and the love of the female character. These factors may serve to disinhibit the respondents in reporting their own AH levels, an outcome predicted by cognitive neo-associationism. (2001: 167)

This complicates the criticism that experiments find contrived effects. Scharrer wanted to know how 'attractive' violence – violence perpetuated by likeable men for noble causes – affected young viewers when they reported their own aggressive tendencies. This study was therefore about performed identities rather than involuntary behaviours that subjects neither controlled nor understood. Answering the survey was itself a performance, if we accept that respondents may have been thinking about what they should say as women and men who have just seen models of gendered behaviors. The point here is that where experiments are often criticised for trying to abstract media from the social, the key to understanding the validity of studies such as Scharrer's is to appreciate them as social events.

Scharrer's study is pertinent since she is an expert on youth-specific effects. In a contribution to Mazzarella's *20 Questions about Youth and the Media* (2007), Scharrer argued that the effects of media violence come in many forms which are frequently difficult to see. Although we worry most about behaviour, media violence also desensitizes audiences to human suffering, or induces the fear that the world is far more violent than it really is. In short, the most profound effect of violence is that it affects what young people believe about how the world works, which is why the *Miami Vice* study treated violence as a narrative that appeals to the young by offering identities that are pleasurable, powerful or both. In short, effects researchers accept that the effects question is deeply cultural.

To acknowledge the space between experiments and society is one thing, but quite another to conclude that there is *nothing* social about experimental media research, and that its results says *nothing* about how young people experience things.[6] If nothing else, practical issues in experimental studies at least show why it is difficult to do meaningful research among the young. Steven Kirsh defended experimental methods on the grounds that they *'approximate* rather than *mimic* real aggression'* (2007: 17; italics in original). It is inaccurate to say that experimental settings are nothing like the real world, because the aggression seen in both is motivated by ideas. Punching someone in the face *is* different from administering a fake electrical shock, but both reflect perceptions of right and wrong. Returning to Scharrer's study, answering a survey on past aggression would be influenced by what the respondent thought he or she should say under the circumstances, where answering a survey means making private thoughts and histories public. What is being 'measured' is the propensity to think aggression is acceptable, and the extent to which people exposed to intense media violence are more likely to think this than those who are not. In Kirsh's opinion, this means that experimental measures of aggression are an effective approximation of the real thing. There are better defences of these methods that are based on evidence rather than argument, which I will discuss further. But the point here is that the gap between experiments and the real world may have been overstated.

EFFECTS RESEARCH AS POLITICAL PRACTICE

There are also political objections to effects studies. This is because selective readings of effects research make it easy to blame complicated social problems on the media. James Anderson (2008) noted that, since the 1970s, North American social scientists have eagerly appeared before the US Congress, bearing testimony to the 'fact' that media were damaging society. Craig Anderson's comments on gaming was the latest example: 'Children who are exposed to a lot of violent media learn a number of lessons that *change* them into more aggressive people' (C. A. Anderson, Congressional testimony, cited in J. Anderson, 2008; my italics). Based on a meta-analysis of recent studies, James Anderson concluded that these arguments endured because they were expedient. The state and the corporate world continued to fund Craig Anderson and others because it is easier to blame conflict on media than unemployment, under-education and engineered social despair. This suited academics whose careers depended on traditional questions, regardless of their relevance to social reality. James Anderson believed that effects research was endemically conservative because it ignored the evidence that the main cause of real violence is disadvantage. Effects research was little more than a 'cottage industry', where scholars colluded with corporate and state funding groups to recycle knowledge in the name of self-interest (2008: 1276). This becomes political when behaviorist misgivings are used to justify infringing the rights of young people to access the things they enjoy (Jenkins, 2006b). But although effects *research* may be used to support these anti-democratic trends, effects *researchers* do not think that their work necessarily implies censorious outcomes. Given this accusatory flak, it is necessary to reconsider exactly what they *are* trying to say.

Anderson's essay appeared in a special edition of the scholarly journal *American Behavioral Scientist*, which clearly signposted exactly where effects research was in the early twenty-first century, and also identified flaws in the political critique of its work. John Murray (2008) defended effects researchers who favoured experiments studies against the charge that they lacked curiosity. To scholars such as he, the finding of consistent associations between screen violence and real aggression was more of a puzzle than a fact. That is, why this happened and what it meant for social policy remained an open question. Craig Anderson's co-authored work on video games reached the same conclusion; although the association between playing violent games and being an aggressive person over the long term was now established, this did not imply censorship, because researchers had yet look for other sorts of effects, including the possibility that gaming is good for some people (C. Anderson et al., 2010). If James Anderson was right to identify Craig Anderson as the icon of twenty-first-century effects research, it matters that the latter acknowledged the ambiguous social consequences of his findings. However certain Craig Anderson was about the bad things that gaming did to gamers who played a lot, he was equally certain that the social effects of gaming in general were likely to be far more varied in nature.

George Comstock (2008) pointed out that although a review of experimental and survey research on television violence and aggression did indicate that exposure to a heavy diet of media violence led to long-term increases in aggression, this data also showed that these negative effects were most apparent among poor, poorly educated, socially disenfranchised groups of people; in other words, media violence was mostly a risk for people for whom life was already difficult. Surveys proved that social groups, not individuals, were vulnerable to influence (Comstock, 2008). Comstock thought the most compelling question about media violence was how it triggers aggression when catalysed by unstable social conditions. What this amounted to was an acknowledgment of the need for more research on the precise sociological conditions that cultivate the potential of media violence to cause the same things.

According to Barry Gunter (2008), many of the criticisms of effects were more practical than political, since these appraisals simply recognised that responsible researchers are obliged to seek alternative explanations for the evidence they find. Whatever the deficiencies of the undergraduate-packed laboratory, the search for natural effects evidence is limited because real-world studies cannot make inferences about causation. To make his point, Gunter referenced Phillips and Carstensen's 1986 survey on the relationship between media reporting of teen suicide and 'copycat' behavior: did statistics show that these stories were followed by a rise in suicide attempts among teenagers? Even if they do, Gunter noted, there is no way of telling if those who took their lives following these stories had actually seen, read or heard about them. Even so, Gunter felt that effects researchers had taught valuable lessons about how young people learn from media, and the same researchers also knew that effects were intimately tied to culture, narrative and interpretation. Learning from media was evidently a complex process resistant to uncomplicated notions of cause and effect:

> There are several stages therefore involved to cognitive processing of media violence. Viewers must be aware of its occurrence, comprehend its purpose in the wider context of a narrative, evaluate its role, purpose, and outcomes for those involved, and absorb its details into their social knowledge, where new behavioral events may be compared with other experiences and modified in the process. (2008: 1089)

Included in this are the effects that different content and audience attributes can have on 'effects'. Responses to media violence are shaped by how 'real' it seems to the viewer, how the consequences of that violence are shown (if at all), whether or not the violence is justified and how viewers feel about the characters who are being violent. And all of these things are also affected by the motivations that make people want to watch or play with violence. Gunter's account is highly useful in interpreting Pieslak's contribution to the effects debate.

Looking at Comstock and Gunter, and adding a positive reading of Craig Anderson's gaming work, early twenty-first-century effects studies were characterised by a commitment to explaining effects as social phenomena, knowing that the political consequences of the findings defy straightforward conclusions about what is to be done; the truth, if anything, is that effects researchers know that there is much more to know. The finding that media violence leads to various sorts of *aggression* actually *increases* the need for research on the *diversity* of media's social effects. Aggression and violence are not the same, and the idea that media do have general effects does not imply that these effects are *uniform*, leading everyone in the same direction, regardless of circumstance. Effects studies are therefore not endemically hostile to cultural accounts of how young people use media.

The commitment to complex social explanations of media power has become stronger since 2008, as demonstrated by the 3rd edition of Bryant and Oliver's *Media Effects: Advances in theory and research* (2009). This volume identifies five positions in effects research that cultural studies can use. First, no one believes in direct media effects. As Oliver and Krakowiak put it, 'the notion that media have powerful, direct effects on individuals is arguably more accepted by the general public than by scholars in media effects' (2009: 517). Second, the influence of media is often determined by the motivations of audiences and users. Petty et al., who have developed models that systematically chart how media inputs lead to 'outputs' in the audience, state that 'most current analyses of attitude change hold that it is not the amount or direction of the information per se that produces persuasion, but rather people's idiosyncratic reaction to this information' (2009: 126). Third, if young people are influenced by media, this is perfectly sensible in a world where media are common-sense resources for 'self-developing, proactive, self-regulating and self-reflecting organisms, not just reactive organisms' (Bandura, 2009: 94). Fourth, there are reasons to think that young people's actions are influenced by industries that tend to depict social reality in ideologically loaded ways; for example, young women are bombarded with images of thin, hypersexualised female bodies, and it is at least worth asking if this affects how they understand themselves (Levine and Harrison, 2009; Smith and Granados, 2009). Fifth, social-science methods have to be used selectively and in an interpretative fashion; effects researchers recognise that their methods are directed at things which cannot be studied scientifically, in the purest sense.

The last position is outlined in Sparks et al.'s explanation of the difference between statistical and social significance (2009). The confidence of effects researchers comes from the fact that experiments and surveys consistently find small but statistically significant differences between people who are exposed to violence and pornography and those who are not. However, thinking statistically, so many people have so much access to content with sex and violence that it is almost impossible to explain how there could not be some effect, so the small changes that researchers find are uninteresting because they are inevitable. In short, *statistical* significance is not the same thing as *social* significance. On the other hand, the reverse may be true – 'small' effects can be devastating; Levine and Harrison (2009) discussed the huge impact that the flood of 'perfect body' images directed at teenagers is likely to have. Even if the *percentage* of teen audiences who directly buy into the desire for that perfect body is small, this still translates into huge *numbers* of youths who end up suffering. The conclusion is that data always has to be placed in a social context, and can never speak on its own.

And so a close look at what effects researchers really say helps to explain the complexity of how power works through media. Effects researchers seek social explanations for the patterns of aggressive responses that their surveys and experiments consistently find. They understand aggression as a phenomenon whose forms and outcomes change in the particularities that affect certain groups of people. Noting a general increase in aggressive tendencies across sample populations who are exposed to violent media, effects research has established a research agenda that looks for how media violence affects different *groups* in different ways. Nothing here contradicts cultural explanations of media effects. In fact, the reverse is true; we can illustrate in controversies on the anti-social influence of rap music.

PUTTING EFFECTS THINKING INTO PRACTICE: WAR AND RAP

When media influence is discussed in public, it often feels like we have to accept or reject the case for direct effects, with no space left to explore the territory in-between (Jenkins, 2006b). Faced with sensationalistic stories about young people who have done dreadful things after listening to music, it is often tempting to dwell on how the tragedy in question had nothing to do with media. When the families of Raymond Belknap and James Vance sued the heavy-metal band Judas Priest, accusing them of writing a song that had encouraged their sons to enter a murder/suicide pact, the defence rested on the argument that the pair were depressed alcohol and drug abusers who saw no future, and that the soundtrack to the tragedy was incidental. Yet we might still ask why, when setting this scene, was *this* album chosen?

Asking this isn't implying that musicians are responsible for how their work is used. But as technology allows access to music in the strangest of places, the question of why people listen to certain genres in harrowing situations that they would rather not be in, with unhappy outcomes, is relevant. Nor can we dispense with the idea that music does things to young people, because they tell us that it does. Nevertheless, the model of influence I am outlining is different from

that assumed in public debates on effects. To show this, I will contrast a controversy surrounding rap duo Insane Clown Posse (ICP) with Pieslak's study of
what rap means in war.

Imagine you were asked to form an opinion on Detroit's ICP. As the name suggests, the pair (stage names: Violent J and Shaggy 2 Dope) paint their faces like
clowns, a style their hardcore fans (known as 'juggalos') copy. According to their
own website, ICP 'emerged from the darkness surrounding Detroit's underground music scene in the early 90s', and since then have inspired nothing less
than a multimedia cultural movement (Insane Clown Posse, 2010a). Today's ICP
experience embraces the worlds of 'music, films, wrestling and festivals'. The
highlight of the ICP year is its annual 'Gathering of the Juggalos', a four-day carnival which recently celebrated its 10th anniversary. ICP have never been shy about
their love of fantasy violence. Having established 'Juggalo Championship Wrestling' as part of their 'Dark Carnival' Emporium, Violent J and Shaggy 2 Dope
announced the following in December 2010:

> It seems that the superstars of JCW felt that this holiday season was miss-
> ing two very important things: Brutality and bloodshed! So, they've
> decided to remedy this by bringing those things and more to The Modern
> Exchange on December 22nd in Southgate, MI at an event they are calling
> VILENT [sic] NIGHT! (Insane Clown Posse, 2010b)

Their lyrics frequently detail vicious fantasies. In 'Another Love Song', Violent J
plays the role of a man who locks his girlfriend in the trunk of his car and tells
her he is going to stab her to death as he drives to the murder scene.

In 2001, ICP were interviewed by conservative American television com-
mentator Bill O'Reilly. O'Reilly warned parents to worry if their teenagers pos-
sessed ICP music, because the pair made other rappers 'look like Shirley
Temple'.[7] In the interview, O'Reilly took Violent J to task, having filmed him
advising a 14-year-old fan to 'go home and smoke something'. ICP argued that
their fans were far worldlier than O'Reilly imagined. Teenagers knew better
than to take *clowns* seriously. Besides, if there were any villain here, it was
surely their own record label, who agreed that their music was offensive and
harmful but went on distributing it anyway.

A decade later, disquiet about the group had intensified because their aspirations to launch a counter-cultural movement had succeeded. On 9 March 2009,
ABC *Nightline*'s Martin Bashir reported on a series of murders associated with
'horrorcore', the rap/horror fantasy subculture that ICP had inspired. Police now
classified 'juggalos' as criminal gangs in parts of Arizona and Pennsylvania.
Bashir didn't think that ICP music made murderers, or that all juggalos were psy-
chopaths; he simply wondered what sort of responsibility the murders implied
for the group. The Bashir interview ended in a stand-off: Violent J said that the
killings were the act of murderers who happened to listen to ICP, among other
things, and more to the point 'I don't believe in the evidence of which you speak'.

Experimental studies of rap effects support the defence that music cannot
make people do things in and of itself, but it stretches credibility to claim that

men who have built a spectacular leisure experience netting millions of dollars every year have no power to affect their young fans; at the very least, they clearly monopolise much of their time and money. We need to be able to maintain a capacity to think about influence in non-reductionist terms. This starts by recognising that the question of whether or not ICP encourages murder misses the point that effects research has no interest in extreme cases; effects research focuses on what a general increase in aggressive tendencies might mean across populations and within socially disadvantaged groups (Comstock, 2008). To explain the difference, consider this: what if we change the question from 'Can rap make a killer?' to 'How do listening choices fit into cultures of violence?'

Can something like 'another love song' inspire feelings that lead, one way or another, to violence? Jonathan Pieslak's work on how US troops use music in Iraq finds an example of where this happens, but explaining how and why it does is far more complicated – and this is the real research endeavour. Like effects studies, Pieslak's interviews with soldiers are grounded on the observation of general patterns of media use, where aggressive music is now a semi-official weapon of war. Pieslak notes that, 'given that the technology allows music to be heard more frequently and in a greater variety of settings, including military vehicles, music's role as an inspiration for combat seems stronger than in previous wars', and that 'almost every soldier I interviewed said that they listened to music before leaving the military bases to go on patrols. Within this listening context, metal and rap appear to be the predominant musical genres of choice' (2007: 127). Eminem's 'Go to Sleep', another song about murder, featuring the line 'Die, motherfucker die, bye, bye motherfucker, bye, bye!', was a popular choice. A young veteran described why:

> War is so ugly and disgusting ... It's unnatural for people to kill people. It's something that no one should ever have to do, unfortunately, someone does. And we happen to be that someone sometimes. And so listening to music would artificially make you aggressive ... when I needed to get aggressive, I'd put some aggressive music on. (Pieslak, 2007: 140)

Gunter (2008) cautioned against mistaking association for causation. Pieslak's data shows that the effects of 'Go to Sleep' in theatre have little to do with the song's narrative, or any desire to find pleasure in the fantasy it weaves. Some of the interviewees did not actually like the rap, objected to its language, and couldn't bear listening to it away from the firing line. Perhaps more interestingly, they also noted how the aggressive effects of music had nothing to do with lyrics. Heavy-metal music was often used in interrogation of Iraqi detainees. Here 'More than any one of these elements in isolation, the distorted guitar sound and vocal articulation appear to be the most significant in causing the desired reaction of frustration and irritation' (Pieslak, 2007: 144).

Pieslak therefore provides a cultural explanation for the effects processes that Gunter described in 2008, adding some crucial modifiers. Effects are real, but highly conditioned by social circumstances and the needs of young people who want to be affected. The soldiers knew that that rap often conjures violent fantasies, but the 'context of the wider narrative' has more to do with *their* story than what 'Go to Sleep' is about. Listening to the rap reflected group needs, not individual desires and pleasure. The soldiers knowingly visited Eminem's 'negative' effects upon themselves under conditions of extreme pressure that were not of their own choosing. It is one thing to speak of tragic cases where young people have decided to end their lives, but quite another to think about how music fits into situations where thousands of young people are looking for something to help them through structured political violence as they struggle with the personal impact of US foreign policy. Policies they did not make created an international situation that they were tasked with solving. To cope, they listened to music that induced the temporary insanity they needed to do horrible things. In this instance, discussing media effects is not about deciding if young people are hapless media dopes, or savvy operators who control their media world.

Pieslak showed why neither the discourse of 'direct effects' nor the discourse of 'individual interpretation' or 'choice' sufficiently explained what makes rap a phenomenon that 'does' something in the world. He took the diffuse anxieties that motivated O'Reilly and Bashir – and recall, Bashir wasn't exactly sure what his problem was – and created a study finding the exact conditions that associate rap and real violence. Pieslak was careful to address a central validity criterion in effects studies: establishing the connection between exposure and action. His achievement was creating a complex cultural narrative which explained the processes that Gunter described. With rap, this involved defining behaviour as performance, investigating how performances are affected by political economies and cultural histories.

Good effects research recommends looking beyond obvious anxieties about media risks, looking for alternative explanations for how effects come to be, appreciating that they assume many forms and allowing that media do good things. Quantitative studies of rap content and effects ignore behaviourist concerns as expressed by O'Reilly and Bashir. Conventional effects studies indicate the importance of understanding rap and violence within the sphere of commodified gender relations. Effects and cultural studies agree that we can't make simple assumptions about rap and violence, because rap is a multifaceted art form whose meanings can be obscure, either in terms of what its artists mean or its audiences hear and see. Both fields think rap matters as a genre that blends business, culture, violence and performance in unique ways; in what follows, I explain why this blend that might explain Eminem's status as a 'weapon of choice' in Iraq. Quantitative data on rap content and effects complements cultural studies of why rap matters. In combination, these literatures explicate the 'effects' that Pieslak observes. This explanation creates an intriguing parallel between performer and listener.

There are studies that show negative outcomes of listening to rap, but these are about attitudes, not behaviours, and sex, not violence. Kistler and Lee (2010) conducted an experiment using – you guessed it – male undergraduates, showing that young men who are exposed to rap videos with high levels of sexual content are more likely to express sexist stereotypes and more accepting of rape in post-testing. Other researchers, however, argued that rap violence is different from that found in other genres. In a content analysis of 203 videos, Jones (1997) found more violent *speech* than action. Jones' findings are significant because they connect with a central theme in cultural explanations of rap, which define it as an oral narrative performance. We will return to this shortly.

Other studies have emphasised rap's commercial effects. Rappers provide unique stories about connections between economics and lived experience. Schemer et al. (2008) thought there was more product placement than violence in rap videos, and set out to study how audiences transferred positive and negative attitudes to rappers onto the commodities that they celebrated in their music (like Courvoisier cognac). De Gregorio and Sung's study of product placement in 3476 top-ten songs from 1954 to 2002 (2009) showed rap to be the most popular genre for such promotions. These studies defined rap as a celebration of commerce and consumption. They did not find this affected audiences directly; Schemer et al. discovered that evaluation of the product depended on attitudes to the performer. Their conclusion reflected the broader effects' consensus that audiences interpret media content in ways that seemingly confound what that content is 'about' in its most obvious sense.

For example, the theme of rap misogyny is often discussed,[8] but Dixon et al.'s (2009) survey of 141 African-American university students found listening to rap associated positively with self-esteem, and that rap fans were less likely to think it misogynistic. That doesn't mean that some rap isn't misogynistic, but effects research does provide evidence that rap's influence cannot be simply deduced from obvious places where it does glorify violent sexism. Even if rappers do have 'preferred meanings' – things that they really mean to say and want to be understood – these can be irrelevant to audiences. On this theme, Bill Yousman (2003) noted that popularity of rap among young white listeners co-existed with racist attitudes.

Qualitative researchers have used the observation that rap content is often about business to explore the idea of *performative* effects. Some have argued that male rappers' macho posturing reflects their understanding of themselves as entrepreneurs. Academics agree with Violent J; the main issue is the music industry, not the things that come out of rappers mouths. Sköld and Rehn defined rap as a narrative on how entrepreneurialism is lived beyond business schools and the sorts of corporate setting that conventionally appear in management literature:

By paying attention to 'the hustler' as an entrepreneurial figure in a specific oral tradition, the impossibility of sticking to a general definition of what 'entrepreneurship' is, is highlighted and thus also the way in which certain localities have been ignored in the study of entrepreneurship. (2007: 53)

Rap bravado is an entrepreneurial strategy befitting an art predicated on spontaneous public displays of rhetorical skill. According to Sköld and Rehn, this is why successful rappers rhyme about making money as much as they do about violence and sex.

However, rap's business ambitions clash with the rapper's need to 'keep it real': to remain faithful and connected to the community from which he or she hopes to escape with success. 'The hustler', the artist like Jay-Z, 50 Cent and Ice-T who admits that his commercial acumen was honed in a life of crime, is a virtual figure. What Sköld and Rehn mean by this is that verisimilitude of the 'hustler' rapper depends on how he performs, not what he is or was:

> The contradictory discourses of rap lyricism can be viewed as ideological moves stemming from a wish to stabilize the lacking subject. The reality of keeping it real is in such a perspective not a question of accurate depiction ... not a move closer to some immutable truth, but an acknowledgment of ... a commoditized virtual reality, inhabited by fairy-tale-like heroes ... and the entrepreneurial or hustling rap artists (among those) packaging and capitalising on these commodities. (2007: 73)

The successful rap *performer* creates a media persona that holds two different worlds together, converting criminal capital into consumer products – music, clothing, video games and movies – that are palatable to the corporate world. Violent rap converts one to the other. The most substantial effects of this conversion are probably political. Balaji (2009) argues that successful rappers make Faustian pacts that end up having negative effects on racial politics. Ultimately, the rapper's tales of mayhem must be sellable, because that is what they are for. However 'real' the artist's experiences are, they are only valuable in so far as they can be packaged and sold within familiar media narratives. One outcome is that in some circles rap complements other negative representations of young black men:

> Framing Black men as the Other has reaped economic benefits for corporations that have capitalised on the 'thug appeal' of Black men in rap music while helping to legitimize policy decisions – such as the repealing of welfare, ending affirmative action, and cutting funding for education and job training – that have had adverse impact on African-American communities. (Balaji, 2009: 23)

This is why Violent J's observation that the real issue in rap effects is how the industry makes controversial messages popular among the public was telling. Like it or not, ICP are part of an elite cadre of rappers who understand their business as well as their art, but who are torn by an inevitably antagonistic relationship with a corporate mainstream who exploit them as they seek to exploit it. If effects studies analyse violence by 'comprehend[ing] its purpose in the wider context of a narrative, evaluat[ing] its role, purpose, and outcomes for those involved, and absorb[ing] its details into ... social knowledge'

(Gunter, 2008), then it follows that these industrial concerns are relevant because they explain why rap violence comes to the attention of the public in the first place.

And so we return to soldiers in Iraq listening to Eminem before combat. When explaining effects, there are parallels between Eminem's public persona and the 'temporary insanity' that the solders describe. Eminem's availability as a source of inspiration to violence has much to do with the music industry and cultural prejudices against rap as art. O'Reilly and Bashir both rejected ICP's defence that they presented fans with entertaining fictions, not literal instructions on what to do. This refusal to acknowledge rap creativity is a key factor in understanding why the genre is so controversial, in terms of its cultural politics. Gil Rodman (2006) explores this point in his work on Eminem, and through this we can see what the ICP controversy has to do with the Pieslak study. Eminem and the soldiers share something: they play public roles in knowing ways.

It is obvious that Pieslak's soldiers listened to Eminem because he is one of the best-selling rap artists of all time. Rap's reputation as an injunction to *violence*, according to Gil Rodman (2006), comes from cultural prejudices. Rodman observes how critics happily accept that Bob Dylan and John Lennon play roles when singing songs about killing people, but assume rappers like Eminem are incapable of speaking in anything other than the first person. When Tom Jones wails 'Why, why, why, Delilah?', having stabbed his girlfriend to death, we know the senior Welsh sex symbol wouldn't really do such a thing, but when Eminem paints the same picture, some think he means it. Rodman is more disturbed by this reaction than any of the clearly offensive things that Eminen says:

> At the root of the widespread, collective inability to see Eminem as an *author*, as an *artist*, as a *performer*, we find a cultural bias at least as disturbing as the goriest of his musical fantasies: a bias that rests on the prejudicial notion that 'some people' are wholly incapable of higher thinking and artistic creativity – and that their ability to create 'fiction' is limited to making minor modifications to their otherwise unvarnished personal experiences. (2006: 105)

Rodman uses this observation to discuss race,[9] but here I take another direction. That is, the idea that Eminem revels in mindless violence, and that this content simply transports its way into the minds of people who use it in functional ways to become pugnacious, vastly underestimates the complexity of the performance of *his listeners*. Moreover, this claim is in keeping with concepts and evidence in both effects and cultural studies.

Rodman interprets Eminem's lyrics as showing awareness that he is indeed a 'virtual' figure whose performance has taken on a public life that he no longer controls. 'The Way I Am' is about the impossibility of pleasing the industry and different audiences, frustration at the constant pressure to reveal the 'real' Eminem (where the fact that he uses three public names shows there is no such figure), and an exasperated 'whatever' conclusion: *I am whoever you say I am*. Eminem, Slim Shady and Marshall Mathers are all masks for a man who just wants to raise his daughter by doing what he loves (Rodman, 2006). There's a parallel here with Pieslak's soldiers, who are also playing a public role. Just as Eminem would say 'I'm not who you say I am', the soldiers are keen to distance themselves from the 'inhuman and disgusting' things that they must do. In the end, it's foreign policy that makes them kill. So why listen to Eminem?

Given the literature, we can argue that 'Go to Sleep' is made effective by the commoditisation of rap as a statement of 'reality' rather than an imaginative art form *and* the way that music is now commonly deployed as a weapon of war. Moreover, there's a parallel between the distance rappers place between their real lives and their encoding of these lives in rhyme, and the accounts that the soldiers give of their actions, which create a space between the things that they do, as soldiers, and what they are, as people. Or at least that seems a possibility. Does rap appeal because it is commonly recognised as a way of creating this gap, that the soldiers need to maintain their sanity and sense of self-worth? This is more of a question than a conclusion, but it makes sense within the literature, and what it does show is that there are many questions that remain to be asked about what media violence does.

CONCLUSION: EFFECTS CULTURE

The purpose of contrasting the ICP controversy with Pieslak's study is to show that journalistic concerns about the former miss the point of both effects and cultural studies, and in fact divert attention away from the complex processes that explain media influence in its most dramatic forms. Media violence is clearly a force in the social world. It matters and it does things, but why and what and how remain unclear. Qualitative and quantitative scholars agree on this.

We need to know about effects research to make academic comments about the youth media events that frequently appear in the news. Fundamentally, it's crucial to understand that effects research is not the enemy in trying to paint more complex pictures of influence than commentators like O'Reilly and Bashir afford. Quite the reverse: effects research is mainly concerned with the less spectacular consequences media exposure has on social groups, and seeks social explanations for these effects. Therefore, effects research does not contradict the importance of cultural accounts of how the young engage media. With rap, effects studies are comfortable with the idea that influence expresses economics more than it does the deranged psychologies of either performers or listeners.

Effects and cultural studies share an interest in 'ordinary' youth. To appreciate media influence in its deepest form, we have to spend less time worrying about aberrant cases, and more time pondering how access to media has multiple effects on how different sorts of young people live. When it comes to rap and violence, it is clear that, for most youth, it is more relevant to consider how the reading of rap as violent genre is at least supported by a series of cultural biases against it, which work in league with the commercial pressures to produce hyper-masculine performances for audiences. The idea of influence as emerging through *ordinary performances* is useful in describing how we can select and analyse youth media case studies in a global context, which is the topic of Chapter 4. But first, it is necessary to understand the idea of media effects from a historical view that pays more attention to technologies rather than content.

CHAPTER SUMMARY

- Surveys and experiments on media effects have created valuable insights for cultural, qualitative approaches to studies of youth media.

- Effects researchers are interested in how media affect *social groups*.

- Effects researchers define *behaviours* as *actions* that are caused by the interplay between media messages and social *context*.

- *Effects* researchers see young people as *active participants* in the production of media effects; sometimes young people are affected by media because they want to be affected by media.

- This doesn't mean that young people control media effects, because their use of media is often determined by social factors they cannot control; the topic of how US soldiers 'use' rap music in Iraq is a case in point, describing a situation where young people grudgingly visit negative effects upon themselves.

- Negative media effects are best understood as things that are visited upon the socially vulnerable.

NOTES

1   See, for example, John Murray's chapter in Sharon Mazzarella's *20 Questions about Youth and the Media* (2007).

2   See Alan McKee's criticisms of experiments on pornography (2006).

3   Bandura's infamous 'Bobo Doll' experiments are often presented as exemplars of everything that is wrong with effects research; see Ruddock (2001).

4   As an example, in 2010 I was asked to comment on a report from the Australian Hotels' Association that claimed pub violence was caused by young men who had played too many video games.

5   The purpose here is to simply show the emphasis on youth in this database using these search terms; wider searches manipulating the terms and utilising other databases would likely have found hundreds more studies.

6   Indeed, Martin Barker, a key critic of the effects tradition, has himself used an experimental style in research on sexual violence in film, which also used a student sample (2005).

7 Shirley Temple was a child film star in the 1930s, famous for the song 'On the Good Ship Lollypop', which explored the pleasure of anthropomorphising candy.

8 For example, Tyree's (2009) analysis of the apparent contradiction of male rappers who love and respect their mothers but dismiss their sexual partners as worthless, and Conrad et al.'s (2009) content analysis showing that women are more frequently sexualised than men are in videos.

9 The thing that makes Eminem so controversial, according to Rodman, is his identity as a white man who situates himself entirely within a black cultural repertoire. For example, Rodman argues that Eminem is crucially different to early 1990s sensation Vanilla Ice who, as the name suggests, drew attention to his whiteness.

3

UNDERSTANDING THE INFLUENCE OF MEDIA TECHNOLOGIES: YOUTH, DISSENT, SOCIAL MEDIA AND SOCIAL HISTORY

Research Question.
What does looking at the role of social media in youth-led protests tell us about the influence of media technologies?

Lessons for understanding media influence.
The technology question is an important component in cultural history

Underlying question about media influence.
Why is it useful to think of media studies as a form of social history?

Outcomes.
Social media 'work' by connecting media industries and audiences through media practices.

Relevant literature.
Social history (E. P. Thompson) Critical studies of protests movements that have used social media Historical accounts of media forms (muckraking journalism)

Exemplifying case study.
The death of Rachel Hoffman: how do economic and historical forces encourage media industries and young people to connect through social media?

This chapter considers the effects of media technologies from a historical point of view. When contemplating the significance of events like 2011's Arab Spring, where young people used mobile media to confront powerful political regimes, it's useful to frame the role of media devices in terms of culture and history – particularly the history of how ordinary people have sought to intercede in public life. Popular protest has been a popular topic in social history, and it is clear that such events are increasingly media dependent. It makes sense, then, to consider the intersections between history and media studies as disciplines.

This chapter does so through three steps. First, it identifies the core research questions in social history. Second, it shows how these core themes have influenced critical media research on youth, social media and dissent. Third, it selects a case study where particular form of youth protest was activated by the application of digital resources to established media conventions, illustrating how a sophisticated understanding of contemporary youth protests demands an understanding of history and *media* history. Drawing on investigations and protests surrounding the murder of Florida student Rachel Hoffman, the chapter explains how regional journalists in Tallahassee, the state's capital, energised young activists by practising 'muckraking journalism', a genre that has been highly influential in American journalism since the turn of the twentieth century, using social media.

The Hoffman study illustrates a simple point about the relationship between history and media studies. Social history explores how social change is affected by the way that culture and institutions bring people together in common interests and activities. Discussion on youth and protests, and the Hoffman case study, show how media practices and organisations have come to adopt that role. Through this discussion, you will come to understand that the best way to study the effects of media technologies is to examine the social and organisational factors which determine how they are used. You will also be able to explain why much as media studies needs history, history now also needs media studies.

WHY MIGHT SOCIAL MEDIA BE BAD FOR THE WORLD?

In April 2012, United Nations Secretary-General Ban Ki-Moon used Google+ Hangout to chat with young people from around the world on a variety of topics, including security, human rights and the role of media technologies in education. The UN's top official 'said he wanted to use the social media tool to connect with people and hear ideas' (United Nations Radio, 2012). In doing so, Ban expressed a familiar utopian conviction: the technical capacity of social media meant young people could, for the first time, literally 'hang out' with the people who would determine their futures.

Ban's actions were born of the UN's belief that free access to media is a precondition for a just world. This commitment is expressed in article 19 of the UN's Universal Declaration of Human Rights, which reads:

> Everyone has the right to freedom of opinion and expression; this right includes freedom to hold opinions without interference and to seek, receive and impart information and ideas through any media and regardless of frontiers. (United Nations, 1948)

Google+'s capacity to conquer challenges of time and space seem to make it a powerful tool for making article 19 a reality. However, at around the same time as the UN was drafting its founding principles in the late 1940s, the Canadian economist Harold Innis warned that, if anything, history taught that faster, more widespread communication could actually make the world a less democratic place:

> Enormous improvements in communication have made understanding more difficult. Even science, mathematics, and music as the last refuge of the Western mind have come under the spell of the mechanized vernacular. Commercialism has required the creation of new monopolies in language and new difficulties in understanding. (Innis, 1947)

Had he been able to speak to Ban, Innis may well have cautioned that the outsourcing of global communication to a privately owned company was unlikely to solve the problems of global democracy. Innis believed the technology question wasn't about technology, but history: the history of peoples, cultures and empires and businesses. So, when faced with events such as 2011's Arab Spring, where young people took an unprecedented role as agents of political change, apparently helped by the capacities of social media to instantly attract global attention, it is important to ask why particular media genres and businesses become involved in particular forms of youth activism for particular reasons at particular times. In this sense, the question of how social media have changed the world continues a long-running theme in social history; understanding how social disorder is deeply ordered by culture.

To justify the value of a historical approach to media technologies, this chapter outlines the main themes of social history, connects these themes to scholarship on social media and student protest, and explores a case study where it is possible to trace how the historical development of journalistic business practices has allowed specific modes of engagement with specific modes of dissent.

TECHNOLOGY AND MEDIA INFLUENCE

The discussion on effects research in Chapter 2 focused, for the most part, on the matter of how young people may be influenced by media content. We saw that this influence depended on the context in which it is encountered; the question of technology thus becomes a factor, since the context of exposure depends, to a great extent, on the devices that make content available in different social spaces. At any rate, when it comes to the matter of what media technologies do in society, the social and political understanding of media influence developed in Chapters 1 and 2 mean it's useful to follow Innis' advice in thinking of technologies historically.

Technologies matter because they enable media practice, a term that describes 'what people are doing in relation to media across a range of situations and contexts' (Couldry, 2004: 119). The idea being expressed here is that media technologies are society's 'rhythm section'. When we watch a musical performance, we tend to pay attention to vocalists or lead guitarists, but the whole thing falls apart without the bass section, even if we rarely take the time to really listen to what they are doing. Similarly, when considering protest and political change, it's easy to think that events are driven by social concerns and powerful personalities, but as society becomes more mediatised, as media use becomes a more routine part of daily rituals, so these concerns and personalities need a 'rhythm section', a network that coordinates communication around the issue at hand. In this sense, mobile media, and the factors shaping how they are used, have the 'effect' of 'keeping the beat'. This is a historical matter, in so far as it is important to tell the story of what these factors are, and how they come together under specific social circumstances.

Technologies don't just appear from laboratories, and their effects often have little to do with their technological capacities or intended uses (Williams, 1974). To appreciate the value of this broadly historical position on media technologies, it is useful to connect debates on social media, youth and political dissent in the period 2009–11, with the famed social historian E. P. Thompson's work on public protest. Thompson's *The Making of the English Working Class* (1963) was a groundbreaking study on the politicisation of culture during the Industrial Revolution. Thompson believed his study established a number of questions about the relationship between culture and power that should inform studies of media influence. In doing so, he made it possible to see social history and media studies as closely related disciplines. This is because Thompson's analysis of culture and power frames media technologies as devices that synthesize social and media change, such that it is now often difficult to imagine one without the other.

Defining the topic of youth, protests and social media as a continuation of Thompson's project casts the technology issue as an investigation into how new media devices 'keep the beat' by constituting communities around common goals and interests. This is important because when it's framed as a historical matter, the technology topic makes the case that social history can no longer be written without considering how the publics are made when they use media.

This is why the Hoffman story is about much more than a tragic murder. In 2009, Florida's *Tallahassee Democrat* pursued audiences, profit *and* social change by grafting social media onto the American tradition of muckraking journalism. The newspaper revived its commercial fortunes by encouraging students in the state's capital to agitate for policing reform. Rachel Hoffman was a graduate of Florida State University who was shot dead in a bungled drug sting. For good or ill, *Tallahassee Democrat* journalists used social media to capitalise on established media conventions and social relationships. The Hoffman case study highlights two important points. First, it gives empirical evidence on how exactly technologies and conventional media practices facilitated effective dissent through social media, as such offering a grounded perspective on the distinct role of media in social change. Second, it emphasises the eminent 'researchability' of the technology theme: that is, whereas extensive attention has been justifiably devoted to landmark global events like the Arab Spring – complex, ongoing historical events whose meaning may be unclear for decades – it is also possible to explore themes of technology, history and social change through smaller-scale case studies.

The case for a historical approach to media technologies, as developed through the theme of youth, media and dissent, is made through the following stages. This chapter:

- considers how a social understanding of media influence implies a set of historical questions about culture as a political force;

- explains Thompson's ideas about the relationship between culture and dissent, and why he thought media studies needed a more determined historical focus;

- shows how media scholarship on social media and political insurrections responds to his criticisms – consciously or not;

- uses the Hoffman case study to explain how social media participate in exploitation and change;

- reflects on the status of social history and media studies as cognate subjects.

MEDIA INFLUENCE: FROM THE SOCIAL TO THE HISTORICAL

A historical approach to technologies concentrates on how media devices create 'political actions spaces' where young people reflect on the meaning of their social situation and, given the right conditions, do something to change it. Pieslak's work on music and war illustrates how media content, media technologies and history collaborate to make these spaces real. It doesn't mean much to look at the effects of rap on soldiers in Iraq, for instance, without first asking why those soldiers are there. Before considering how digital technologies allowed soldiers to carry vast musical libraries into war and access them at any time, we have to know something about why they were placed in a position where this was something they felt compelled to do. At the same time, we can also say that music played an active role in shaping the experience of war, because the way that Pieslak's soldiers were brought together as rap audiences affected how they saw themselves as soldiers. Rap helped the soldiers manage their situation by giving them a language to express how they felt about it. Putting a well thought out playlist together, then carrying it into battle is a technical achievement, but it is also a meaningful act – something that expresses a view of the world. Media technologies are therefore important not because of what they can do, technically, but because of how these capacities are used to create spaces where people can contemplate their situation. We need to pay attention to media as historical formations, but we also have to consider how these forma-tions come to act as material forces – things that don't just create the space to talk about change, but also become the vehicle for that change. Here is the first connection with Thompson; the notion of culture as a driving force for political change was a key theme in his study of how ordinary people influenced the political social and political outcomes of the Industrial Revolution

E. P. THOMPSON: WHO WAS HE, WHAT DID HE WRITE ABOUT AND WHY DOES HIS WORK MATTER TO MEDIA STUDIES?

The matter of how culture expresses the desire for social change was a funda-mental concept in Thompson's *The Making of the English Working Class* (1963), one of the most influential social histories to be written in the twentieth century. Thompson's oeuvre on the history of public protest in the late eighteenth and early nineteenth centuries helps to outline a historical approach to media tech-nologies because it allows a particular view on contemporary debates about youth, social media and dissent. Reading Thompson frames the question of what media technologies do as an extension of the interest in how culture becomes political when it congregates groups of people around sets of ideas and practices.

Thompson was interested in the institutions and cultural activities that brought the working poor together. His point was that it was only when they were gathered together in workplaces, schools, churches and trade associations that working people could recognise common experiences and interests. More impor-tantly, it was only when the working poor began to communicate these interests and experiences *as* common that 'the working class' became a real force that changed history. Writing in the 1960s, Thompson thought an understanding of how the working class came to be through culture was vital to the newly emerging discipline of media studies. Thompson believed that the Industrial Revolution, and the emergence of working-class consciousness, set the foundations for under-standing culture in political terms. Thompson saw the Industrial Revolution as a cultural metamorphosis that changed how ordinary people thought about their rights. In the late eighteenth century, profound economic transformations led to an unprecedented politicisation of culture where everything that working people did – eating, sleeping, playing, going to school, going to church, and even rioting for no particular reason they could explain – had some foundation in the systemic political conflicts of the inchoate capitalist order. Thompson was convinced that these changes were the prequel to the questions that media scholars had started to explore in the 1960s. As Thompson put it himself:

> Those writers today who rightly expose the human depreciation result-ing from the commercial abuse of the media of communication, seem to have matters out of proportion when they overlook the extent and char-acter of mass indoctrination in earlier periods. (1963: 378)

Thompson had a Marxist view of culture; he believed that there was a relationship between being and consciousness, where culture was the conduit between how people existed and how they understood their existence. Once again, this can be explained in reference to Pieslak's work: the idea of rap violence as a performance helped Pieslak's respondents to imagine a distance between what they were and what they did, and this capacity to imagine was a real help in reconciling a series of contradictions. However, this imagination only went so far since, in the end, as the soldiers said, 'war is disgusting'. Such statements are indicative of culture's inherent ambiguities, as an entity that contains and provokes unrest at the same time. On the one hand, music played a functionalist role for soldiers in the field (and US foreign policy). Rap energised, placated, passed time, and even served as a weapon of war. On the other hand, it confronted the soldiers with contradictions that could not be explained away ('Why am I listening to things that I never listen to at home, because I don't really like rap that much? Why am I being made to kill people when I really don't want to?'). The tension here is, when does popular culture stop being doing things that re-creates the world as it is ('Rap violence is just pretend, but it temporarily pumps me up, kills time and generally gets the job done), and when does it encourage people to stop conforming and change that world ('This isn't right; this isn't me')? Another way to put this is to say that media influence is determined by how media practices – the way that people live their lives in relation to media – set in train contradictory processes that reconcile some people to how things are, and encourage others to change things.

This is a historical matter, because Thompson believed that these sorts of experiences, where culture presented ordinary people with a series of contradictions on the meaning of their life, became common during the Industrial Revolution. The speed of social change in this period meant that, for the first time, people were routinely compelled to wonder why life had become so systematically miserable. Thompson observed that religion was one of the places where people were given the space and the tools to find the answer to this dilemma. For this reason, he understood religion as a cultural practice that ended up creating a language that ordinary people used to make sense of the world. Thompson's relevance to media studies is best appreciated through his analysis of religion as a political and cultural force.

THOMPSON'S VIEW ON CONFLICT AND DISSENT

In this aspect of his work, Thompson developed a conflict model of culture. Religion had always been a political force, but in the Industrial Revolution, Thompson believed religions began to prototype popular culture. Methodism, for example, was an enormously popular faith among working people that established ideas and cultural practices which contained popular resentment against the inequities of the time, while also creating the spaces and the language that allowed this same resentment to fester. Thompson was especially interested in unpacking how Methodism had cultivated a generation of important socialist thinkers when, if anything, it set out to do exactly the opposite. Thompson defined Methodism as a politically expedient form of 'psychic exploitation' (1963: 375). Methodists were devoted to understanding the mechanics of salvation, and this distracted attention from the desperate poverty and exploitation of the time. Methodism was counter-revolutionary because, as life seemed to be getting worse for working people (longer working hours under intolerable conditions, shorter life spans and the removal of paternalistic social welfare measures that had protected the agrarian classes), the church encouraged the poor to concentrate on the afterlife. Methodist schools taught young people that they deserved to suffer because they were sinners who could only be saved through silent penitence.

Thompson believed that Methodism favoured the capitalist industrial order because, by deliberately instilling the fear of God from the cradle, Methodist preachers and teachers cultivated sensibilities that helped those who would deny the working classes political representation. Methodist schools indoctrinated the young with a sense of fatalism toward the short life of pitiless toil that lay before them. John Wesley, the Church's founder, ordered Methodist teachers to beat any hint of free expression from the young:

> Break their wills ... let a child from a year old be taught to fear the rod and cry softly ... break his will now and his soul shall live, and he will probably bless you to all eternity. (Cited in Thompson, 1963: 375)

But Methodism also encouraged popular politics simply by creating places where the working poor could congregate and talk about the corporeal world – and what could be done about it. Thompson thought that this explained the popularity of charismatic evangelists among Methodist congregations in the late eighteenth century. Methodism was so good at focussing attention on the next life, that when prophets arrived in working-class communities with tales of the impending Day of Judgment (spurred on, for example, by the idea that the French Emperor Napoleon was satanic, and the Napoleonic wars signalled the ultimate clash between good and evil), they caused mass hysteria – people rejoiced at the prospect of an end to their suffering. Seeing their power over the masses, some of these preachers stepped into the political ring. Johanna Southcote, who attracted a following of tens of thousands of Methodists with her vision of the end of days, rebuked landowners for raising bread prices in the name of profit: 'my charges will come heavy against them, if they starve the poor in the midst of plenty' (cited in Thompson, 1963: 386). Despite its intentions, implicit and explicit, Methodism's evolution as a cultural form set the grounds for collective expressions of discontent that registered, very visibly, the chaos and despair that industrialisation was visiting on the working class in the name of progress.

Thompson believed there was a connection between this and the fact that Methodists would eventually take leading roles in the working-class political movements of the nineteenth century. He thought of Methodism as a political action space that illustrated a new, political take on ordinary culture. Methodism had no explicit political agenda, but in the end it had powerful political effects that worked in two directions: pacifying some, encouraging others to demand social justice. In any case, in creating places where people could come together and discuss the nature of sin in forensic detail it became a vehicle for the expression of political world views, as such epitomising how the things that people did regularly in their leisure time had become central to the operation of society. Poor Methodists had two things: the experience of exploitation, and a medium to express that exploitation in a way that demanded radical reform. Methodism provided a language and a place to articulate the desire for a fundamentally changed society where ordinary people, for the first time, would have a political voice that mattered. In this sense, it exemplified the political role of culture, establishing ideas that had become the foundation of studies of media power.

THOMPSON ON MEDIA STUDIES

Thompson thought events like this should inform the then growing interest in the social power of advertising and the popular press (1961). Thompson's take on media power was ambiguous. On the one hand, as has been mentioned, be believed that mass media were far less effective than earlier forms of social control. On the other hand, he suspected that media *were* blocking further socialist reform in the UK, because they had colonised the national popular imagination and dictated the terms through which reality was expressed. His criticisms were particularly directed at youth audiences. Where, in the end, Methodism let Methodists imagine a radically different world, youth reactions to the mass media seemed far more conservative: 'it is one of the paradoxes of the critical younger generation, that one may hear on every side voices deploring the effects of advertising and of the centralised media, but scarcely a voice which goes on to say: we must combine to produce, finance and sell an independent paper' (1961: 28). Worse still, Thompson believed the lack of attention to historical detail in the media analysis of the time created the impression that these 'centralising forces' where the product of inevitable 'impersonal forces' rather than the outcomes of specific struggles between particular groups of people in conflict. That is, Thompson thought that no study of media power could afford to ignore the particular people and conditions that produced the particular outcomes of particular media practices.

STUDENT ACTIVISM AND 'TWITTER REVOLUTIONS'

So, Thompson thought that his work was relevant to media studies, even if it wasn't about media as such, because history and media studies are both fundamentally about how culture either helps or hinders ordinary people as they seek to take control of their own lives. Looking at the things at stake in contemporary debates on youth, social media and protest, it's easy to find places where Thompson's ideas about culture help to explain controversies around media and politics. In the UK youth riots of 2011, apparently organised via Twitter and Blackberry Messenger, there was a great public controversy over whether what looked like an orgy of looting had some kind of political motivation, and how far events had escalated thanks to the anarchic congregating potential of instant messaging. Commenting on the alleged role of mobile media in the riots, Prime Minister David Cameron publicly pondered legislation that would allow the authorities to shut down sites like Facebook and Twitter in the face of mass disorder (Halliday and Garside, 2011) while also lauding a Facebook page that was organised to show support for the police officers who had confronted the rioters (David Cameron: The fightback is underway, 2011). Anyone who had read *The Making of the English Working Class* (1963) knew that Thompson had already offered a valuable perspective on 'senseless' rioting. Thompson pointed out that the English had been rioting for reasons that they barely understood for centuries, but that irrational outbursts (such as the popularity of anti-Catholic rioting in the late seventeenth century among crowds of people who had virtually no understanding of the political and theological differences between Catholicism and Protestantism) always reflected genuine tensions around inequality. But Cameron's ambivalent stance on social networking reflected a basic lesson from Thompson: throughout history, the cultural forms that bring people together – be those forms churches, trade unions or Twitter – have promised order and threatened chaos at the same time. This is why culture matters, and this is also why Thompson believed that media studies needed a historical focus, so that it could be specific about the significance of media power vis-à-vis other forms of culture.

Looking at critical studies of the role that social media have played in fostering political dissent among young people, it is clear that many writers have followed Thompson's lead by tempering euphoria about the democratic power of Twitter et al. with some sober analyses of the particular histories of particular 'revolutions' where, superficially, young social media users were credited with affecting political change.

As the twenty-first century moved into its second decade, it was easy to find media commentary arguing that Twitter and the like suddenly offered a solution to a problem of political inclusion that has been around for centuries. On 9 December 2010, thousands of students from English universities converged on London, protesting against the new coalition government's plan to triple university fees. The demonstrations were controversially violent,[1] but social media allowed protesters to instantly publicise the view that police had aggravated the day's disorder. Journalist Laurie Penny, who specialised in youth issues for the *New Statesman*, argued that student tweeters proved that the police, the authorities and the news media could no longer fabricate stories about unruly youth unopposed:

> In the Parliament Square 'kettle'[2] on 9 December, I happened to be standing next to Jody McIntyre when the police began to baton him and his brother, who was pushing his wheelchair. Within seconds, I had pulled out my phone to tweet about what I had seen; within minutes, the backlash had begun as outraged citizens all over the country found supporting evidence of the assault and let each other know what had happened. By the time I

arrived home, bloody and bruised from further police violence, the assault on Jody had made the national press. December 2010 will surely be remembered as the month when the global ruling class lost its monopoly over information. (Penny, 2010)

The idea that social networking gave people unprecedented opportunities to write history as they were making it came to global life again in 2011, when citizens in Tunisia, Egypt, Libya, Bahrain, Jordan and Syria took to the streets to demand regime change. In Egypt, the protests had a definite youth and social media flavour (Kirkpatrick and Slackman, 2011). *Egypt Independent* (2011) reported that youth groups had marched on Hosni Mubarak's presidential palace to force the Army to side with them. When Mubarak addressed Egypt and the world in his speech of 11 February, he directed his appeal for support to the nation's youth, recalling how his own experiences as a young man had shaped his presidential career. In a Whitehouse press briefing on the Egyptian crisis, Barack Obama called upon Mubarak to restore public access to the Internet and social networking (YouTube, 2011), and it was certainly true that even schoolchildren could make telling points that the world would notice, thanks to new modes of circulation made possible by social networks. In an act that was far more calculated than Florence's, an Egyptian schoolgirl delivered a devastatingly succinct admonition to Mubarak that was shared across the globe:

> Also much the same as ever is the Egyptian sense of humour – and it's on display back in Tahrir Square ... the jokes are aimed at getting President Mubarak to pack his bags. A young girl was seen wearing a badge urging him to do it quickly. 'Make it short,' the badge said. 'This is history, and we'll have to memorise it all at school!' And in the land of the Pyramids, I guess there's already way too much history for kids to learn. (Johnston, 2011)

Initial academic analyses of events like this portrayed the enthusiasm for digital activism as a sort of giddy false-consciousness. Studies of Moldovan and Iranian students, for example, built on Thompson's observation that change requires a means of expression *and* the right material conditions. These studies showed how revolutions 'fail' when social media do not foster empathy because of insurmountable political and economic divisions. In April 2009, high-school and university students marched alongside activist groups to protest alleged electoral fraud that had returned the ruling Moldovan Communist Party (PRMC) to power in the election of that year (Mungiu-Pippidi and Munteanu, 2009). The protests were the latest in a series of 'colour revolutions' that had swept Eastern Europe. The first had taken place in Serbia in 2000 when OTPOR!, an organisation arising from the Serbian student movement led by the then 25-year-old Srdja Popovic, successfully agitated for the end to Slobodan Milosevic's authoritarian regime (Stack, 2010). Popovic's media strategies became something of a blueprint for protests against regimes who clung to power through intimidation, media control and vote-rigging in the former Soviet States of Lithuania, Georgia, Kyrgzstan and, finally, Moldova. The Moldovan experience was the first to use Twitter, but according to

Mungiu-Pippidi and Munteanu's analysis (2009), no amount of Twittered calls for democracy could overcome sober economic exigencies. Mungiu-Pippidi and Munteanu argued that students were not able to achieve their immediate goals because economic and political realities prevented effective cross-generational alliances; unlike students in England, Moldovan students were unable to persuade older Moldovans that their interests were one and the same. Older people, who feared Russia's capacity to damage the economy, especially through its alliance with the heavily armed breakaway state of Transnistria, did not share young Moldovans' antipathy toward the Communist Party. Twitter could not affect these economic and military realities, which was fatal to the protests in Europe's poorest nation (Mungiu-Pippidi and Munteanu, 2009).

Eyvgeny Morozov's work on Iran's 'Twitter revolution' (2009) added a more pointed media angle to 'Twitter cynicism'. In 2009, people took to the streets in Tehran to protests the results of a national election. They believed that the landslide victory of the incumbent Ahmadinejad regime were the results of electoral fraud. The *Washington Times* dubbed the protest a 'Twitter revolution' since

> Iran is a highly computer-literate society with a large number of bloggers and hackers. The hackers in particular were active in helping keep channels open as the regime blocked them, and they spread the word about functioning proxy portals. Hackers also reportedly took down Mr. Ahmadinejad's Web site in an act of cyberdisobedience. (*Washington Times*, 2009)

Morozov argued that even if Iranians were highly computer literate, the people in the West who followed their actions were less sophisticated. As a result, the challenges facing the protestors were exacerbated by the interventions of international youth audiences who did not understand the nature of the political space that Twitter provided. Morozov thought that international social media users unwittingly helped the Ahmadinejad government, and that subsequently social media were of more value to international news agencies than they had been to the protestors. Morozov condemned 'slactivists' (social networkers who did more harm than good) because they failed to understand the industrial and political realities that underpinned how social media worked in Iran. Slactivist's didn't really try to cultivate deep social relations with the protestors on the ground, and therefore could not see that social media were more valuable to Western journalists than the young Iranians who tried to stay one step ahead of the Basij.[3] Morozov thought local bloggers made life easier for foreign correspondents – blogs helped journalists to affect an ear to the ground. Twitter was better still, slicing through the fat of the blogosphere to the meat of what was happening. Things were harder for the protesters. The trouble was that Ahmadinejad had Twitter too, and distant digital supporters of the protest actually helped make the network a surveillance tool. Liking a Facebook page or retweeting a protestor placed that person on the authorities' radar. 'Denial of service' attacks on official Iranian websites slowed down the whole national system. So if the students were using social media to organise, they suffered too (Morozov, 2009).

Moving on to 2011's Arab Spring, Jack Bratich argued that close analysis of the role that social media played in Egyptian activism only underlined their 'containing' power. His work on this topic is important because his point was that the images which most television audiences saw around the ouster of Mubarak misrepresented a true picture of who the real power brokers in the event where. Bratich (2011) hinged his argument on the story of how young Egyptian Google executive Wael Ghonim emerged as the face of youthful resistance to Mubarak. *Time* magazine celebrated Ghonim as a 'typical' young Egyptian who had cleverly used social media to capture the sentiments of his generation.

> Wael Ghonim embodies the youth who constitute the majority of Egyptian society – a young man who excelled and became a Google executive but, as with many of his generation, remained apolitical due to loss of hope that things could change in a society permeated for decades with a culture of fear. Over the past few years, Wael, 30, began working outside the box to make his peers understand that only their unstoppable people power could effect real change. He quickly grasped that social media, notably Facebook, were emerging as the most powerful communication tools to mobilize and develop ideas. (Elbaradei, 2011)

Bratich countered that Ghomin's fame did not depend on his access to social media; it depended on his access to social media *administrators*. This become clear when considering how Facebook lent Ghonim unprecedented support:

> When his first page was shut down for not using a proper email, he was given a loophole to overcome the impasse by Richard Allan, Facebook's director of policy for Europe. Allan also noted that Facebook 'put all the key pages into special protection' so that they would not be closed down by Mubarak's forces. The mysterious Ghonim admitted that he had an 'open line' of communication with Facebook throughout the 18 days of the uprising. While many can become friends on Facebook, few can be friends *with* Facebook á la Ghonim. (Bratich, 2011)

Bratich's point was that Wael Ghonim's apparently spontaneous emergence as the face of a grassroots youth protests was in every respect an illusion. Facebook was his 'rhythm section'. He did not operate 'outside the box', because 'the box' was using Facebook and the like to reconfigure powerful new alliances between media and political power. Ghonim's access to Facebook administrators was no accident; it was the end result of deliberate US-based efforts to find ways of using social media as a foreign-policy tool. The sort of advice available to people like Ghomin was there because of the Alliance of Youth Movements (AYM), the brainchild of Google executive Jared Cohen. While working for the US State Department, Cohen had founded the AYM with the help of his employer, the Obama administration, MTV, NBC, CNN, Google and Facebook. The operation provided 'free' advice on using social media to organise grassroots movements, including tips on how to circumvent official efforts to block online actions. Ghonim was a beneficiary of this operation (Bratich, 2011).

Bratich painted the impression of Egyptian youth proactively, using social media to assemble into a self-directed political force as a myth disguising an ingenious new blend of state and corporate power. The story of Egypt's Facebook-driven youth revolt was fundamentally about the media practices of media businesses and governments. If Ghonim indicated anything, it was the 'containing' power of media culture. Powerful new forms of counter-insurgency were possible because social media disguised terrifyingly complex partnerships between digital media businesses and the US military–industrial complex. Together, new media, old media and the state created the impression that grassroots movements were spontaneous, when in fact organisations like Google were working with the US State Department and many other partners to foster dissent in the right places. In this respect, Bratich's study confirmed Thompson's early suspicion that the main effect of media industries was their power to reconcile young people with the view that existing corporate media structures were the only viable means of public expression.

Looking at academic studies on social media and dissent, two things become apparent. First, scholars have taken on board Thompson's challenge to be very specific when writing the particular histories of media insurrections. Second, if we look at Bratich's rich account, it is clear that it is no longer possible to write material histories of dissent without considering how a variety of media practices from the state and ordinary users intervene in the historical unrolling of media events. The difference here is that where, for Thompson, culture was a force that either disguised or revealed real exploitation, studies on social media and dissent show how media practices are themselves exploitative. They are part and parcel of the political and economic inequalities that drive dissent. Thompson was ultimately interested in how the organisation of labour affected consciousness. Often, using social media is work that produces profit. Morozov warned that enthusiasm for the democratic potential of Twitter ignored how the technology made life easier for news agencies. Social networking created new means of exploitation, where young people literally worked for free for news organisations that could not penetrate events in Iran. The idea of free labour is one of the key points of misrecognition that others feel is endemic in digital media. Social networks privatise the profits of common creativity; young people save media organisations costs by making content, then signing over the rights to that content for free, which organisations like Google then sell to advertisers (van Dijck, 2009). Bratich painted a more sinister picture still: social media were making activists in the Middle East de facto undercover agents for the US State Department.

But something is missing from this picture. Thompson was not a relentless pessimist. He believed that working-class history proved that radical social change is possible. Moreover, he believed two other things that are significant when reflecting on youth, social media and dissent. First, he was convinced the story of the working class was incomplete without considering how ephemeral, unconsidered, ill-considered and even reactionary movements eventually helped the working class to think of itself as the working class:

> I am seeking to rescue the poor stockinger, the luddite cropper, the obsolete hand weave loomer, the utopian artisan, even the deluded follower of Joanne Southcote from the enormous condescension of posterity. Their crafts and traditions may have been dying. Their hostility to the new industrialism may have been backward-looking. Their communitarian ideas may have been fantasies. Their insurrectionist conspiracies may have been foolhardy. But they lived through these times of acute social disturbance, and we did not. Their aspirations were valid in terms of their own experience. (Thompson, 1963: 12–13)

Given this quote, it is reasonable to assume that Thompson would have cautioned against dismissing those ordinary young people who did feel empowered by social media: 'Their aspirations were valid in terms of their own experience' (1963: 13). Had he been writing today, Thompson would perhaps have been less condemnatory of 'slactivists', or those who believed in Wael Ghonim. Even if slactivists caused more harm than good, they still announced the sentiment that young people should care about their peers in distant cultures. Suppose Laurie Penny's account was an empirical misrepresentation of how Twitter worked most of the time in 2010; this would not alter the fact that the idea that young people could use social media to effect change became a public idea. Comparing Thompson's treatment of Methodism with Bratich's exemplary work on Facebook and Egyptian youth, the lesson of the former for the latter is that even if events in Egypt were engineered to further the interests of a new digital media/ military–industrial complex, we can't be sure that this is all that happened.

CASE STUDY: REGIONAL NEWS, DIGITAL MEDIA AND YOUTH

From this perspective, one of the problems in using Moldova, Iran and the Arab Spring to make general judgements on the politics of digital activism is that the hopes of the protestors were highly ambitious, and the outcomes of their actions would play out in numerous ways over years rather than months. An alternative way to reflect on how young people and social media change society is to look at smaller-scale examples, where digital activism can be viewed from a longer historical perspective. This is the value of the Rachel Hoffman case, as a story that could be viewed within a longer view of journalism history, and engages with Thompson's observations about the power of media systems to absorb any potential criticisms by making it appear that they are the only places where social reality can be expressed, largely under organisational arrangements that are already in place.

Hoffman was a 22-year-old Florida State University alumnus and police informer who was murdered during a botched police drug sting in 2009. Hoffman had been arrested for drug possession, and agreed to become a police informant as part of a plea-bargain deal. She was sent to buy drugs from two suspected deal- ers, but during the operation her handlers lost track of her movements. Hoffman was shot dead. Florida's *Tallahassee Democrat* (*TD*) used social networking to draw the attention of local students to the case. The newspaper believed that the story would appeal to the city's student community; Hoffman was one of their own, and a tale of how recreational drug use had ended in tragedy was likely to resonate (Thompson, 2009). For the *TD*, the story offered access to a student reading audience that had been difficult for them to penetrate. Sensing an opportunity, its journalists established a website for the story (Rachel Hoffman Case, 2009a), accompanied by a Facebook page (Rachel Hoffman Case2009b), YouTube channel (RachelHoffmancase's Channel, 2009d) and Twitter feed (Rachel Hoffman Case, 2009c).

Hoffman's story put a twist on Thompson's approach to media criticism. On the one hand, it could be seen as an example of 'containment', where the desire for justice suited commercial needs. On the other, it was an example of how the combination of traditional journalism, social media and community outrage at an incident that seemed a clear injustice did combine to make a substantial change to the organisation of community life. It thus invites us to consider if new combinations of media forms and community organisation do create situa- tions where commercial media can be the vehicles for social justice.

This story exemplified how social media extend Thompson's interests by affecting the production of spaces where contradictory forces and histories meet one another, facilitating, among other things, new alliances that can produce change, given compelling circumstances where material conditions and forms of expression work hand in hand. The expression of outrage felt by local students over Hoffman's death was, in many ways, expressible because it suited the goals of the local press, and also suited their access to social media and the muckraking tradition that has been influential in American journalism for over a century.

This is not a conspiratorial take on media power; it is an empirical one: beneath the Methodist case study was the idea that a cultural practice designed with an ostensibly apolitical purpose in mind ended up having effects that were deeply political; in this case, religion and concern for the soul in the next world eventually had an influence on industrial social relations. The Hoffman case is similar in so far as we see how a story motivated by commercial interests affected community activism. Added here, however, is an example of how this was related to media-created spaces, as they come to be through the interplay of production conventions and technologies. This 'new' strategy was consistent with the history of American journalism, particularly in the influence that the muckraking era continues to exert over how journalists understand their role as social commentators. The Hoffman story consequently affords reflection on how 'old' and 'new' combine in digital production.

'Muckraking' was a style of magazine journalism dedicated to exposing cor- porate and political corruption that became hugely popular in the period 1901–12 (Feldstein, 2006; Reaves, 1984; Stein, 1979). During this time, magazines such as *McLures*, *Harper's Weekly*, *Arena* and *Lady's Home Journal* (Thornton, 1995) featured exposes of corporate excess, government corruption and the plight of working people forced to live and work in squalid urban conditions. President Theodore Roosevelt coined the term 'muckraking' in 1906, when criticising what he saw as the fanatical pursuit of political 'dirt' regardless of the consequences for the country (Feldstein, 2006). However, histories of muckraking have also suggested that it was inspired by commercial ambitions to attract readers. The *TD*'s strategy came from the same combination of conscience and commerce.

Although the muckrakers were as publicly zealous as Johanna Southcote had been about chasing down corruption, the motivations for their actions is a matter of controversy. They were certainly encouraged by a large urban reading public willing to buy scandal. It has been suggested that muckraking was simply a device to generate new interests, following a period where the same magazines had relied on stories about the success of the very business entrepreneurs that they now attacked (Endres, 1978). The extent to which these writers really wanted to reform anything has been questioned (Reaves, 1984), and doubts have also been cast over whether or not the public read these stories for political reasons (Thornton, 1995). At any rate, the muckraking era is deemed to have ended with the election of Woodrow Wilson and the collapse of the Socialist Party of America as a meaningful political force in 1912. Nevertheless, this period provoked a debate on public-interest journalism that shaped how investigative journalism is understood (e.g. Fee, 2005), and the Hoffman story inherited this history. It is not actually possible to fix the meaning of what this case study was 'about' by attributing it to conscious professional motives or the natural outcomes of social media – and that is the point about understanding influence historically.

It is no real surprise to find that the *TD*'s main webpage provides an archive of stories on the Hoffman case and a forum for those who want to discuss it – for a price (The Rachel Hoffman Case, 2009a). The gateway page featured a well-organised introduction to the story, its issues and why it mattered vis-à-vis broader themes of law and social justice. The site was divided into themes: What had happened? Who was responsible? What were the legal arguments surrounding the trials of the alleged murderers? How should the police treat informants. What duty of care do they have to them? However, as soon as a reader clicked on one of these links to discover more, he or she was directed to a payment page, and given the option of either subscribing to the *TD* for a day or a month, at a cost of $2 or $9.95 respectively.

Having said this, the *TD*'s championing of the Hoffman cause was not a case of simple, cynical manipulation. Those who marched for 'Rachel's Law' did understand the issues at stake (unlike the working classes who protested against the Papacy in the late seventeenth century without knowing that they were protesting against Catholicism) and the *TD*'s turn to social media was partly reactive. Pre-trial motions in the prosecutions of the accused killers sealed official evidence, so the police could give no details to reporters. It was only then that local journalists turned to memorial Facebook pages that Hoffman's friends had already established to glean new angles on the story. *TD*'s strategy thus capitalised on things that local students were already doing with social networking

(Thompson, 2009). Tallahassee's digital youth audience became 'real' in a rally at the headquarters of the Florida legislature in May 2009 in favour of 'Rachel's Law'. This community presented itself as a community by wearing the colour purple, together with memorial T-shirts. Their presence contributed to the passage of the law, and the disciplinary action against some of the officers involved in the debacle. The rally showed how muckraking has continued as an idea in public journalism, which also aspires to make communities around particular issues with the goal of affecting change (Fee, 2005).

The Hoffman story underlines the contention that we can find the roots of today's media issues in the nineteenth century. *TD* journalists saw the Hoffman case as an opportunity to reach young readers, but this is an offshoot of the fact that regional news has always been challenged by the tendency towards national consciousness, first fostered by the railroad and telegraph (Feldstein, 2006). More positively, their pursuit of the Hoffman case reflected many 'muckraking' qualities: the determination to expose particular cases of injustice with the goal of attracting a paying audience *and* affecting social change. In this sense, we cannot tell how this is about youth and technology without asking how the story was also about the evolution of a genre which, for all the controversies surrounding it, continues to exert an influence over American journalism and academic writing on the same.

CONCLUSION: WHY HISTORY NEEDS MEDIA STUDIES

The *TD*'s treatment of the Hoffman story and the consequences that followed reminds us that new media practices have histories, but also underlines the case that new media technologies do have identifiable social effects in so far as they help determine the exact form that political action spaces take on. For this reason, the way that the Hoffman tragedy was transformed into a media event which helped social activists achieve their goals connects the matter of what social media do to social histories of dissent, also demonstrating how media have become part of that history.

The Hoffman case became a news story because of traditions in American journalism, general commercial challenges directed at regional journalism, and students' penchant for social networking. The key to the Hoffman case was *interaction* between new technologies, traditional production and business practices and localised, experience-based, *politicisable* sentiments. The story told how media technologies become effective when they connect existing people and social trends into new coalitions. Starting with its understanding of the issues that young people cared about, and the media they tended to connect with, the *TD* built a movement and an audience by deploying interlocking digital resources.

The key here is to understand that the *TD* did much more than simply address social groups that already existed. Where we might assume that a regional paper speaks to (and for) an existing geographic community, digital regional journalism makes communities by connecting people, organisations and businesses that are *not* already in touch; its main power lies in the capacity to make a space for public action. Here, media become historical drivers, constituent elements in change. This is true everywhere: Tallahassee, Cairo, Chişinău, London or Tehran.

The common issue here is how communication makes coalitions; just as, according to E. P. Thompson (1963), talking about salvation in public eventually led to agitating for the rights of the working poor. Technologies and their social uses are indivisible from the analysis of dissent, conflict and change that has always fascinated political historians. The role that social networking played in London, Iran, Egypt and Moldova can be disputed, but the fact that Twitter and the like will factor in how those events are remembered, and how they affect the future, cannot. This is better appreciated by considering communications technologies as historical practices.

Having said this, when the US Library of Congress announced in April 2010 that it had began to compile a Twitter archive, it also announced, in effect, that history was no longer possible without media history:

> Even though tweets, as messages on Twitter are called, can only be 140 characters long, the amount of information to archive is significant. There are 50 million tweets per day and the total number of tweets already number well into the billions. The Library of Congress plans to focus on the 'scholarly and research implications of the acquisition.' Certainly the daily thoughts of millions of people worldwide would make an excellent source of sociological information. (Hope, 2010)

There are dangers in endeavours like this that show why history now needs media studies. Recognising that it is impossible to transform 50 million daily tweets into a manageable research tool, the Library of Congress stated its intention to focus on those of clear historical significance – like President Obama's Twitter announcement of his 2008 election victory (Hope, 2010). Clearly, this raises again the question of how scholars make judgements about what things are worth remembering, but there is an added technological and sociological component here, where we must question how tweets gain public attention in the first place, before we consider if they are worth preserving.

Media scholars have complained that historians tend to regard media as things that *register* historical events instead of phenomena that *participate* and *influence* them (O'Malley, 2002). When the histories of the Arab Spring are written, they will have to include what media did and what people *thought* media did because, as projects like the Library of Congress Twitter archive show, the presence of media also affects the accounts on which future historians will base their judgments. To put things another way, media affect how history creates the reality of the past.

This strengthens the case for seeing history and media studies as cognate because both are interested in how competing narratives about social reality drive political conflicts. James Curran (2002) noted that most media scholars drew on stories about the genesis of social conflicts; particularly relevant here is his comparison between radical and populist histories, where some authors concentrate on how capitalism consistently derails media's capacity for democratisation, while others prefer to detail how ordinary people have always used popular culture to foster their own interests. According to O'Malley (2002), media studies and history had largely failed to explore common ground because the in the 1960s, scholars in the former thought their colleagues in the latter spent too little time thinking about what history is for. Transparently, this criticism could not be directed at E. P. Thompson. However, in the opposite direction, where Thompson warned in 1963 that media scholars had to pay attention to history, it is also true that historians of popular dissent have to pay attention to how media industries, technologies and practices give voice to that dissent. This said, appreciating the historical dimensions of studying media influence places us in a position to consider how technologies do play a distinct role in influencing history and society. The next chapter explores this distinct influence in relation to debates over youth, international media and propaganda.

CHAPTER SUMMARY

The power of media technology can only be properly evaluated if it is historicised in the history of culture, power and conflict. To study media technologies is to study the history of peoples and media practices. Social networking seems to have ushered in a new era of global youth activism, where youth groups are quite deliberately seeking to intervene in national politics, strengthening their hand by using Twitter, Facebook and the like to attract global attention. The nature and significance of these movements has to be assessed in the context of earlier forms of popular dissent. Seeing media studies and history as cognate disciplines helps us to explain the impact of media technologies while avoiding the error of technological determinism: thinking that new technologies have the power to change the world simply because of their technical capacity to conquer space and time (Williams, 1974). We need to understand how media studies and history are related before we can identify the distinct contributions that new media forms make to social change – a question taken up in the next chapter on youth and Chinese media.

NOTES

1 Protesters attacked the Treasury building and a Royal car carrying Prince Charles and Camilla Parker-Bowles to the theatre. Eighteen-year old Edward Woollard was jailed for 32 months for throwing a fire extinguisher from the top of a building, narrowly missing a police officer.

2 'Kettling' was a police tactic that involved confining protestors in a small pocket of space for prolonged periods of time.

3 An Iranian militia group who conducted a series of attacks against protesters.

4

UNDERSTANDING GLOBAL MEDIA INDUSTRIES: CHINA, REALITY TELEVISION AND MEDIA GOVERNANCE

Research question.
Why are reality talent shows so successful and controversial in China?

Underlying question about media influence.
What does the international flow of media content have to do with international politics and national identity?

Relevant literature.
Audience theory, studies of media and cultural imperialism, Chinese Media Studies

Exemplifying case study.
Super Girl: Why so popular with audiences? Why so unpopular with the state? Why did the state keep changing its mind?

Outcomes.
Audience participation in *Super Girl* reflects the subtleties of a state-managed experiment in liberalised media policy, allowed by convergent media platforms

Lessons for understanding media influence.
Super Girl explains why the way audiences consume media might be more significant than how they interpret the meaning of media content

Global popular media – blockbuster movies, children's cartoons, prime-time soaps, reality television and the like – have worried nation states for a long time now. The controversies that broke out around the spectacular success of reality talent shows in China were the latest incarnation of fears about what happens when stories, ideas and images from one culture become popular in another. The fear has been that those ideas and images might also popularise the values of the authoring culture, and this is a big problem when content circulates between countries that have opposing political views.

So when reality talent shows like *Super Girl* were enthusiastically received by young Chinese audiences, they also triggered a set of longstanding fears about the power of Western media content to undermine national identities in other parts of the world. This presents an opportunity to reflect on why global popular culture can be conceived in political terms, as outlined in the literature on cultural imperialism. It also allows us to explore how the effects of global media vary according to how audiences interpret and use them – a question that is especially interesting given the size and complexity of Chinese audiences. At the end of this chapter you will understand why apparently trivial media content can assume intense importance in the world of international relations, how global media depend on a series of complex negotiations between businesses and governments, and how audience researchers' conception of media influence has changed over the last century.

WHY REALITY TELEVISION IS POLITICAL

In 2011, China's state media regulator decided to ban *Super Girl*, a *Pop Idol*-style television show, because it was too long. Many suspected ulterior political motives. Developed by the semi-autonomous Hunan Satellite Television (HSTV), some believed the regulator envied the show's enormous youth audience – far bigger than any drawn by fare from official state channels. Others argued the objections were ideological, that official opinion regarded *Super Girl* as a vulgar celebration of consumerist individualism that was anathema to the ideals of the state. Certainly, HSTV responded as if the latter were true. It promised to replace the show with more edifying alternatives, including a show on how to do the housework properly (Bristow, 2011).

At face value, this was an especially clear example of the political fears that popular culture causes, especially when it is popular with the young. When 2007 winner Yang Lei delivered a giggling performance of 'America the Beautiful' (freeflowing-wind, 2008), it was tempting to see this as a triumph for Western commercial television in an ideological media battle against China that has been waged since 1949. Perhaps this is why HSTV decided effectively to tell budding Yang Leis to shelve their pop-star dreams and get on with the ironing. Certainly, *Super Girl* showed the interactive effects of content and technology. Fears about the implicit messages of popular culture become acute when that content is globally distributed.

However, a closer examination of the *Super Girl* case – the things that made it possible within China's media system, that factors that made it wildly popular among young audiences, and crucially the interactions between the needs of audiences, the state and media industries – shows that global media are about much more than ideology. Indeed, the show's story offers the tantalising possibility that the question of what young people think about the media they consume may be far less important than we often imagine it to be. Certainly, *Super Girl* dramatised changing modes of international media management, becoming popular in a period when China was re-creating itself as a global media power. To explain why *Super Girl* was special, we need to consider how reality music television fits within literature on propaganda, global media and audiences.

SUPER GIRL: ACADEMIC CONTEXT

The topic of social media and youth activism indicates that media technologies affect society by articulating groups of people to the goals of media organisations. This chapter uses this idea to explain how global media industries attract youthful audiences while negotiating the political sensitivities of different cultures, paying special attention to the success of international reality television formats. The recent Chinese experience of reality television suggests that media technologies have international effects when they allow governments and businesses to appropriate the everyday routines of media users. In China, changing technologies, genres, business models and political philosophies have allowed the state and media industries to capitalise on the pleasures young audiences find in participatory media events. The topic of Chinese reality television therefore offers a media technology perspective on how ordinary people make history; in this case, how young Chinese television audiences complete the circuit of global media when they vote for their favourite reality stars by text message. Such 'trivial' actions in fact reconcile a number of historical tensions between the Chinese state and Western media formats.

This argument is illustrated by using Chinese media studies and audience theory to explain *Super Girl*'s notoriety. Enormously popular among young audiences, *Super Girl* almost immediately provoked the wrath of state broadcaster China Central Television (CCTV) and the State Administration for Radio, Film and Television (SARTF), who were both deeply suspicious – in their public statements, at least – about the moral damage inflicted by global reality-television formats (Zhong, 2007). Despite its eventual demise, the show initially survived because it was an important testing ground for new methods of state-run, business-friendly media management (Zhong, 2007, 2010; Huang and Chitty, 2009). Here, the habits of its fans were a key factor. Scholars agree that the practice of voting by text message, and organising events that encouraged others to do the same, was connected to youthful desires to participate in society, and the ambition of the state and business to channel that desire in functionalist directions (Zhong, 2007; Huang and Chitty, 2009).

This was significant in a country where youth have always been the vanguard of political change (Weber, 2008), where young people, to some eyes, have brokered a complex deal with the state over social freedom (Donald, 2011), and where changing media business arrangements, afforded by convergent media platforms, provide political spaces where new forms of public expression can be tolerated. Scholars have disagreed on the nature of *Super Girl*'s political impact, but agree that, whatever its outcomes were, the meaning of China's complex media economy is ultimately secured in the things that ordinary people do when they want to be entertained (Yu, 2011). Thus, *Super Girl* represents the argument that media power only becomes real when it is lived by its audience.

Super Girl is an interesting case study in the nature of international media power because it marked a shift from conflict to cooperation in relations between China and commercial media. It was a multimedia event, unprecedented in Chinese television history, that forged strategic partnerships between parties who otherwise held significant political differences. Exploring how these partnerships came about connects *Super Girl*, reality television and Chinese youth with the history of thought on propaganda, transnational media and the effects of media practices that turn publics into media audiences. *Super Girl* was an index of how audience theory and Chinese media studies interact to produce new perspectives on how power flows through international media circuits where audiences are participants. To make this case this chapter:

- explains how the *Super Girl* phenomenon came to be (paying particular attention to the work of Yong Zhong on the political economy of Chinese television);

- frames the show as a case study in why Chinese media studies is breaking new ground in conceiving media power (with a special focus on Haiqing Yu's work on 'anti-functionalist' power);

- contextualises this discussion in the history of research on propaganda and the role that music television has played in that history;

- explains why *Super Girl* develops audience theory by encouraging a focus on audience habits (as opposed to behaviours, beliefs and/or performances).

THE *SUPER GIRL* STORY

Super Girl is a remarkable success story from a unique television operation. The regional station Hunan Satellite Television (HSTV) commissioned the show in 2004, as part of its efforts to gain a foothold in a market dominated by CCTV, the main state-owned operation in China (Zhong, 2010). Since then, HSTV and *Super Girl* have embodied new forms of market-friendly state media power. In its first season, *Super Girl* drew 150,000 contestants, and captivated an enormous audience whose attention was 'sold' to advertisers at a record rate (Zhong, 2007). When HSTV's website proclaimed that the original show, which ran from 2004 to 2006, was the most successful Chinese television programme ever – being viewed by over 400 million people, who cast somewhere in the region of 60 million mobile-phone text votes during the period (Hunan TV, 2007) – it was actually being extremely modest about how much of a media landmark *Super Girl* was. *Super Girl* was nothing less than a paradigm of how internationally recognisable media formats achieve success by negotiating political challenges peculiar to specific markets.

The show exhibited the distinct power of media technologies in two respects. First, multiple-media platforms complicated production of the event by introducing an ever-growing number of stakeholders into the mix. *Super Girl* ended up arbitrating between the state and the television, mobile phone and online media industries. Second, technology helped antagonistic bodies to get along by creating an agnostic space that could accommodate conflicting interests. *Super Girl* was a fascinating exercise in détente, brokered because the technological architecture of reality television allows for the production of depoliticised action spaces, which are attractive to the government and private business interests alike as China promotes state interests by engaging with media markets.

This diplomacy was not always successful; in 2006 *Super Girl* was castigated by CCTV for morally corrupting young Chinese audiences (Zhong, 2010). However, this controversy was not just about the show or reality television, but also the media business arrangements that made it possible. Since 1989, China has sought to 'rebrand' itself by engaging with international commercial media on its own political terms. However, the success of this operation has varied, because it always demands some compromise. *Super Girl* is the progeny of an experiment in centrally controlled marketised media practices. The intentions and consequences of these practices are difficult to judge because they are subject to constant negotiations between a changing cast of stakeholders, where no one has absolute power to impose their view of what 'proper' Chinese entertainment should be in the People's Republic of China (Zhong, 2010). This fluidity, however, is not a threat to the state, in any simple sense.

This is illustrated by the fact that, in 2011, the Chinese online portal television company PPTV Live announced it was to revive *Super Girl* through the website kuainv.pptv.com, partnered by HSTV and computer company EE Media. The website offered viewers 24-hour access to the performers on PC, iPad and mobile phone. The resurrection of the show online, in a modified form, illustrated the range of creative options afforded in a commercialised media market where content must still be controlled by the state, and producers are obliged to reflect national values. In China, the questions of what content is, how control works and what values are are all in flux (Zhong, 2010). Understanding *Super Girl*'s fate means moving beyond simple 'top-down' models of media power.

HUNAN SATELLITE TELEVISION

Ironically, *Super Girl* was only controversial *to* the state because of the autonomy that HSTV had been granted *by* the state. HSTV could pursue a more aggressive commercial policy because although it was 'state owned', inasmuch as its largest stakeholder was the Provincial Radio TV Bureau (PRTVB), 79 per cent of shares are held by private equity interests and individual investors. Subsequently, Yong Zhong used the show as the basis for his analysis of recent development in Chinese media industries (2007, 2010). Zhong notes that *Super Girl*'s popularity prompted CCTV, 'the primary mouthpiece of the Party State'

(2010: 653), to convene a summit with propaganda officials, where the show was condemned as 'evil' and where the state broadcaster determined to start its own talent show called *Dream China* as a better reflection of 'healthy' social values. CCTV executives likened *Super Girl* to the Japanese attack on Pearl Harbor. Such fears became policy matters in 2007, when the State Administration of Radio, Film and Television limited, by statute, the production of reality shows to one per broadcaster per year, and to prohibit the telecasting of live audience events without the approval of that office (Zhong, 2010).

Zhong believed that *Super Girl* was controversial because it created a space in which its youthful audience could imagine what it would be like to have more of a say in public matters (2007). Administratively, however, this was the inadvertent outcome of a planned experiment where HSTV was allowed to function as a commercial venture with less formalised relations with the state than is typical in Chinese television. The first point that Zhong makes is that the rapid growth of Chinese television means that regulation is largely reactive. The fundamental driving force behind television policy is China's capacity to use the medium as part of a multi-platform device to reach huge national and international audiences. Questions of content and control are often quite deliberately considered after the fact. CCTV is a state-owned enterprise, governed by a political appointee from the State Administration of Radio, Television and Film, that has evolved into a sophisticated, vertically integrated business. Its 17 channels broadcast in English, Spanish, French and numerous Chinese dialects to 120 countries (Zhong, 2010). Its production capacities include film studios, equipment-leasing companies, media-planning organisations, transport services and even a theme park. Zhong stressed that such a complex operation demands a dispersed 'leadership' model, since it depends on a fine division of labour. Broadly speaking, what this means is that while the bottom line remains political, daily operations separate political leadership and commercial development for the sake of broadening China's international media footprint.

As such, the 'turmoil' around *Super Girl* was probably predictable. According to Zhong (2010), the fuss around the show overestimated the scale of the policy challenge it posed. HTSV's subversive power was always more theoretical than actual because of the nuanced nature of state ownership in China's liberalised media economy. Although the majority of HSTV shareholders are not state bodies, Zhong pointed out that many of these companies are still likely to have their own formal arrangements with the state. Shareholders could theoretically unite against the PRTVB, but in practice it would be near impossible to coordinate such a diverse range of interests to agree on coherent action against state power (Zhong, 2010). Zhong's argument was supported by HSTV's quick action to counter the claim that *Super Girl* was a corrosive influence by ensuring, for example, that auditions were held outside of school hours to discourage truancy. So the *Super Girl* controversy only happened because of a state-organised experiment in commercial broadcasting and proved, if anything, the state's ongoing capacity to rein liberalised media relations in and out as it searched for a balance between political principle and audience reach. The controversy was, in this respect, an exercise in acceptable chaos.

CHINESE MEDIA STUDIES AND YOUTH

The unique nature of media management in China is one reason why Chinese media studies has emerged as a discipline in its own right. It is possible that CCTV's alarmist warnings about the insidious implicit messages of *Super Girl* were, in fact, a canny strategy using the language of propaganda to protect market share in an increasingly competitive television market that sought to profit from the vast opportunities afforded by Chinese-speaking audiences. At any rate, it is certainly true that Chinese media, society and political culture are too complicated to be explained by propaganda models (Khoo, 2011). Yet to make this case, we have to explain what these models are, why Chinese media scholars have rejected them and why this theme matters to media studies in general.

The temptation to think of China simply in terms of the Chinese Communist Party's (CCP) ambition to control public discourse reflects the relative lack of research on the empirical details of how media industries actually work on the ground (Yu, 2011). According to Haiqin Yu, China is a paradigm of the general idea that 'state control' cannot be explained by notions of functionalism, centrism and spectacularism: functionalism being the idea that media are always motivated toward the preservation of a pre-existing social balance; centrism being the idea that this preservation is the simple projection of the interests of those already in power; and that these processes are best addressed in the study of major media events, such as the Olympics (spectacularism). Eventually, this paradigm is about audiences and everyday life, because the 'propaganda' focus also ignores how mobile media count in the things ordinary Chinese people do to make their lives feel better in ordinary places like 'railway stations, subways, taxis, worksites, dormitories and tourist zones' (Yu, 2011: 71). Which is not to say the power of the state is simply there for audiences to take or leave. For Yu, Chinese state media policy works because it *does not* depend on an immutable party line. The first return of *Super Girl* online showed official opinions wavered, partly because the show was an enormous hit and its appeal could not be denied.

China's media policy is better understood as an intricate balancing act where forces that *could* be in conflict at least find points of agreement in daily media operations where pragmatic concerns place political ones at a distance. Before we get to media policy, Olivia Khoo points out that we have to recognise China as a multicultural society that has experienced enormous shifts in its political structure, such that matters of 'national interest' are subject to negotiation:

> Think outside the nation state idea and think instead of compound states, including the 'one-nation two systems' schema applied to Hong Kong's return to China, or as a way of thinking through China's relationship to Taiwan or Tibet or Xinjiang – that is, having consideration of minorities within, and of members peripheral or external to, a nation state. (Khoo, 2011: 134)

Within these general conditions, Stephanie Donald (2011) argued that young Chinese audiences have also brokered a complex 'deal' with the state, where the desire for change is tempered with the recognition that Chinese youths have many privileges that their parents did not enjoy. This 'deal' announced itself in global pro-state demonstrations by Chinese students studying in Europe, the US and Australia. Donald notes the incredulity Western commentators have shown towards the fact that exposure to Western media, and indeed Western media studies, has encouraged overseas Chinese youth to become more nationalistic, as opposed to more resistive to the power of the CCP.

> Youth alienation and dissent exists, but the overwhelming result of a carefully managed media economy is just that; a managed system with reasonable acceptance of the rules as a fair price of national growth and wealth-creation. Students overseas are precisely the contingent that has benefitted from new wealth. (Donald, 2011: 60)

The conclusion from all of this is that beneath the alarmist rhetoric about *Super Girl* anarchy there was a more complicated debate about the political role of popular culture, where the state stood to profit from the chaos it publicly condemned. To appreciate this, we need to explore how politics moves from propaganda to entertainment, and how music television has served as a medium for this transition.

PROPAGANDA: FROM PERSUASION TO MTV

Super Girl was an exercise in articulating an international genre and twenty-first-century Chinese politics. Analysing international media influence involves three things: considering the global flow of technology, content and ideas; analysing how these flows are influenced by negotiations between media business, national governments and media audiences; and, crucially, trying to understand how these processes work as a whole. The topic of how young people in China engage with music television demonstrates that 'globalization and the "question of the transnational" go beyond the theoretical reach and scope of the old imperialism theory, thus forcing us to think of a new fabric of actors and territories, of contradictions and conflicts' (Khoo, 2011: 282).

'Going beyond old imperialism theory' means appreciating how *Super Girl* sits at the end of a historical trajectory, where media, technology and politics interact to move from a conflict to cooperation model of international communication that involves audiences in the production of the events they behold. The history, and the model, can be mapped in the following way. Beginning with propaganda, and American efforts to foster discontent among Chinese audiences and the socialist world in general, it moves into the politicisation of popular culture as a tool of cultural imperialism, where 'persuasion' came wrapped in the guise of entertainment, with the Disney corporation as an early example. The model then moves towards music and television, as MTV inherits the Disney mantle in Asia, and acknowledges how the MTV experience in China signalled a sea change, as the Chinese state sought to further national goals by engaging with marketisation. Finally, it shows how the mechanics of reality music television create a politically agnostic space, where different groups can interact without having to reference the political differences that continue to divide them.

We can explain this transition by thinking about an artefact from South Korea. An innocuous scrap of paper sits in a glass case in Seoul's Korean War Museum. On it, a cartoon: Joseph Stalin is pushing Mao Tse-Tung; Mao, in turn, is pushing a Chinese soldier toward the flames of the Korean War. The message, dropped onto Chinese troops sometime between 1950 and 1953, is that they are fighting for Stalin. The intention of the message was to dismiss the idea that their sacrifices were for their own people. The leaflet is a testament that there was a time when the US did try to turn Chinese people against communism. According to Noam Chomsky (1997), anti-communism was a founding principle of the US media system that sought to undermine socialism wherever it threatened to blossom, at home or abroad. In *Manufacturing Consent* (1988), Edward Herman and Chomsky argued that anti-communism was a fifth 'filter' in a 'propaganda model' where the US news media systematically championed capitalist free-market principles in their coverage of international politics. This was not because media companies represented big business; it was because they were big business:

> In the cases of NBC and the Group W television and cable systems, their respective parent, G.E. and Westinghouse, are themselves mainstream corporate giants, with boards of directors that are dominated by corporate and banking executives. (1988: 8)

So, when CCTV and SARFT executives argued that *Super Girl* was an insidious plot to overthrow party principles, they would have found much in Western political economies of media to support their case. After 1945, new American transnational media set out to 'promote ... a capitalist 'American way of life' ... The result was an 'electronic invitation', especially in the global South, which threatened to undermine traditional cultures and emphasize consumerism at the expense of community values' (Thussu, 2006: 48). Here, entertainment was quickly deployed in place of overt propaganda because persuasive messages were more effective when they didn't look like persuasive messages. Dorfman and Mattelart's study of comic books in Latin America concluded that Disney was an innovator in the field:

> Even if some foreign country like Cuba or Vietnam should dare to enter into open conflict with the United States ... Disney makes them run a gauntlet of magazines. There are two forms of killing; by machine gun and saccharine ... According to Disney, underdeveloped peoples are like children, to be treated as such, and if they don't accept this definition of themselves, they should have their pants taken down and given a good spanking. (1984: 48)

MTV: FROM CONFLICT TO COOPERATION

By the 1990s, it seemed as if MTV was doing the same thing (Banks, 1997). Capitalising on the opportunities created by the international spread of cable television and global deregulatory sympathies, MTV stood as the (then) latest incarnation of cultural imperialism, consisting overwhelmingly of American and British artists or of international artists who mimic American styles. Offered via Star TV to over 40 countries, the channel favoured Western performers, attracted substantial advertising revenue from companies such as Nike, and was credited with making Whitney Houston's 'I will always love you' the fastest selling Asian single of all time (Banks, 1997). MTV was, in essence, an extended commercial for Western media products, whose intention was to coax audiences into a 'global consensus' on consumption (Banks, 1997). The articulations of youth style and propaganda represent 'the communication hegemony of the market [and] the transformation of communication into the most effective device behind the unhitching and insertion of all cultures – whether ethnic, national or local – into the sphere of the market' (Martin-Barbero, 2006: 279–280).

Yet MTV's Asian success was not unqualified. Japanese television networks dropped it in the 1990s because audiences preferred Japanese singers. This early lesson on the importance on indigenising was quickly applied to Chinese markets. MTV diversified into MTV Mandarin and MTV Asia. MTV Mandarin embraced Deng Xiaoping's 'spiritual civilisation' movement, which aimed to integrate individualism, Confucianism and socialism (Weber, 2003). The lack of tension around MTV was down to cooperation that was once unimaginable: 'The authorities seem to have ... given special permission to trial collaborative ventures with global capital to create a new youth culture, which combines a sense of Chineseness with a Western modernity stripped of any strong political values' (Fung, 2006: 77). The truth was MTV Mandarin had to work with CCTV; CCTV in turn was willing to do this because partnerships with 'foreign globalizing capital' provided opportunities 'to promote the nation's image and culture' (2006: 85). The 2004 CCTV–MTV Music Awards stood as an example. The spectacle had to be seen as both distinctively MTV and distinctively Chinese. Awards had to be presented by Chinese celebrities. Chinese performers had to take precedence. Hip-hop, MTV's lingua franca, was welcome, but only in depoliticised forms (Fung, 2006).

This example shows that the international musical and stylistic language that MTV has enabled has also been a vehicle for projecting Chinese themes and identities onto a world stage, delivered to global audiences speaking Mandarin and Cantonese (Zhu, 2008). The idea that MTV content offered something to Chinese national interests is illustrated by the actor and singer Wang Lee Hom's 'chinked out' appropriation of hip-hop culture. Wang's decision to describe his style as 'chinked out' fits the picture of a nation that is determined to use international media forms to develop its own identity:

> Derived from the historically derogatory racial slur 'chink', used to out-down Chinese people, 'chinked-out' repossesses the word, turns its negative connotations upside-down, and uses them as material to fuel the

new sound of this music. The term describes an effort to create a sound that is international and at the same time Chinese. In this album, I decided to implement some of China's most precious and untapped resources, the musics of its 'shao shu min zu,' or ethnic minorities ... This is NOT one of those 'world music' CDs. It's an R&B/hip-hop album that creates a new vibe the whole world can identify as being Chinese. (Wang, 2004)

Engagement with Western media content has become a strategy in the construction of new Chinese national identities, as China seeks to 'rebrand' itself internationally. But this is not simply a matter for the media elite. It has also become a regular facet of life for young Chinese audiences.

CHINA AND GLOBAL MUSIC TELEVISION: AN AUDIENCE'S VIEW

The research discussion propaganda and the politics of international media has, so far, focused on 'elites': media corporations, governments and performers. But let's remember the young Chinese soldier, shivering in a foxhole in Korea in 1950. Now, as then, international media flows seek to shape what young media users do, and for this reason it is important to approach the topic of global media genres from an audience's perspective. This is all the more so since Wang's 'reimagining' of national identity describes a process that many young audiences regularly engage in. In their 1999 book on media audiences, Abercrombie and Longhurst argued this sophisticated combination of media resources in the construction of identity was a common feature of ordinary life in mediatised societies. Their work was premised on a simple observation: in media-saturated societies, we are all audiences almost all of the time, even when we are not exposed to media in any obvious way. Mediatisation means we are constantly 'on call' as audiences, because the people we meet in daily life frequently reference media content in performing their public identities.

Another Korean example illustrates the point. Tourists on Untied Service Organizations (USO) tours to the Korean Demilitarized Zone (DMZ) are advised not to wear 'baggy, gangster style clothing' because North Koreans consider it provocative. When reading this advice, the visitor to the DMZ is invited to think of him- or herself as an ambassador of global hip-hop style, and is asked to consider what sort of identity he or she wishes to project. The simple request – please don't wear baggy jeans – demands that the ordinary tourist sees him- or herself as a participant in the circulation of global media images, as a performer who might act out hip-hop culture for an audience of North Korean soldiers, whose resolve might crumble thanks to inadvertent exposure to Western media culture. Moments like this show why, according to Abercrombie and Longhurst (1998), the analysis of media power has to begin with how and why the public act out media messages; we start with the fact that someone would want to dress like this at the DMZ, then retrace steps to ask how this situation comes to be, and what, if anything, media have to do with it.

However Abercrombie and Longhurst also remind us that this sort of 'effect' is different in kind than that which Korean War propagandists desired. The idea that a persuasive leaflet could literally drop an idea into a person's head, immediately changing their behaviour, was something that belonged solidly in what they termed the 'first age' of audience research. By the late twentieth century, the most powerful media messages weren't messages: they were events that audiences participated in, because their content was presented as a malleable social resource which audiences could use to be the people they wanted to be. Abercrombie and Longhurst argued that although global media still aspire to direct audiences, this ambition no longer involved using specific messages to induce particular responses.

There are two reasons for considering the *Super Girl* controversy when using Abercrombie and Longhurst's (1998) work on audience theory. The first is that the various anxieties around the show illustrate different ways of conceiving the impact of media content on audiences, characteristic of the three 'ages' of audience studies. The second is that the shows' fans did invite us to consider a 'fourth stage' of audience research, centred on the political and economic capital to be made from audience habits and the compromises that are possible when what audiences are doing is more important than what they are thinking. Abercrombie and Longhurst's paradigm raised a series of research questions whose prescience became clearer with the rise of reality media, and this significance is amplified through the case of *Super Girl*. This is why *Super Girl* was a global television landmark.

UNDERSTANDING *SUPER GIRL* WITH AUDIENCE THEORY – AND VICE-VERSA

Each of Abercrombie and Longhurst's (1998) 'ages' in audience studies had a seminal thinker, a main research question, a main research finding and a general political position. If we look at why China found *Super Girl* so enthralling, we find reasons that fit into these categories, and also new questions that indicate new directions in audience studies, leading to the importance of understanding the politics of audience habits.

The first age of audience research was represented by the behaviourist era (the early period of experiments and surveys, explored in Chapter 2), which looked for short-term and immediate effects that media had on audience attitudes and behaviours (Abercrombie and Longhurst, 1998). Convinced that the US mass media could foster democracy, this research set out to help business and government communicate their aims and values to the public with greater efficiency (see also Ruddock, 2001). The behaviourist paradigm started with Lasswell's *Propaganda Technique in World War I* (1971). Lasswell defined propaganda as the conscious attempt to use media messages to change the thoughts and behaviours of a target population. This became the defining feature of early experimental effects research, where by the late 1940s Carl Hovland was defining communication as 'the process by which an individual transmits stimuli to modify the behaviour of other individuals' (1948: 371). At the time, the

Stalin/Mao leaflet was being dropped on Chinese troops in Korea; the behaviourist paradigm had come to focus on how messages like this could produce immediate, short-term effects by changing what audiences bought, whom they voted for and whom/what they feared (Defleur and Ball-Rokeach, 1989). Certainly the SARTV's concerns about *Super Girl* – and HSTV's measures to placate these concerns – drew on behaviourist thinking. When HSTV pledged not to hold auditions during school hours to stop young people from skipping school, they were defining the show's negative appeal in direct short-term behaviourist terms. This demonstrated the practical appeal of behaviourism to the state, as it sought to control an errant operation.

In contrast to behaviourism, the incorporation/resistance paradigm (IRP) used qualitative methods to study media's long-term ideological effects. The IRP assumed that media generally reflected the interests of those who already had power, particularly conservative political interests and big business. The approach therefore tended to be on the side of audiences. Beginning with Stuart Hall's encoding/decoding model (1980), the question here was how media constructed subtle yet powerful political messages, and how audiences interpreted these messages by making a series of aesthetic and political judgements about that content.[1] If we apply this model to *Super Girl*, the idea that the show was a sugar-coated attack on socialist values, and in this sense part of a long-term campaign of ideological warfare against the Chinese state, was a key theme in the CCTV summit of 2006. The view that *Super Girl* was a 'cultural Pearl Harbor' signalled the move from persuasion to ideology as the main index of media power.

Originally, the IRP assumed the interests of media and audiences were generally opposed (because media justified inequalities that made life worse for most of the audience), and therefore 'active' audiences who found pleasure and empowering messages in media did so 'against the grain' of the intentions of media producers. This was because the model was conceived at a time of intensive class struggle in the UK as conservative political forces sought to win public support for attacks on organised labour movements (Glasgow University Media Group, 1976). This political project manifested itself in terms of encoding/decoding because, generally speaking, British television tended to represent middle-class interests as national interests, and its success in doing this depended on the viewer's wherewithal to 'decode' this as a political message, using what they knew about media and the world.[2]

According to Abercrombie and Longhurst (1998), this context meant that the IRP still assumed a 'transmission' perspective where power flowed from industry to audience, even if it experienced a few roadblocks and diversions on the way. *Super Girl* exemplified these misgivings, as a show that didn't clearly 'represent' anything in the context of a media policy that is in flux. *Super Girl* was better conceived as an intermediary between two different power blocs: an international reality media, and a state-governed media system with vast production resources and an equally vast global audience for its programming. Also, the questions about the show's political meaning were really about what audiences were prepared to *do* to be *part* of the show; whether that be skipping school to audition, taking part in fan groups who actively campaigned for their favourite performers, or just spending money every week to take part. In this sense, *Super Girl* seemed more at home in Abercrombie and Longhurst's 'spectacle/performance paradigm', focused on the growing number of media events where public participation was needed to complete the spectacle. The 'SPP' shifted the emphasis from what people think back to what they do, although 'doing' came in the form of 'performances' rather than 'behaviours', implying a more knowing, less involuntary aspect to audience action. The main idea was that the public used media to project public identities by staging their own performances that attracted attention, either from the media or from other people. This remained on the side of the audience, in so far as the underlying concern was how participation in public culture was governed by the terms on which media industries offered that participation. Abercrombie and Longhurst were driven by the observation that in consumption and leisure people were being increasingly treated as audiences, such that 'being a member of an audience is intimately bound up with the construction of the person' (1998: 37). This tempered any notion of political resistance, since any action that was possible was 'imagined' in a universe whose limits were decided by access to media practices. This observation is absolutely crucial to understanding why the 'disruptive habits' of *Super Girl* fans are in step with China's ambition to generate more political capital from global media.

Abercrombie and Longhurst summarised their typology in a diagram (1998: 37) that can be modified with *Super Girl* in mind. In Figure 4.1 we see that the concerns that typified each paradigm were echoed in the concerns voiced about what *Super Girl* might 'do' to its audiences. We also see a progression in thinking about the role audiences play in completing media events, represented by the fact that no single paradigm could embrace all of the shows' 'effects'.

AUDIENCES: FROM BEHAVIOURS TO HABITS

The implication of the move to performance and spectacle is that effects emerge through identities, and political ambitions depend on negotiations between people, groups and organisations as they meet in media practices. In this sense, we should see the evolution of audience typologies as developing an 'anti-functionalist' power model. What this means is that while the ambitions of the people who ostensibly control media industries are very important, their success or failure in achieving their goals ultimately depends on what ordinary people do with media. Abercrombie and Longhurst's typology moves from behaviours, to meanings to performances, which we can think of as meaningful behaviours. The fourth stage afforded by *Super Girl* is media habits, which we can think of as behaviours with meaningful outcomes.

The key here is to displace what people think they are doing as the starting point for the analysis of power, be they audiences or powerful people who do make decisions about what gets made and who gets to see it. This, in fact, was a grounding assumption of early propaganda studies. Lasswell had been keen to point out that the goals of propagandistic messages were not always clear or coherent, and so their outcomes could be unpredictable and even counterproductive. Lasswell did not believe that functions could be reduced to what

Behaviourist	Incorporation/resistance paradigm	Spectacle/performance paradigm
	Research question How do media encourage audiences to accept social inequality, how do audiences fight back by rejecting or reinventing political messages?	**Research question** How do media become essential to identity, and how do they collapse the boundaries between different sorts of identities (consumer /citizen/audience)?
Research question Can media produce immediate changes in thought and action?		
Political question What are the post-Great War US concerns about power of propaganda and the rise of Communism?	**Political question** Does UK television side with middle-class anti-union interests?	**Political question** The politicisation of everyday life; we are constantly 'reading', 'responding to' and 'making' political messages – how is this manifest?
Super Girl *question* **Anti-social behaviour** When semi-autonomous TV stations are allowed to import Western formats, does this present an *immediate* threat to social order?	Super Girl *question* **Political resistance** When semi-autonomous TV stations are allowed to import Western formats, does this present a *long-term* threat to social values?	Super Girl *question* **Performance** How do Chinese audiences perform as consumers, does this affect their performance as citizens?
Evidence The fear that teens would skip school to audition.	**Evidence** *Super Girl* as 'Pearl Harbor'.	**Evidence** Action: '*Super Girls* has constituted an enormous "NGO Political space" that has afforded new possibilities in thought and action. It has also created new relationships between audiences, and new types of audience function' (Zhong, 2007).

Figure 4.1   Analysing the 'effects' of *Super Girl*
Source: Adapted from Abercombie and Longhurst (1998: 37)

key people thought, but were subject to negotiations throughout the entire media system:

> Properly conceived, the problem of organization in propaganda extends beyond the forms and mechanics employed within propaganda agencies for the production of political communications. It also embraces the extra-governmental effort by government to structure and relate groups and private persons in ways that will allow propaganda to obtain maximum reverberation throughout the social system or systems addressed. More than any other category of content, the propaganda of war aims is the catalyst of transnational political action. (1971: xxiv)

Lasswell's concerns, then directed at propaganda, actually described why *Super Girl* initially survived official efforts to secure its demise. As much consternation as the show caused, it was also an 'extragovernmental tool' to secure public consent for new modes of state media management. Technology collaborated here by concentrating attention on audiencing practices that avoid ideological questions.

This is the point that Huang and Chitty made in their explanation of *Super Girl*'s success. The 'performances' seen around *Super Girl* mostly took the form of viewers aggregating themselves into online advocacy communities named after snack-food companies, who generated and attracted revenues by voting for their idols and encouraging others to do the same. These communities illustrated a fundamental shift in commercial media, where the communication of business became the business of communication (Huang and Chitty, 2009). As well as attracting audiences, whose attention is then sold to advertisers, *Super Girl* immediately exploited the financial potential of 461 million telecom subscribers. More precisely, the presence of this huge market meant that HSTV, in partnership with Wireless Service provider Linktone, could fulfil a 'traditional' service of selling audiences to advertisers at a record advertising rate while also using the presence of live performers and audiences to encourage television audiences to participate through paying to vote. As the authors put it:

> The value of audiences is redefined by media while selling participation to them. In traditional studio-based broadcasting, the target audiences for advertisers are judged by purchasing power, need and wants as potential consumers. In broadcasting as transaction, within the particular transactional venue of an extended studio space, participation is reduced to a commodity that sells at 1 yuan per shot. (Huang and Chitty, 2009: 131–132)

This is why there are significant distinctions to be made between how a more liberalised media economy could work in China, theoretically, and the sober analysis of how liberalisation *does* work in Chinese media (Zhong, 2010). With *Super Girl*, there was no necessary contradiction between a reality format based on audiences who express their desires, and a political system that is keen to avoid social turmoil. Audiences have to pay to speak, and when they do so 'the content of "say" is not what one would associate with the public sphere, so while there is a modality of participation ... it is apolitical participation' (Huang and Chitty, 2009: 131).

Huang and Chitty's point was that the simple act of sending an SMS to vote for your favourite singer inserted the *Super Girl* fan into a modern circuit of media production that was the outcome of almost a century of conflict through propaganda, regardless of the motives of the user and/or the pleasures involved – just like wearing baggy jeans on the 38th parallel. The pleasure of voting was not irrelevant, but there was another dimension to be considered regarding how this 'habit' appeared from political and technological history. SMS votes perform an economic function for China's media economy that has little to do with the satisfaction experienced by the sender.

There is no reason to accept this reading as a 'fact' which dismisses the possibility that Zhong's more positive reading of what *Super Girl* might mean for participatory democracy is anything more than a fantasy – we would need more research on what voters think they are doing, and how this shapes their future identities. However, the point is that the ways young audiences performed did not disrupt business as usual for the state or commerce, even if those audiences did imagine what this sort of voting might say about the pleasures of another. In this sense, technologies created spaces where power could be 'time-shared'. This reconstituted the 'involuntary' aspect of audience action that the behaviourists looked for, bringing research back to the matter of what audiences do, not what they think. Instead of meaningful practices, we have habits with meanings.

YOUTH AND INTERNATIONAL COMMUNICATION: FROM ACTION TO THOUGHT TO HABIT

The challenge from the last chapter was to explain the distinct effects of media technologies as 'cultural drivers', phenomena that work in partnership with other forces to catalyse social change. One way to do this is to look at successful international genres that have capitalised on the access to audiences enabled by mobile technologies. There are few finer examples than China's *Super Girl. Super Girl* saw collaboration between interests that have been hostile under different circumstances – and media technologies have helped make those circumstances different. This *is* a question about technologies, in that platform convergence in China produces catholic 'power spaces' that, because they do not belong to squarely to any single interest, can serve transnational commercial interests and national political goals. Technologies and practices work together to produce a space that can accommodate alternative ideologies, and this is extremely valuable as China seeks to reinvent itself through developing media policies. *Super Girl* has been openly criticised as a show that threatens to derail national development by 'poisoning' Chinese youth (Zhong, 2007). Desperate to save a show that has been an unprecedented commercial success, HSTV took steps to make *Super Girl* adhere to Chinese state principles (Zhong, 2007). Yet aside from this, it survived for a long time by using convergent technologies to move further into the everyday habits of its audience with no particular message in mind.

Super Girl inherits a history of thinking on international propaganda; its story fits the observation that propaganda is not only about persuasion, but also seduction through entertainment, where music television has been an important vehicle for this struggle. The point, however, is that this is about the capacity to place media practice, as distinct from media meanings, at the centre of social life.

What is at stake here is the power to corral the audience in a media space, where the habits that make the space are more important than any meaning its content might carry. This shifts the emphasis from what the audience is thinking to what the audience is doing, and as such represents a fourth 'moment' in audience theory. *Super Girl* was an exercise in 'vertical branding' (Huang and Chitty, 2009), a form of transmission that succeeds because it lives in every aspect of Chinese life, from policy, to state-managed media events, to youth experiences.

The Chinese experience of reality television suggests that media technologies have political effects, because they enable cooperation between powerful interests who can exploit the media practices of young audiences to different ends. Voting for *Super Girl* contestants generates profit, fosters dreams of a more liberalised political system, and performs a political 'containing' function, all at the same time. The thing that makes it possible for all three goals to co-exist is the fact that the things young Chinese audiences do are more important than what they think; whatever their motivations, their actions make political and economic capital for others.

The notion that media power happens even when young people cannot be told what to think or believe is an important concept to grasp; it also, for example, helps explain the influence of marketing and advertising, as we shall see in the chapter on binge drinking and social media. Chinese reality music television is a phenomenon where fluid state/business operations exploit technologies to affect the *social outcomes* of *audience habits*. This represents a fourth transition in understanding what media do to the public: from behaviour, to ideological thought, to performance, then to habit, cultural actions which media structures make appealing and easy.

These effects are powerful because they are apolitical: that is, cultivating easy habits is a strategy that belongs to no defined political interest. This is why the study of how media technologies allowed co-existence between opposing interests in China carries important lessons across the discipline. The basic idea is that media saturation creates media habits that are flexible power resources because they can be turned to numerous ends, and it is the flexible model that explain how media serve as cultural drivers in media events, marketing practices, politics and celebrity culture.

CHAPTER SUMMARY

- The Chinese experience of reality talent shows exemplifies important shifts in understanding international media flows.

- These shifts involve the transitions from propaganda, to the politics of popular culture, to the politics of media practice.

- Audience theory provides a valuable way of conceiving the connections between the state, media businesses and the public.

- Focussing on audience habits suggests that the matter of how state, business and audience interact in media practices is more important than the meaning of media content.

- This locates international media power in the fact of media saturation, rather than particular ideologies.

- The 'controversy' around *Super Girl* was the predictable outcome of the negotiations demanded by China's emergence as a global media power.

NOTES

1 For a useful typology, see Michelle (2007).

2 The role of class in influencing audience reception was described with particular clarity in David Morley's *The Nationwide Audience* (1980).

5

UNDERSTANDING MEDIA USERS: GIRLS, MOBILE PHONES AND IDENTITY

Research question.
How do young people make identities by using media?

Underlying question about media influence.
How do media create meaningful social spaces and meaningful ways of living in those spaces?

Relevant literature.
Feminist media studies and subcultural studies.

Exemplifying case studies.
Ethnographies of how young women use mobile phones in private spaces.

Outcomes.
These studies tell us that private media use is a reaction to formal and informal regulation of gendered identities

Underlying thought on media influence.
Studying why girls use mobile phones when they want to be left alone shows how feminism has updated the idea of 'defensive space', found in subcultural studies, to the analysis of mobile media.

Although the last chapter was about 'big' identities – national ones intended to affect widespread control – it also explored the importance of how young people encounter and use these identities personally – as things they feel and use. The way that young people experience and even author identity through media use is another enduring theme in media research. It is especially useful in analysing the significance of mobile media. Researchers have always argued that one of the main 'effects' of media technologies is that they are devices societies use to negotiate the relationship between public and private. The central idea here is that the use of media in intimate places – like the home or the bedroom – is always structured by external forces, including social policy. Subcultural studies set the agenda here, in establishing that studying *where* young people use media is as interesting as looking at *what* they do. Feminist media researchers developed this by establishing that the most interesting forms of media use often take place in the least public spaces, when media users believe – or hope – no one is watching.

This insight set an important foundation for studies of mobile media, as established by fascinating ethnographies of how and why young women use and value mobile phones. By the end of this chapter, you will be able to see how feminism continues to make innovations in ways to conceive and study the connection between media use and identity. In seeing this, you will also appreciate the wide range of social settings where mediated identity building can be seen in action.

WHY DO GIRLS JUST WANT TO HAVE FUN?

Sometimes, journalists ask media academics for their views on media culture – usually when spectacular events place media effects in the public eye. The busiest I have ever been, on this score, was when *The X-Factor* winning boy-band One Direction hit Australia's shores in 2012. Crowds of teenage girls spent the night at Sydney airport waiting for their idols, only to be disappointed as the band left without bothering to say hi. Didn't the girls feel duped? Why had they expended so much effort and emotion on a bunch of generic, indifferent foreign pop stars? Wasn't it time the girls woke up to their cynical manipulation at the hands of the most commercial wing of the music industry?

These are some of the questions I fielded in that week. I was invited to speak on two radio programmes, where the presenters were keen to investigate how 'directors' were different to their grandmothers, who wept at site of The Beatles in the 1960s and the Bay City Rollers in the 1970s. Both bands had evoked similar chaos when touring Australia. Seen that way, One Direction fans seemed to be following in a tradition, which begged interesting questions about why teen-girl hysteria was a recurrent feature of cultural history. This was the crux of the matter that radio broadcasters wanted to explore.

A tabloid journalist who interviewed me, however, was more pugnacious. Hadn't the girls at the airport been in danger? Shouldn't these girls be protected from themselves? After all, wouldn't they be terribly embarrassed about all of this when they grew up? Imagine a 40-year-old you watching a 15-year-old you gushing about Harry's hair?

I was taken aback by the concern. It didn't really matter that the girls hadn't met the band, I argued, because they still got to have the fun of hanging out with their friends all night – not something that teenage girls get to do that often. As to later regrets, many previous generations of women had survived the 'shame' of having screamed at a pop idol. Also, the girls who greeted One Direction seemed to know that *they* were onstage; most seemed able to swoon on cue, as if they knew perfectly well what the watching adult world wanted them to do. When the editorial was published – as part of a two-page spread, which also featured a couple of my quotes, lengthier reactions from other celebrities, and lots and lots of pictures of the band itself – the pejorative tone was unmistakable: One Direction were talentless clones who sang bad songs, and their girl fans should simply wise up to the fact that they had been very publicly taken for fools. The argument that the fans were making too much about a band who, in the pantheon of musical greatness, barely made the foothills, seemed more than a little disingenuous, given the amount of column inches devoted to the visit.

The brouhaha around One Direction's Australian fans showed a couple of interesting trends. First, teenage girls seemed comfortable in the knowledge that their hysteria was being avidly consumed by a watching public. Second, news organisations put a lot of time and space into using this 'hysteria' to make critical observations on the nefarious effects of other aspects of media culture. In any case, the controversy did show a peculiar paradox: society is fascinated with the inconsequential things that 'silly' girls do with meaningless media.

Actually, this makes a lot of sense. Consumption has become a central part of being a girl, and research on how teenage girls use media to *be* teenage girls makes compelling points about the accelerating role media play in defining social identities, especially as they are embedded in a burgeoning range of social settings. In fact, work on girls and mobile media encapsulates the significance of feminism, when considering how identities rely on media. This research suggests that events like the One Direction incursion appear meaningless because the meaning of social identities regularly depends on media routines practised in ordinary places.

FEMINISM AND MOBILE MEDIA

In the last chapter, we saw that in China, voting for a reality-television star by SMS is a habit that involves young audiences in public performances of identity. Yet mobile phones are also important grounding points for less conspicuous social identities. As such, research on mobile phones inherits a long academic tradition; this chapter explains how, using feminism and subcultural studies to outline the role that mobile phones play in identities practised in 'private' places. Seen from these perspectives, mobile phones have the effect of weaving young people into public life, even when they want to be left alone.

Another way to put this is to say that when young women use mobile phones, they are performing gendered identities that reflect social and political histories, even when seeking privacy. Ultimately, this question explains how media become influential as part of a physical world whose textures and dimensions are guided by political decisions. The topic of girls and mobile phones underlines the importance of feminist media studies within research on media, social policy youth and identity. When girls use phones to be left alone, they alert us to the fact that private spaces are regulated by social policy and cultural convention, and media technologies have come to play a role in how those spaces operate. This can only be appreciated because feminist media research has developed a number of powerful insights and methods for connecting 'private', 'nowhere' places with social structures. Feminist scholars started researching 'bedroom cultures' of the 1970s (reading teen magazines, listening to records and the like), seeing these 'passive' activities as reactions to the policing of gender in post-war social policy (McRobbie and Garber, 1978). This work established a foundation for reflecting on the political significance of 'mobile' identities, premised on an interest in the relationships between media, policy, space and identity. For this reason, it isn't possible to understand how mobile-media cultures operate without understanding feminist media theory, particularly as it has developed around studies of what teenage girls do with media. This case is made by:

- returning to subcultural studies, and explaining how its idea of 'defensive space' created an interest in how media interacted with other phenomena in the material social environment to compel or enable actions that had a social meaning;
- explaining how feminist scholars developed the understanding of the relationship between media, space and identity in their analysis of bedroom cultures;
- explaining why important feminist scholar Angela McRobbie's thinks that the essential lessons of early British subcultural studies on the relation between media, culture and political reality still apply in a world where media continues to support the continued, global exploitation of women;
- using studies of young female mobile-phone users to connect private media experiences with social policy and social history.

SUBCULTURAL STUDIES AND THE IDEA OF DEFENSIVE SPACE

Feminist media research encapsulates the best ideas from the history of youth media studies on how to explain the relationship between media use, culture and identity. Feminist media scholars have been especially sensitive to the significance of the 'private' spaces, like the bedroom, that are increasingly important within the analysis of mobile-media cultures. Feminists valued subcultural studies for connecting studies of young media users with the broader analysis of material cultures. Subcultural studies established the idea that youth identities were made in social spaces that reflected history, tradition, social policy and economic change. Feminists simply thought that these ideas needed to be pursued by paying greater attention to the things that girls did for pleasure.

British subcultural studies was grounded in the idea that music and fashion gripped British youth with a particular intensity after World War II as 'imaginative' responses to dramatic changes in national life that announced themselves in changing social geographies, particularly the dissolution of traditional working-class communities brought on by shifts in industry and urban planning. This thesis was most clearly articulated in Hall and Jefferson's *Resistance through Rituals* (1978). They set about studying how youth made identities that expressed understandings of history and place in the world. Teds, mods, rockers, skinheads, glam fans, punks and new romantics might have looked different, and even hated each other, but they were all about making sense of a world where old certainties about class, race, gender and sexuality were in flux. Subcultures reflected the enduring need for people to 'give expressive form to their social and material life ... Social and economic conditions "limit" ... how groups live and reproduce their social existence' but also formed a 'historical reservoir – a preconstituted field of possibilities which groups take up, transform and develop' (1978: 11).

Subcultures showed that young people experimented with identities because social policy and changed infrastructures meant they had to. Working-class youth were particularly affected, because post-war urban renewal had physically changed their communities. Before 1939, working-class people lived, worked and played in the same area, and were constantly reminded of collective identities as they moved through ordinary everyday spaces. This was no longer true. Young people went elsewhere to make a living, and when they got home, it was to communities that weren't really communities because they had no shared spaces where people to gather and share their day (Hall and Jefferson, 1978).

Resistance through Rituals saw subcultures as efforts to control these shifting circumstances. The music and fashion choices that young people made somehow articulated how they felt about society. Skinhead style, for example, was read as an effort to preserve a traditional working-class look in the face of a history that was encouraging everyone to be middle class. However, Hall and Jefferson thought that, in the end, these were exercises in self-deception. The idea that shaved heads, heavy work boots and braces were a meaningful antidote to the dissolution of working-class communities and the evaporation of jobs in heavy industries was laughable. And those who did embrace social mobility, like the 1960s mods who were only too happy to give up boots and braces for suits, ties and Italian loafers, ended up materialising an argument that simply wasn't true – that young people could now be anything they wanted to be in the new age of prosperity, when in fact class distinctions were as deep and rancorous as ever (Hall and Jefferson, 1978).

Feminists agreed that youthful media pleasures reflected material cultures and political histories. The problem was that works like *Resistance through Rituals* had not been thoroughgoing enough in contextualising media pleasures in social spaces, because its authors had only considered public displays of identity. Feminist media researchers thought that that media power was most effective when it 'worked at home'. Researchers in the women's studies group at Birmingham University's influential Centre for Critical Cultural Studies felt that the relative lack of attention paid to girls in subcultural studies betrayed a failure to analyse the importance of private places in reproducing social structures:

> The historical separation out of the domestic sphere ... articulated through ... class specific ideologies of domesticity, femininity and personal life, which have contributed to the representation and understanding of the home as a private sphere, undetermined by the capitalist mode of production. (CCCS Women's Studies Group, 1978: 39)

The essential idea of subcultures – that the things young people did for fun had something to do with the economic and legal structures that made the places where they had fun – was sound. The problem was that the focus on public spaces as the locus of culture and power ignored the economic burden placed upon British women, who were expected to work at home. To connect power with private spaces, the group argued that one of the reasons why teenage magazines had become so popular among girls in the 1970s was because they liked reading magazines in their bedrooms, which is where post-war social policy had decided to put them. This was exemplified by the history of 'family allowance', a post-war Labour Party initiative, supported by trade unions, and designed to support working-class families by supplying a wage for domestic work. Founded on the 1942 Beveridge Report, the family allowance explicitly engineered a division of sexual labour by codifying the home as the primary sphere for women's work. As the report itself stated, 'in the next 30 years housewives as mothers have vital work to do in ensuring the adequate continuance of the British race'. Yet burgeoning industrial demands also conscripted women as a 'reserve labour army', ready to fill vacancies as and when required by economic expansion. These circumstances were credited as the inspiration for British feminism, as 'the managed contradiction between woman's role as a waged worker and as a domestic worker and reproducer, and the concomitant rise of female part-time work has itself accelerated militancy among women' (CCCS Women's Study Group, 1978: 53).

ANGELA MCROBBIE: CONNECTING BEDROOM CULTURES WITH MOBILE MEDIA

Feminist writing of the social aspects of domestic spaces was vital in two respects: first, it shows how apparently personal media tastes often reflect public histories; second, it defined the domestic sphere as a 'defensive position' for feminist politics. McRobbie and Garber (1978) argued that girls were absent from early subcultural studies because the field researched places where girls had no physical or emotional investment. Girls *were* marginal in public cultures precisely because they were absolutely central to the production of the domestic, and it was here that they made their stand. For this reason, McRobbie and Garber began a feminist tradition of 'bedroom studies' that set out to explain how the ways that girls consumed media at home told a lot about the societies in which they lived.

McRobbie and Garber wanted to overturn the implicit cultural hierarchy of subcultural studies, in which the only young people who counted were distinctive subculturalists who confronted social norms in very obvious ways. In the 1970s, girls were more likely to be fans than subculturalists. Teenage girls, who seemed inexplicably devoted to 'pin-up' pop stars of the day, made sensible use of the resources at hand (girl magazines, records, television) within the confined spaces where they were allowed to do as they pleased (the bedroom). Girl cultures were more about collecting and arranging than doing things in public, if for no other reason than their being more restricted than boys in their chances to be in public. Yet if these pastimes tended to be directed at romantic fantasies which ended in conventional expectations about love and marriage, this did not obscure their potential for showing how popular culture could give a voice to feminist politics.

McRobbie believed these studies remained relevant to understanding contemporary media. She remained convinced that digital, post-broadcast, mobile cultures still exercised distinct ideological effects disguising the global economic exploitation of the female workforce. The truth of global sexist exploitation is, in her view, masked by repetitive media stories about women who can be anything they want to be. Assessing girl cultures in the early twenty-first century, McRobbie adopted a '*plus ça change, plus c'est la même chose*' philosophy. Some girls are more visible, but others – particularly girls in the developing world who haven't the time or the money to experiment with identities because they are too busy making cheap consumer goods for those who do – aren't. She acknowledged that it is now much easier to find girls making culture, and media images of upwardly mobile young women who can create their own futures in a world replete with choices. However, she saw this as a patina disguising that what had been 'created' was actually a 'recreation', and a repetition of the same conditions of inequality that grounded feminist media research in the 1970s. This recreation was secured though a sexual division of labour, and thus women's bodies. The mechanics of the family allowance case study are repeated through a new, global, 'sexual contract' which

> permits the renewed institutionalisation of gender inequity and the re-stabilisation of gender hierarchy by means of a generational specific address which interpellates young women as subjects of capacity. (McRobbie, 2007: 718)

McRobbie thought that this was about 'capacity' rather than agency (2008). 'Capacity' expresses the opinion that women who seem to do as they please are very often making the best of a bad deal in a world that places unprecedented economic and social demands on their time, and that media play an ideological role with stories that depict women's duties as choices. Shows like *Sex and the City* create the impression that girls can have it all, but the global economy commands women to 'do it all'. Media images of women who 'have it all' have convinced many young women that gender inequality is a thing of the past. This is not true; many women, especially those in the developing world, face the same sorts of discrimination that inspired feminist media studies in the first place.

McRobbie therefore believed that, when it came to young women, media played the same sort of legitimating role that had been criticised by subcultural studies – disguising economic oppression with stories about young women who could be anything because they could consume as they pleased. The task remained to consider how media and ordinary expression feature in a political project to maintain inequality by appearing to solve it in culture. McRobbie reiterated the view that youth is a sort of false consciousness, achieving imaginary solutions to material contradictions which actually exacerbate those conditions. As in the 1970s, the problem was the intersection of patriarchy and capitalism. The feminist project is to establish an alliance between 'the new "career girl" in the affluent west ... [and] the "global girl" factory worker, in the rapidly developing factory systems of the impoverished countries of the so-called Third World' (McRobbie, 2007: 718). This is difficult when the former live the reality of choice through consumption and the body. These acts are made possible by two things: the sweat of the latter, and the repeated celebration of the choice/consumption nexus in popular culture. So, McRobbie felt that the pleasures of popular culture helped a vicious campaign to widen the gender gap. Young women had come to occupy the same analytic space held by young men in subcultural studies, notwithstanding changed times and technologies. This criticism raises questions about method, and particularly the role of qualitative methods that look at media cultures from young users' points of view.

INDIVIDUALIZATION AND METHOD

Recent qualitative studies on how girls use media clarify how media influence the physical experience of being a girl, in conjunction with other forces in their world. Rebecca Coleman's research on the effects of sexualised images (2008) places these images in the world of 'meaningful objects' that girls use to make sense of their bodies. Coleman asked a sample of teenage girls to write biographies by collecting and narrating images of bodies that they came across every day. The biographies confirm that mediated images sometimes make the girls 'feel bad', but only in relation to a wider set of anxieties about looks. Often, commercial images are easier to dismiss than family portraits. Coleman's respondents know that even the models shown in glossy-magazine advertisements do not possess the bodies on display. Despite this, such images remain a source of anxiety; but so too do family photographs that capture them in unflattering poses, or at times when they were embarrassed about their looks.

It has been argued that the increased mobility of media has amplified the commodification of the female body, such that the volume of images which women *have* to deal with has vastly increased. The porn industry is a case in point, tying the question to matters of space. Anne Reading (2005) observes that pornography's exploitation of the internet and digital media, together with its integration with the leisure industry, means that it is no longer quarantined to shady urban areas. Beth Eck (2001), in noting a highly bargained relationship between women and what they understand as different genres of pornography, agrees that sexualised images have come to matter more in recent years, since pornography no longer lives in magazines and videos that can be hidden, and has also infiltrated advertising – a context where it is often seen as being more offensive. In other words, sexualised images are a part of everyday material culture for women. On the basis of this evidence, Coleman concludes that sexualised images are important because they force their way into how women make sense of who they are and what kind of world they live in. She argues that we can only understand influence, which *does* manifest in the stories that girls tell about 'feeling bad' by viewing 'bodies and images ... [as] entwined ... [in] constitutive relationality' (2008: 174). This is to say that power is best understood in the context of a world where girls are constantly 'on call' as sexual citizens, where acts of biographisation are demanded as the body is presented and foregrounded as a cultural text, to be written and rewritten in relation to identity.

The manifestly political ramifications of this position can be found in scholarship on young Muslim women, the role of 'modesty' in European debates on multiculturalism, and the deployment of mobile phones as a means of managing the lived realities of these conditions. Pnina Werbner (2007) presented style, the body, choice and identity as key factors in British and French controversies around veiling. Noting the altercations around moves to ban the *niqab* in both countries, Werbner defined the veiling issue as 'loaded with higher order symbolic elaborations ... [with] ranges of contradictory messages ... [which] endow or deny agency to young South Asian and Muslim women in highly ambivalent ways' (2007: 162). While acknowledging the gravity of honour-killing and forced-marriage issues, Werbner argued that the variety of veiling practices were not simply imposed upon young Muslim women. In any event, whatever the complexities of the issue, veiling debates showed how bodies and styles mediate ethnic, national, gendered and generational identities. Veiling had, after all, created unlikely alliances. Rowan Williams, the UK's Archbishop of Canterbury, opposed injunctions against the *niqab* as examples of secular bigotry. Werbner argued that many young Muslim women used veiling to 'make their own histories' under conditions that they do not choose: 'what seems ... to be an extremist Islamic ideology of veiling and purdah for women ... empowers these young ... women with the right to choose their own marriage partners, even against the will of their parents' (2007: 171).

MOBILE PHONES

So, veiling is another cultural practice that mediates public and private identities. Hijazi-Omari and Ribak's (2008) research on mobile-phone usage among Palestinian teenage girls explored how the gendered and generational relations implied in veiling issues are also lived through a medium that has always occupied the space between private spaces and collective female identities. In this, biographies of users and the technologies themselves are crucial.

Perhaps no other technology better captures the politics of the ordinary and intimate than mobile phones. They are used, most of the time, to transmit intimate or banal messages from one sender to one receiver. Yet this disguises a number of macro dynamics. 'Mobile meanings' are partly conditioned by the commercial narratives that make us want cell phones and understand what they will do in our lives (Aguado and Martinez, 2007). The economic significance of the mobile-phone industry cannot be underestimated. In Jamaica, the mobile phone is a multi-functional everyday tool. So indispensable is this 'private' lifestyle accessory, that it demands a variety of industries to support the technology's multiple social uses. The aggregation of private applications supports a cumulative outcome, where mobile telephony is a vital feature of the Jamaican economy (Batson-Savage, 2007).

None of this dilutes the everyday identity politics experienced by users, a fact particularly highlighted by feminist media scholars. Cecilia Uy-Tioco (2007) applies the argument to demands made by global corporate power on women in particular, showing how the technology is used by migrant Filipina workers to manage what it means to be both a 'good' and 'absent' mother when effectively forced to work overseas. In Hong Kong, girls have created a texting culture that has sparked a debate over new forms of media literacy, and reworked the way we understand relations between individual media use and social connectivity (Lin and Tong, 2007). This should not surprise us, for well over a century women have driven the emergence of telephony as a form of social communication used by and in communities (Kearney, 2005; Shade, 2007). Knowing this, as early as the 1940s companies such as Bell were targeting teenage girls as cultural drivers in the popularisation of the telephone as a domestic device (Kearney, 2005).

In this sense, Hijazi-Omaris and Ribak's ethnographic investigation of how young Palestinian girls obtain and use mobile phones to negotiate gendered and sexualised identities follows an established theme and asks a familiar question regarding identity, negotiation and empowerment:

> These girls' moves are constrained by men, by their parents, and by the community's conservative reaction to the seemingly liberal Jewish hegemony. In this context, the mobile phone both reestablishes these teenage girls' layered subordinations and tampers with them, allowing the girls to develop a mediated and face-to-face community that provides them with essential practical and emotional support. (2008: 150)

This is a great case study because it encapsulates the significance of invisible youths. These girls' use of mobile phones was mostly about secrecy, because they expended more energy on hiding them than on calling or texting. This reactivates the notion of defensiveness, tied to space, found in early subcultural studies.

For the girls in the study, the mobile phone was implicated in modesty and agency as a 'postmodern engagement ring' (Hijazi-Omaris and Ribak, 2008: 156), initially given to them by boyfriends in relationships they had developed without the consent of their families. As a result, mobile phones were actually a source of some anxiety as objects that needed to be hidden from fathers and brothers. Their presence promised both romance and the constant threat of discovery and punishment. Phones and calling cards did not really liberate the girls from patriarchy because they were given to them by boyfriends who jealously regulated how the phones were used: the phones were to be used to call boyfriends, and no one else. Hence, where literature on women and phones has outlined how the technology is used to create communities and thus a public presence, in this case the structures placed around mobile phones worked hard to block these possibilities. This is not to say that this is all they did. The authors also noted that the girls in the study evaded this:

> The girls would lend each other phones and hide them for one other, transfer SIM and calling cards, and collectively secretly purchase used phones as birthday presents for friends who were unable to obtain them from boyfriends. (Hijazi-Omaris and Ribak, 2008: 161)

These stories operate at the interface of gender, sexuality, ethnicity and religion, which all affected the bodies of young women. Mobile phones are part of the material culture through which young Palestinian women manage the political struggles which, globally, are defining what it means to live in multi-cultural societies. Daily, repeated rituals of using and concealing mobile phones in ordinary places – under the blankets and in closets – are creative ways of structuring defensive positions against traditions that the girls do not wish to follow in any straightforward way. Private moments of intimacy are building blocks in politicised identities. Equally, these 'defences' are fragile because the threat of discovery is a constant fear. Recognising the informal networks of friendship that make them possible also clarifies the absence of social structures that would allow girls the chance to form their identities in more public and overtly political ways.

MOBILE PHONES IN PUBLIC PLACES: JUST LEAVE ME ALONE

We have now encountered a number of stories about girls, media, bodies and private moments that intercede in global politics. But what about girls who do not want to act out their identities for audiences? What happens when they want to be left alone, and how does this reflect back on academic practice? This is an important question, since McRobbie's conclusions about post-feminism renders some young women as speechless as they were in studies of boys' subcultures. To explain this point, I will return to the fire study mentioned in Chapter 1. In this I will write in the first person, in keeping with practice in feminist ethnographies where the presence of the researcher must be acknowledged as a factor that generates data (e.g. Hobson, 1980), and McRobbie and Graber's critique (1978) that male researchers sometimes construct projects biased toward boys, such that they cannot hear or interpret what data about girls' cultures actually says. To preserve anonymity, the names used below are not participants' real names.

The study used a combination of creative media research (asking students to write their own newspaper stories about fire offending in Liverpool), participant observation (I worked as an assistant on the course) and interviewing. Interviews were conducted with students who had graduated from the course. I was interested in how students used various resources to make sense of how they fitted as individuals into political discourses about youth and anti-social behaviour, and so asked them to narrate how they had come to be on the course, what their life had been like since graduating, and how they felt their lives had changed, if at all, since taking part. All of this designed to place ideas about media influence in a wider cultural context.

In one-hour interviews with 12 alumnae, questions of style and gender identity were often mentioned by former students. Susan, who had started working for the Fire Service after leaving school, explained how she had come to Beacon (the fire-safety course mentioned in Chapter 1) after getting into trouble with teachers for a series of 'performances' that had been designed to win the approval of classmates. Looking back on at this, Susan felt that she could see why the teachers had been so angry with her, but she explained her behaviour as the result of the pressures induced by the importance of youth style:

> It is, I'd say, right, everything is based on an image thing. Say if you go into school, and you don't look right – this is from a kid's point of view – you get penalised, and that's when the bullying starts. You're not classed as an individual, you're classed as one of that crowd. And it's the same with teachers, if they see you wearing certain sorts of clothes, or any other adults, they penalise you for that, just because you want to be accepted. It's horrible, because if you want to be accepted by a group of kids, you won't be accepted by the teachers because they think you're all the same.

This approaches the question of style from both an individual and a collective position. Susan slipped between wanting to be seen as an individual by teachers and avoid bullying by being seen as one of the crowd by her peers. Much as she was genuinely sorry for some of her past behaviour, at the same time she did see it as an expression of the frustration she felt at her limited chances to explore her identity, to fit into a scene as the person she wanted to be.

Jennifer associated her own Beacon experience with gender. In an otherwise very positive account of her time on the course, she told the tale of how, much to her surprise, she had been made to feel uncomfortable during a first-aid lesson:

> When we were doing mouth to mouth that felt really uncomfortable and I didn't want to do it, so the person that was teaching us got Chris to get them all out the room so they couldn't see me and I done it … I don't feel comfortable with people seeing me on a dummy because they [peers] say I've never kissed anyone. It would be uncomfortable for anyone, wouldn't it?

Here, Jennifer outlined the need for a 'defensive position' because she lives in a world where her gender can be interpolated by institutional settings in ways that she could not control.

Of course, there is nothing especially new about wanting to fit in or be seen as a person, not a uniform. Nor, despite McRobbie's consternation about the clearly sexualised products (thongs and the like) directed at pre- and early teen girls, is there anything new about adolescents being cruel to each other when it comes to kissing. When it came to the girls on the study, media were more distinctly influential as objects that interacted with spaces and bodies. Again, evidence supporting this thesis came from mobile phones and the way that they access issues of mobility.

Chapter 4 outlined a case for seeing centres of media power as fluid and mobile. It follows that defensive positions need to be equally mobile. One reason why bedrooms were important places for girls was that they were barricades to the world, hence the popularity of 'Keep out!' signs (Lincoln, 2005). One of the ironies of new media technologies is that they have compromised youth's power to exclude the adult gaze into their private worlds (Shade et al., 2005). Since the history of youth media studies shows a series of tactical shifts, where youth use media to address new problems, how are mobile media used to confront mobile forms of media and cultural power? Let us consider this question with an incident that happened during the fire course.

We were taking the students on a visit to a fire station that involved a 25-minute mini-van ride across the city. I was sitting next to Ian and in front of Helen towards the back of the bus. Helen was listening to rapping on her mobile's speakerphone. This was annoying Ian intensely, and a row ensued after Ian told Helen to 'shut the fuck up'. Naturally, she responded by increasing the volume and hitting 'repeat'.

I wondered of this was directed at me. Was her behaviour another form of the music-enabled 'venting' noted by Tia Denora (2000)? Denora cites the case of the young women who blasts out Radiohead's 'We Hope You Choke' from her bedroom to express how she feels about living with her boyfriend's parents. I wondered if the girl hoped that I choke. Why might this have been the case?

One reason why I wondered this had to do with method. The participant-observation phase of the study left no time for interviewing the students who were actually participating in the course. I had to get to know them in the course of daily duties, asking questions where I could. For a variety of reasons, this had led to the situation that McRobbie warned about, where I tended to spend more time with and speaking to the boys.

But perhaps Helen was simply trying to carve out a little time for herself in a world that placed her under almost constant surveillance, a world that I represented, somehow. Although some students on the course did want to talk about the political aspects of their identities, and the extent to which this politicisation was driven by media panics, others did not. They were on the course to, as Terry put it earlier, 'make friends and get on with people'. They were there to have a break from school and have fun – to do the things that they wanted to do against a social context where they were rarely allowed to do so. Talking about media, politics and identity was not fun and felt like work. They did not want to perform on this stage. They wanted to be left alone. They had a right to silence.

Did my presence on the course remind students that they were powerless to resist institutional interpollation? The Fire Service had decided they wanted an academic to study the cultural aspects of Beacon, and so there I was – another example of the mobility of power. Against this, did Helen use her mobile phone to fashion a defensive position in ordinary spaces that, ironically, underlined the role that women have always played in defining the social meaning of telephony? If this was the case, then Helen's was a *non-performative* performance, where she would not act like a young person who was determined to correct the media-supported misperceptions of the adult world.

Of course, part of the tension came from the fact that a lot of bodies were packed into a tiny bus, but this was also an institutional matter because Helen, Ian and I all had to be on it. The closeness meant that we all had to think about how we could defend our positions. Helen chose noise, Ian silence. Against the history of feminist media studies, it is possible to hypothesise, however, that Helen's desire to be left alone was at least in part an overdetermined exercise in individualisation and capacity. Her mobile phone allowed her to turn a dreary bus ride into a fun time, but perhaps Helen's desire to do so reflected how rare these opportunities were for her. This reflected individualisation and capacity, as Helen struggled to carve out a place for herself in a context where she could not be alone because of institutions had responded to anti-social behaviour issue by extending the adult gaze to mundane spaces. And so, it would make perfect sense for her to choose these same spaces as the grounds on which she would defend her right to be left alone, using the props available to her, but understanding that, ideally, she would rather be somewhere else. The general lack of interest the students showed in the politics of their lot indicates that Helen would probably not have explained her actions as a conscious kicking against patriarchy. She would therefore count as one of the girls who, Götz fears (2008), feminist scholars have ignored. Yet her reaction *did* indicate the repetitive experience of encountering cultural power in settings beyond the public gaze that requires defensiveness. '*Plus ça change, plus c'est la même chose*'. Hence while the dynamics of mediated power plays around youth may change with media environments, some of the early questions that feminist media scholars asked about space, identity and the body are clearly still relevant.

CONCLUSION: WHY ALL MEDIA RESEARCHERS NEED FEMINIST MEDIA STUDIES

The feminist critique of subcultural studies established a set of observations, research questions and research practices that are well equipped to study how mobile media induce girls into global media economies in their most private moments. All media scholars need to know about feminism, if for no other reason than feminists have led so many conceptual and methodological innovation in the field. The relatively new area of girl studies is especially important here for two reasons: first, it shows how the ideas developed in early subcultural studies still help understand why young people use media; second, it develops 'capacity' as a means of explaining powerful 'ordinary' media influences, finding ways to study young people who are socially invisible, or indeed do not wish to be seen. New research on teenage girls and mobile phones exemplify the political importance of invisible youth. These studies connect media to the analysis of material culture (the world of meaningful objects), where the private use of media clearly shows how political power is felt in intimate moments. This work discerns important connections between media, identity and the body, which incorporates many of the foundational ideas from subcultural studies. Girls studies is a key innovator of these themes, especially in the analysis of mobile media in changing global economies.

In the end, media matter when they are part of our physical environments. When British subcultural studies made this point in the 1970s, it was to claim that young people used music and fashion to occupy public and historical space: to say, 'we are here'. When punk-rock pioneers The Sex Pistols sailed up and down the Thames in London playing their anti-monarchist anthem 'God Save the Queen' during Elizabeth II's 1977 Silver Jubilee celebrations, they meant to be confronting. But things don't need to be this public or political to warrant our attention. Some young people either are or want to be invisible. This is not a matter of 'ordinariness', but dispossession; about youth who are silenced, more or less deliberately, or who want to be left alone in societies that are rather too interested in what they say, do and think.

Girl studies has developed a language and method for discussing invisibility through its analysis of individuality as a social experience. Perhaps the fundamental point of early feminist scholarship was that invisibility is a species of 'ordinariness', spawned from coherent attempts to control young women's bodies. Because of this, private media moments are exactly where young women feel the full public force of other people's power. Studies of how Palestinian teenagers use mobile phones are a superb representation of this thesis. Case studies like this show how girl studies has updated the idea of 'defensive space' from subcultural studies. Angela McRobbie is a pivotal figure in this regard. McRobbie's notion of 'the new global sexual contract' (2007) is especially relevant because it revisits a number of central conceptual and methodological issues that connect studies of media influence with the analysis of culture in general. McRobbie's 'contract' describes how the politicisation of women's bodies has taken on new public forms, both in terms of how these bodies are represented and, indeed, how women choose to act as women. The global political relevance of gendered identity experiences is sharply outlined by work on women, and the mobile phone as a mediator of politicised identities. Despite new times and technologies, the telephone has always revealed the arbitrary nature of the distinctions we make between public and private identities and places, and so in this sense girl studies inherits a tradition of cultural history and takes it, quite literally, into new places.

This counts because the power of some social groups and institutions depends on what young women do with their bodies. For Anita Harris, girl studies interrogates 'the relationship between popular cultures, material conditions and gendered identities; the role of social institutions such as school and the media in shaping femininities, and the places and voices young women use to express themselves' (2004: xix). Girl studies thus succeeds a history of research on how shifting socio-economic conditions affect youth behaviour on a symbolic level. It approaches this familiar question through the notion of sexual citizenship, most recently articulated in McRobbie's 'new sexual contract' (2007).

McRobbie maintains that bad old ideas about media, ideology and false consciousness still explain much about the social relevance of how young women engage with their own images. This is a serious challenge; McRobbie's point is that the 'problem' of youth is *not* that we are unwilling to listen to what young people have to say. In fact, the reverse is true; studies of media influence have headed in the wrong direction because they have over-invested in listening to the voices of young audiences, at the expense of explaining how media industries encourage girls to think, talk and act gender in ways that actually end up being disempowering. Maya Götz concurs, writing that what is needed 'is an interrogation of how girls are positioned to speak as girls' (2008). Part of the problem is about sampling methods; 'we hardly ever mention case studies of successful femininity in which no explicit critical stance against patriarchy is expressed' (2008: 81).

The case studies used in this chapter are intended to show the sorts of media practices that might correct this balance, by using mobile media to access those whose gendered identities are often about silence; if early subcultural studies were about youth saying 'look at me', mobile media studies are about others who are saying '*stop* looking at me'. Both are worth studying, and so we must understand the common ground shared by subcultural and girl studies.

CHAPTER SUMMARY

- The topic of young people using mobile media in 'nowhere' and 'private' places continues an interest in how young people react to changing social structures by making defensive places.

- Feminist media research is particularly useful in this area, because it began with detailed empirical and conceptual work connecting public policy to the construction of the private, then using this work of explain gaps in subcultural studies.

- Mobile media have made this work particularly important, as media scholars are required to consider how media penetrate almost every quarter of social life.

- Whether texting a vote to have their voice heard in public, or listening to music in an effort to be left alone, when girls use mobile media they are inserted into global economies of cultural production.

6

UNDERSTANDING MEDIA VIOLENCE: SCHOOL SHOOTINGS, MEDIA STORIES AND THE FRAMING OF SOCIAL REALITY

Research question.
Why have school shootings become such recognisable media events?

Underlying Issue about media influence.
What does media violence say about organised media production?

Relevant literature.
Cultivation analysis, agenda setting, myth and media rituals

Exemplifying Case Studies.
Murders at Columbine, Virginia Tech (USA), Jokela and Kauhajoki (Finland)

Outcomes.
School shootings endure as media events because they are pliable; they can be moulded to fit different arguments, representing the enduring value of media violence as a means of attracting audiences

Lessons for understanding media influence.
Media violence is popular because message systems need it to be so. The popularity of media violence is enhanced by young users who make and share it.

Since 1999, debates on media violence and its impact have frequently centred on rampage murders that take place in schools. So common are these tragic events that they force us to ask why global audiences are exposed to so much violence. That is, before worrying about what this violence does to audiences, especially young ones, it is important to ask why that it is there to see in the first place. One of the most significant turns in media research came when scholars defined media violence as a recurring story. As a story, violence appeals because it is a flexible tool that can be used to communicate a number of ideas and lessons about what the world is like, and so can also be relied upon to attract attention; and the profit attention brings (Gerbner, 1998). Following in this tradition, research on school shootings underlines an important point: there is more to the question of why media violence matters than the issue of if violent media content encourages copycat behaviour.

Although school shootings are a relatively new phenomenon, their role as media events can be explained by using academic ideas that have been around since the 1960s. In this chapter, we will see how major theories from quantitative and qualitative media research help explain why school shootings have become a familiar part of the media landscape, and how this familiarity might affect how audiences understand the worlds they inhabit. School shootings raise deep questions about what it means to live in a mediatised world, where media organisations need formulaic narratives, and media users need equally formulaic media 'rituals' to organise daily living. At the end of this chapter, you will be able to explain why media violence is popular and useful to media industries and media users. The observation that media violence is motivated by profit isn't a particularly original, but after reading this chapter you will be able to take it a little bit further, explaining how media violence can affect media professionals and seeing how media users *participate* in the commodification of violence.

MEDIA VIOLENCE: IT'S NOT ABOUT VIOLENCE

Let us start with a news story about school violence that you probably haven't heard of, because it never happened. In 2009, a 21-year-old Canadian student called J. P. Neufeld was surfing the net in Montreal, when he came across a post on a website purporting to be from a teenage boy from Norfolk, England. The teen was boasting that he was about to set fire to his school. Reading closely, Neufeld concluded the boy meant business. He knew cyberspace echoes with idle boasts, but something about the tone here rang true. Neufeld looked up the number for the Norfolk police, and gave them a call. 'Hi, I'm a guy from Canada. There's a guy about to set fire to a school' (CBC News Canada, 2009). The police were convinced, and when they arrived at Attleborough High School, near the city of Norwich, they found a 16-year-old boy armed with a knife, matches and flammable liquid.

Neufeld didn't fit the image of the young male internet user that we commonly find in stories about digital media and school violence. He wasn't a loner bent on destroying everything around him, and he used online resources to *empathise* with others. Placing J. P. Neufeld alongside the likes of Eric Harris,

Dylan Klebold, Cho-Seung Hui and Pekka Eric Auvinen, infamous mass murderers, indicates that school shootings raise a wide range of questions about how young people use media to relate to the world, and the role that media stories play in shaping our basic understanding of what the world is like.

FRAMING MEDIA VIOLENCE

Chapter 2 established that research on media violence has at least shown the difficulties of pinning 'media influence' down as a researchable concept. At any rate, youthful reactions to media violence reveal much about the connections between media and the social imagination. School shootings are noteworthy, in this regard, exemplifying how media violence constructs images of reality that affect what audiences believe to be true about the societies they live in. School shootings raise many different reasons to worry about media violence, other than the behaviourist concerns mentioned in the first and second chapters. These new reasons define media violence as a narrative that exercises a powerful influence over how audiences understand social reality.

Prior to 9/11, the 1999 Columbine High School massacre, where teenagers Eric Harris and Dylan Klebold used a sophisticated arsenal to murder 12 people and injure 20 others, was one of the most reported and revisited stories the media world had ever seen (Altheide, 2009; Muschert, 2009). Coverage of Eric Harris and Dylan Klebold's murder spree was so intense that it established their crime as the yardstick against which all similar outrages would be judged from thereon. For this reason, studies of school shootings as media events have played a major role in explaining the power of media framing, 'framing' being a term that describes how media actively process reality by taking things that happen in the world and presenting them to audiences as events that somehow encapsulate seminal social issues (Carragee and Roefs, 2004). Framing encourages particular patterns of emotional response from audiences and users, and these responses have political outcomes. Violence has always been an important framing device because it can be relied upon to draw audiences. This being the case, studies of school shootings represent an important idea in critical media research – that media violence has ideological effects, because it cultivates beliefs and expectations about what the world is really like (Gerbner et al., 1980). Further, research on school shootings contributes to the view that media violence prospers because of its commercial value.

The idea that media violence thrives because it is a reliable source of profit is an important brake on perspectives that blame the prevalence of media violence on the tastes of young audiences. Media violence is not there because young audiences like it, however much they seem to enjoy making, sharing and celebrating horrific images. They enjoy making, sharing and celebrating horrific images because those horrific images are readily available. Violent images are readily available because they suit the purposes of commercially organised media industries. School shootings have become a genre for a number of social and economic reasons that have all come to rely on different framing practices. Critical media studies have described these practices in terms of cultivation, agenda setting and myth. Here, the school-shooting topic is especially important to media studies because it demonstrates how little the role of violence within media message systems changes when the public become involved in framing processes. This chapter elaborates all of these themes by:

- using the work of cultivation analyst George Gerbner to explain why media violence tells us a great deal about how media industries work;

- arguing that debates on the role that media play in school shootings demonstrate the shift from thinking about the effects of media on society to the role that media play in *media societies*;

- using the work of Glenn Muschert to show that school shootings are media events which exemplify how media influence social reality by defining that reality;

- media frames affect how real-world events are remembered, but this also influences how subsequent events are understood; for this reason, the way that rampage killers use social media is about framing;

- examining the lessons of recent Finnish studies of school shootings as media rituals where young media users recycle violent media narratives.

MEDIA VIOLENCE AND MESSAGE SYSTEMS

On one level, media violence matters academically, simply because it is a perennial source of public anxiety. The rap-case study described situations where young people have used media violence to heighten their aggression, although these 'effects' are often consciously manipulated by 'the affected'. The topic of rap is telling when reflecting on effects, because when performers like the Insane Clown Posse (ICP) claim that their lyrics are inspired by what sells, they reference a history of thought on why there is so much violence in media. Gerbner, famed for his studies of how television violence affects audiences' political attitudes,[1] spent five decades explaining why Violent J was right: media violence is prevalent because it suits the needs of *message systems* (1998).

The concept of 'message systems' expresses the idea that media content reflects the prevailing economic priorities of media industries over and above the creative vision of individual writers and producers or the fantasies of youthful murderers. Gerbner thought that media violence was symptomatic of the social damage created when storytelling, the sort of thing that communities used to do for themselves, was subjected to industrial mass production. Mass-produced stories were told for profit, not pleasure or edification. Ironically, this meant that mass-produced stories about violence *did* end up teaching lessons about the world that were particularly clear, because the stories all had the same structure. Together, stories about violence taught audiences that the word was something to be feared. However, this message was a by-product of the economic goals demanded by the market (Gerbner, 1998).

THE POLITICS OF MEDIA VIOLENCE

Thinking of violence in terms of message systems connects 'old' concerns about film and television effects with 'new' questions about the role of digital media in contemporary cultures of violence, such as the phenomenon of school shootings. Although he wrote mostly about television, Gerbner's true interest was the social production and distribution of messages. Television mattered as the most powerful message system the world had ever seen. Television had organised the common human capacity for storytelling into a narrative production line. Its only goal was to draw large audiences and the advertising revenue that followed. The best way to do this was to rely on standardised stories that already attracted viewers, and violence fitted the bill. Looking at television content across a variety of genres, Gerbner and his colleagues at the University of Pennsylvania concluded that the medium told the same story over and over again, and more often than not it used violence to do so (Gerbner et al., 1980). Violence was frequent and generic on broadcast television because the commercial medium could rely on it to draw a crowd.

If, however, the motives behind violence were economic, the outcomes were political. Gerbner thought the sheer weight of television violence carried a single lesson: the world was a 'scary place'. The main effect of this message was to make people afraid (Gerbner et al., 1980). Television violence made people think society was far more dangerous than it really was. This fear affected civic participation, because those who watched a lot of television were less likely to trust other people. It affected public policy too, in a roundabout way, because media violence made people more receptive to political candidates who favoured punitive approaches to crime. This thinking has been applied to school shootings. For example, commentators speculate links between this perception and penal 'reforms' that have reintroduced physical punishment – boot camps, chain gangs and beatings – as a sensible way of dealing with young offenders (Hogeveen, 2007). Less formally, events such as the 1999 Columbine numbers, widely blamed on aspects of the goth youth subculture, unleashed a wave of suspicion against young people who favoured the style (Consalvo, 2003).

Consequently, school shootings show how Gerbner's thoughts on media violence are relevant to digital media societies. The advent of social media, where images and stories are also created and shared by young media users, connects 'old' ways of conceiving violence with 'new' practices in user-led media. Media professionals and media users participate in school shootings as media events for a number of different reasons: profit, kudos and the chance to connect with communities. But no matter the motivation, the consistent allure of violence says, among other things, that the multiplication of signifying practices brought about by social media does not necessarily imply a multiplication of meanings. Whatever its provenance, media violence is always a commodity that can be traded for attention, and this meaning supersedes all others.

It is the capacity of message systems to secure the singular meaning that audiences will pay attention to media violence (regardless of whether *messages* come from seasoned journalists, experienced film makers, Californian soundstages, rock stars or bedroom-bound teens) that explains why school shootings are tragically familiar media fare – and why they reflect general dynamics in media societies. School shootings are about the economies and technical capacities of public storytelling, not the homicidal tendencies of resentful young men with digital cameras or our appetite to witness them in action. Studies of school shootings suggest that these 'economies and capacities' create profit and cultural capital by sharing the means of producing media content, then encouraging the production of particular meanings from a range of possible alternatives. Meanings are closed through a variety of 'framing' devices that can be analysed both quantitatively and qualitatively. In recent studies of school shootings, the concepts of agenda setting and myth have been used to show how media become powerful when they win public trust as authoritative sources for defining what is important in the world. Media power is about highlighting, repeating and interpreting; school shootings are frequently brought to our attention as common events that represent a series of coherent dangers to social order. The fact that this seems like a simple truth is a function of media's ability to make us see different events as variations on the same themes, because they are presented *and interpreted* as such by media industries, media users and media audiences alike.

FROM MEDIA VIOLENCE TO SCHOOL VIOLENCE

Recapping, media violence is popular because it is a device that media industries have used to monopolise public sense making. Societies have always entertained themselves with violent dramas, but twentieth-century television and film became influential because they appropriated this tradition to political and economic ends, with public consent (Gerbner, 1998). The television age saw a vast homogenisation in public storytelling: audiences were repetitively entertained with the same story, where the same people carried out the same actions for the same reasons to the same ends. Whatever the show, primetime television in the 1970s tended to be about white middle-aged, middle-class men safely negotiating a violent, urban world that preyed on older people, women and other races (Gerbner et al., 1980). Media coverage of school shootings seems similarly generic: no matter the place, time or specific grievance, we see stories of young men who kill their classmates, then themselves, and leave posthumous media messages arguing that they had no choice but to resort to violence. Looking at school shootings, it is notable that people like Pekka-Eric Auvinen, who killed 12 people in Jokela, Finland, in 2009, consciously repeated the narratives that had been built around earlier mass murders. However, such actions also represent the broader effects of message systems, particularly the conviction that social events are not truly social until they have a media presence. This is a belief to which the *victims* of school shootings have also subscribed. Nothing demonstrates this more adroitly than the fact that even survivors of the 1999 Columbine Massacre – that scholars agree formed a template against which many subsequent events would be measured – have used media as a prosthetic to process their real experience and have, in the process, been exposed to uncomfortable questions about what it means to profit from suffering.

So, school shootings are indicators of general media influence for the following reasons:

1 School shootings have drawn attention to the shift from effects, as understood when speaking of media *and* society, to political influence, as it is understood in *media societies*.

2 Agenda setting and myth have been used in combination to explain why school shootings suit the needs of message systems and political interests that benefit from the production of fear.

3 Research from Finland shows how questions about media violence still circulate around profit and methods for attracting audiences under different historical, national and economic conditions and when, perhaps more importantly, most of the framing work comes from young media users.

Generally, then, this topic shows how the ideas and the methods that were applied to the mass-media era, when explaining why violence was such a systemic feature of film and television, can also be applied to digital media. This raises a fascinating research question that crosses over to other topics: How can the multiplication of the means of media production lead to a narrowing of the ideas that are placed before the public? School shootings are therefore case studies that redirect questions on media violence towards more general issues in understanding the nature of media influence in media societies.

VIRGINIA TECH: LIVING IN MEDIA SOCIETIES

When Eric Klebold and Dylan Harris murdered 12 people and injured 20 others at Colorado's Columbine High School in 1999, they set in train a sequence of media processing that would, from thereon, repetitively represent the boys as symbols of why audiences should fear a world where terror could strike anywhere (Altheide, 2009). However, the 2007 murders at Virginia Tech gave a clearer view of why school shootings encapsulate a media society's view on violence and influence, as they catalysed public discussions on how media are *systematically* involved in the production of fear. This is because when discussing these murders, it was immediately apparent that the issue here was how news companies could not simply cover the story, as they were part of it.

On 16 April, Virginia Tech student Cho Seung-Hui murdered 32 of his peers. Two days later, NBC news aired excerpts from a 'multimedia manifesto' that Cho had mailed to the network (NBC News, 2007). Chillingly, the killer had recorded and sent the piece *during* his rampage. Anchor Brian Williams was visibly troubled by an ethical dilemma: would granting Cho infamy inspire copycat killers? However, deeper issues were at play. Cho's preoccupation with how his actions and death would appear to the public showed that media representation is something that media users think about. Years earlier, Gerbner had argued that television valued violence as a reliable means of attracting audience attention. Cho demonstrated that this was no longer a matter for media professionals alone.

This is why Virginia Tech clarified the significance of framing influence in terms of media societies, as opposed to media *and* society. Cho's planning complicated the traditional privilege that usually allowed the news to blame other genres for encouraging real violence. In a study of how news apportioned blame for Columbine, Scharrer et al. (2003) discovered that journalists distanced themselves from popular culture by blaming the massacre on Marilyn Manson, German death-metal, video games like *Doom*, and movies such as *The Matrix* and *The Basketball Diaries*. In juxtaposition, William's dilemma over what to do with the Cho footage demonstrated that this was a false dichotomy; the possibility that Cho had been partly inspired by a desire to speak to the nation through the news showed how the issue was mostly about craving public visibility. If media 'caused' the event in any way, it was equally plausible that this worked through the impression that in media-saturated societies, speaking to the world through international media is an attainable goal.

The lesson of this incident is that to understand why school shootings matter as media events – which they clearly do – we have to consider how media violence *in general*, including the violence we see on the news, cultivates a series of beliefs and expectations of what the world is like among audiences. There is evidence that media violence affects expectations about how the world works, even when audiences know, in abstract, that reality is not as it appears on our screens. This is one of Gerbner's lessons, as his data suggested that television crime dramas cumulatively influenced what television viewers expected from real encounters with police officers, lawyers and the like, even though we know these dramas are fictions (Gross, 2009). The idea here was that media fiction and non-fiction both tended to present violence in the same way, producing an accretion in public common sense about what violence meant socially, which then affected how audiences interpreted new incidents, whether they be in media or in society. Fact and fiction were common drivers of underlying ideological processions, where particular interpretations of violence are turned into facts by simple repetition, and where news and drama told the same basic story about who committed violence, who suffered from it, and what all of this meant about society and its governance (see Gerbner, 1998; Shanahan and Morgan, 1999; Shanahan et al., 2012). Marilyn Manson could tell you this, as he eventually had to accept that his career is for ever connected to Columbine because he, Harris and Klebold were constantly seen together in popular culture. In a 2005 interview, the singer conceded that Columbine was part of his public image, and his only option was to play along: 'in the wake of Columbine – I had clearly become far deeper into the culture that I was criticizing than I had expected' (Interview, 2005). If news coverage of school shootings does create misperceptions about reality, these misperceptions become real, in so far as they direct thought and action. Although the chances of being killed by an armed teen are remote, the danger of being a victim of the fear they generate – or a victim of those whom the fear afflicts – is not. Even if the belief that spectacular school violence is on the increase is incorrect, it has become 'true' inasmuch as many people believe it to be a fact, and this has led to real actions, for example in the formulation of school policies (Muschert and Peguero, 2010).

The question that emerged from Virginia Tech was: How do media users become involved in the cultivation process, where media violence affects beliefs about social reality? The first step to answering this question involves considering how media practices attach particular meanings to school shootings, the effects these attachments have, and finding the ideas and methods that can describe the process. Studies of school shootings have approached these matters by applying the ideas of agenda setting and myth to the broader concept of 'framing'.

SCHOOL SHOOTINGS AND MEDIA FRAMING

Studies using the concepts of agenda setting and myth have defined school shootings as *violent media events that express the values and practices underpinning organised message systems*. Mediated school shootings affect reality by creating politicised narratives that become scripts for action. These narratives emerge from framing processes. The argument that media power relies on 'framing' (popularising particular interpretations of reality against a range of alternative interpretations) is a mainstay of media and communication studies that embraces mass-communications approaches, such as agenda setting (McCombs and Shaw, 1972), and qualitative methods, like semiotic studies of media myths (Barthes, 1993, 1977). Framing is about how messages attach non-necessary meanings to real events with such force and frequency that political arguments become common sense. Framing comes in various guises, as described by Carragee and Roefs:

> Framing research examines how frames are sponsored by political actors, how journalists employ frames in the construction of news stories, how these stories articulate frames and how the audience members interpret these frames. (2004: 215)

Framing helps message systems process reality for audiences in an efficient manner. In news, frames give journalists formulas for writing their stories (Kitzinger, 2004). News media attract audiences by attaching new events to existing beliefs and interests – like the feeling that bad things are extraordinarily upsetting when they happen to good people and the young (Muschert, 2009). Frames help media organisations maintain audience attention because they can be modified to suit new occasions (Chyi and McCombs, 2004). Framing *frames* media influence as the marriage of continuity and change; frames attract public attention to new events by referencing old ones, activating existing values, and then leading beliefs, values and opinions in new directions.

In the last decade, few catastrophes have exemplified the political force of framing better than the Columbine High School Massacre. One of the most reported and followed news items of the 1990s, Columbine has assumed a life that was unimaginable in 1999; post-9/11, it has been represented as an omen on the impossibility of living safely in a terror-plagued world (Altheide, 2009). On the other hand, Columbine stays in the public mind because its meanings are adaptable, which is why it has been reinterpreted across genres: documentary (Michael Moore's *Bowling for Columbine*); teen television (Josh Wheedon's *Buffy the Vampire Slayer*;

Forman, 2004), film (Gus Van Sant's *Elephant*); and literature (Douglas Coupland's *Hey Nostrodamus!*). Even Columbine survivors have fictionalised their ordeal; 2009 saw the release of *April Showers*, a film dramatisation of the massacre by alumnus Andrew Robinson. Robinson's classmates credited the film with helping their healing, indicating *their* feeling that re-enactment affected how the ordeal would be recalled even for people who were there. *April Showers* speaks to the success of message systems, which have created media societies where events must be mediated to be social. No matter *what* we want to say, *when* we speak of Columbine, we use what Roland Barthes (1977) called a 'thick', media-dependent language; it is impossible to talk about it without referencing the media stories that have been woven around the original incidents, and even its survivors feel the need to translate their experiences into stories for the public. Thick media languages make events like Columbine influential because the language and the events work together to produce evocative ideas that are hard to resist when we seek to communicate. The genius is that they work even when we know they spin reality because they are sometimes our only access to speaking of that reality. We may object to specific meanings that have been attached to Columbine, but it is almost impossible to imagine a conversation on school violence that would not mention it. The Columbine shootings are, in framing parlance, an event that is both accessible (a frequent feature of media content) and applicable (i.e. connected to themes that are often used to interpret the significance of subsequent events) (Tewksbury and Scheufele, 2009). In this sense, if these thick languages already exist, then social media simply multiply the numbers of people who can remind us of it.

One way to measure this is by simply counting how often Columbine has been referenced publicly; this was the founding method of agenda setting (McCombs and Shaw, 1972). However, Columbine's political relevance depends on what people remember about it *thematically*, and how they see parallels with things that followed. In part, this is again a quantitative issue, but it is also about how different themes were connected to the same incidents. How, for instance, did Columbine stop being about goth rock and start being used as an index of global terror? These are complicated questions requiring many different types of evidence. Consequently, qualitative and quantitative methods have been applied to studying school shootings, and also why the topic clarifies the importance of framing as a unifying topic across the discipline.

MUSCHERT, MYTH AND AGENDA SETTING

Glenn Muschert's work on the framing of school shootings has demonstrated an important shift in the general argument about agenda setting, and connected this argument to cultural understandings of media power. Agenda setting is a process where the media affect political opinions by presenting particular events or *objects* as being of public interest, and then emphasise *attributes* of those events in defining *why* they are of public interest (McCombs and Shaw, 1972; McCombs, 2005). Attributes take the form of aspects and central themes; aspects are themes that the media attach to events, and central themes are aspects that the media repeatedly present as summarising what a story is about in terms of why audiences should care about it (McCombs, 2005). McCombs thought that Columbine was a case study in agenda setting because media framing transformed a local tragedy into a tale of a dysfunctional American psyche, and it is no longer possible to speak of school shootings at all without referencing it (Chyi and McCombs, 2004). Over time, news stories stopped writing about what Klebold and Harris had done to their community and began stories on what they had done to America (Chyi and McCombs, 2004). Muschert's (2009) analysis of 683 newspaper reports confirmed that Columbine became an *applicable* story because, gradually, stories about Columbine itself became less frequent, while others about reactions to Columbine in other schools became more common. Columbine prompted media narratives that invoked processes of stability and change where fear was amplified. The initial sorrow and pity over what happened in Columbine was transformed, in the news at least, to reasons for fear about what might happen to your own family.

Muschert used agenda setting and myth to describe how news transformed the facts of school shootings into political narratives that are repeated with such ubiquity that they seem to be pure common sense. There were three stages to his project. First, he explained how agenda setting turns shootings into public issues (Muschert and Carr, 2006). Next, he built a typology of school shootings, noting similarities and differences between international events where armed people have killed school children and their carers (2007). Third, he interpreted the political aspects of agenda setting by exploring myth as a special case of 'applicability', where publics are taught what to think about events through the themes connected to those events (2009).

Muschert argued that one of the main effects of framing is homogenisation, and that Columbine could only be seen as an archetypal rampage because media chose to suppress the differences between it and other cases (Muschert, 2007). Harris and Klebold were 'rampage killers', disgruntled students who had deliberately targeted an institution and students against whom they had a grudge. Columbine was different, then, from crimes committed by adults (like Dunblane), or attacks by terrorist groups (like Beslan). The impression that one incident represents them all is more about framing than it is about things that actually happened. This homogenisation explains why school shootings are easy to cover from a message-systems perspective (although not for the journalists who work in them), in so far as new incidents can be swiftly processed in order to quickly attract large audiences (Muschert and Carr, 2006).

On one hand, this marks a divergence between media and the real, since statistics show that young people are more vulnerable to other forms of violence, and that media attention to school shootings does not mirror their real frequency (Muschert and Carr, 2006). On the other hand, this divergence exerts its own reality effect through a two-stage agenda-setting process (Muschert, 2007). Columbine has stayed in the public mind through sheer repetition, but this repetition is helped by its plasticity, as a real occurrence that could be interpreted in many ways, and re-purposed to suit the anxieties of a changing political world. At base, Columbine's salience is explained by the operations of message systems that naturalise non-necessary meanings.

Muschert showed how news about Columbine created a general climate of fear by creating and emphasising one central attribute of the story: the myth of the 'juvenile super predator'. This was a 'crime myth' that presented certain criminals as particularly alarming threats to the order of things:

> First, a myth requires the identification of innocent and often – helpless victims. Second, a myth requires the appearance of brave and virtuous heroes. Third, there must be a threat to legitimate and established norms, values, or lifestyles. Finally, a crime myth needs the identification of a deviant population responsible. (2007: 252)

Muschert found that most of the news stories written about Columbine were 'mythic' because they concentrated on victims who were obviously heroic, or whose deaths were especially tragic because they had overcome severe challenges in their lives. Examples were: teacher Dave Sanders, who selflessly tried to save as many of his charges as possible; Cassie Bernal, a young Christian who allegedly refused to renounce her faith even when facing the barrel of a gun;[2] and Isaiah Shoels, an African-American athlete who conquered a heart condition only to be murdered. These deaths *were* deeply tragic, but they also helped journalists as they immediately activated emotive 'scripts' that quickly told audiences why these deaths were *especially* upsetting. The unequal attention given to certain victims expressed the newsworthiness of violated social norms and expectations (Muschert, 2009).

Muschert's work on myth supports the view that school shootings are public events because of message systems, not morbid publics. In the essay 'Myth Today' (1993), Roland Barthes described how myths happened when the media used signs to convert debatable political opinions into truth. Media processing connected material objects, like news photographs (signifiers), to a series of contingent political arguments (signifieds), naturalising these connections such that they passed into common sense because it became practically impossible to separate the two. The myth of the 'juvenile super predator' is one such phenomenon. Harris and Klebold were undoubtedly responsible for a tragedy; they undoubtedly used popular culture to express their disdain for the classmates they ended up killing, and succeeding 'rampagers' have modelled their own crimes on Columbine (Larkin, 2009). However, it does not follow that Harris and Klebold were harbingers of psychopathic youth hordes who have been whipped into a homicidal frenzy by goth rock, first-person shooters and bastardised readings of Nietzsche. These conclusions depend on how their story is told and repeated.

Myths have always been the stuff of culture, but Barthes argued that mass media were particularly good at making them quickly and giving them a real force through 'compact' languages where the constant availability of media texts as resources for making social meaning made it near impossible to speak without referencing them (1977: 168). Media mattered politically because the only truths that counted were those that could be widely expressed and popularised. 'Citation, reference, stereotype' became inescapable devices in political speech

(1977: 168), such that even if we could see through myths, it was much harder to see through *myth making* because society is invisible without it. Audiences need myths, because myths are valuable road maps that help people to grasp social reality in its totality. This becomes a problem when 'map-making' is handed over to industries that tend to produce the same maps for economic reasons.

Columbine was a vivid exemplification of Barthes' point that media have power because it is hard to separate *experienced* truth and language. It was difficult to distinguish between the reality of the Columbine deaths *as* tragic and their representation as *mythologies of tragedy* because they *were* heartbreaking. The murders of Sanders, Bernall and Shoels were terrible injustices; Sanders' reward for his dedication was a lonely death on a cold floor, but his life and death lent itself to conveying a sense of tragedy in a particularly effective way. This, for Barthes, was the power of myth. Barthes believed media power was unassailable because it is impossible to conceive society without mythological processes. This all too easily tips over into ideological outcomes, such as the feeling that the level of tragedy in an event depends on who the victim is. Muschert applied this idea in making the following point: it is not that the deaths of Sanders, Bernall and Shoels were not poignant – they were. However, the reality of their lives lent themselves to frame processing, and this is one of the reasons why Columbine and its victims are remembered and represented more than other shooting incidents.

For these reasons, Muschert's connection of agenda setting and myth to understanding Columbine is a statement on the history of thought on the politics of signification. The next logical question is: How do these ideas apply when social media and media users participate in setting agendas and perpetuating myths? Finnish studies of school shootings, centred on murders in the towns of Jokela (2007) and Kauhajoki (2008), explore this question. These studies develop scholarly thought on framing and reality by showing how violence, profit, media technologies, media businesses and media users still connect in ways that Gerbner would have recognised under different national and political conditions, where much of the framing comes from the public.

FINLAND: WHAT HAPPENS WHEN SOCIAL NETWORKS LEAD THE NEWS?

Muschert's research concentrated on news stories, which means his assertion that commercial interests drove myths and agendas was assumed, rather than argued, empirically. Sumiala and Tikka's (2010) study of Finnish shootings was then complementary as a grounded example of how a very particular set of production and media practices impacted negatively on how events at Jokela and Kauhajoki were explained. At face value, both of these events were different media wise because social media users started to frame what had happened long before professional journalists started their work. If anything, online framing affected media professionals, forcing Finnish news organisations to desert principles of public service as they fought to recover their readers. Although social media challenged the framing monopolies of powerful media organisations (like the influential newspaper *Helsingin Sanomat*), the functioning of profit-driven 'thick' languages that interfaced between entertainment, information and the ethics of profiting from violence remained determining factors. This indicated that democratised media production does not necessarily change the questions we ask about what inspires media violence, what it means and what it does.

Just before the lunch hour on 7 November 2007, Finnish teenager Pekka-Eric Auvinen posted a clip called 'Jokela High School Massacre' on YouTube, cycled to the eponymous institution, shot and killed the head teacher, a nurse and six students, then committed suicide. Less than a year later, on 23 September 2008, Maarti Saari staged an almost identical mass murder: he downloaded photographs of himself pointing a gun at the camera to Finland's IRC-Gallery message board, made his way to the Kauhajoki School of Hospitality, killed 11 people, shot himself, and died the next day. Auvinen saw his actions as part of a historical continuum that started with Klebold and Harris. In doing so, he showed why social media could supplement mythical processes that are already in place. The fact that anyone can get involved in framing does not imply that events will be framed in numerous ways if we are all bound by thick languages (represented by the conviction that it is impossible to speak of any school shooting without referencing Columbine). The Finnish case study is internationally relevant as a paradigm of why this remains true under different conditions, where effects do not start in established media organisations. That is, the *differences* between the Finnish and American cases indicate the presence of common underlying dynamics. So, explaining how Auvinen and Saari acted out narratives that were already in place means starting with how their actions departed from other incidents. These differences revolve around how social networking led news agendas in a nation where media technology is close to national identity, factors which eventually amplified the mythic properties of media.

Jokela and Kauhajoki differed from Virginia Tech because both were media events before the shooting began. Auvinen joined an online chat community dedicated to Klebold and Harris months before his attack. Jokela's framing as a Columbine-like occurrence was from the inception a public event, because Auvinen left evidence about his motivations that anyone could gather before any professional news organisations could dictate what the public should and should not know. By the time steps were taken to sweep traces of Auvinen and Saari from social networks after their crimes, their words and images were already in the public domain, never to be recaptured and sealed (Sumiala and Tikka, 2010).

When Pekka-Eric Auvinen framed himself as part of Columbine's legacy, he distracted attention from the uniquely Finnish characteristics of the Jokela story. There are reasons to think that such an event could have been especially troubling in a nation where digital media are fundamental to an international commercial identity that rests on the production of smart mobile technologies. Debates about mobile media and national identity were especially sharp in Finland because they were also about leveraging economic advantages for Finnish products – including Finland itself – in competitive international market-places. Nokia has played a key role in speeding Finland's transition from a producer of raw materials to a manufacturer with a reputation for design excellence that reflects national characteristics (Ryan, 2008). Nokia developed Finland's manufacturing reputation by establishing itself as a producer of quality first, and then beginning to explain its qualities in terms of national characteristics. The marketing of national identity was also important in a nation whose tourist industry helped turn a huge national deficit into an equally huge surplus between the 1960s and 1970s (Haahti and Yavas, 1983).

So, we can see why, if Serazio was right in designating these murders as a 'disconcerting dystopia of user-generated content gone wrong at a moment of much Web 2.0 hype' (2010: 416), Jokela was especially disconcerting in a country that has prided itself as being the European vanguard of the digital transition (Aslama et al., 2002). The tension between information and entertainment, endemic in any representation of school shootings, was likely to be close to the surface in Finland, where fears about what commercialisation was doing to the idea of public service was felt by audiences and media professionals alike, not only in the news (Hujanen, 2009), but also music radio (Kurkela and Uimonen, 2009), sports media (Nylund, 2009) and political campaigning (Isotalus, 2001).

Young Finnish social media users aggravated these fears, giving the national newspaper of record an excuse to set professional standards aside as they battled to recover audiences that were being lost to 'citizen journalists'. News about Jokela reversed the process we saw in Chapter 3 around the Rebecca Hoffman case. In Finland, newspapers like the *Helsingin Sanomat* and broadcasters like MTV3 ran to get ahead of online communities who were already framing what had happened before professional journalists could get to the scene or even figure out where Jokela was (Sumiala and Tikka, 2010). As the news broke first across message boards like MURO BBS, professional newsmakers also deployed their online resources as the frontline of their coverage, meaning that Jokela was primarily an internet story from inception to dénouement (Sumiala and Tikka, 2010). The public challenge to professional news framing made for more competitive conditions where violence's ability to draw a crowd was even more important, meaning profit triumphed over public service. Worse yet, the notion of responsible journalism was dealt a severe blow in the rush from 'deadline to online' journalism that was a response to a news story which was already breaking through online media. This came at the cost of conventional due process, with less time for troubling details like fact checking:

> In competitive media environments, digital communication technology offers new possibilities to fight for the audience. Circulation of authentic visual material – killer images – becomes an easy, low-cost and effective strategy for the media business. (Sumiala and Tikka, 2010)

So, here was another illustration of the argument that although dramatised violence has always enthralled, media violence is about profit. The comparison between the USA and Finland shows that this underlying principle remains constant across immense cultural differences.

CONCLUSION: VIOLENCE, DIVERSITY AND SOCIAL INCLUSION

When media violence entertains, it operates as a sort of deep common sense that unites business and politics in unintentional yet effective ways. The idea that violence, profit and storytelling go hand in hand is finally supported by the fact that even Columbine survivors have had to associate the processing of their ordeals with the financial realities of media production. Once Andrew Robinson decided that his was a story to be told in film, he was forced to consider who would pay for the telling and how. Robinson was publicly disconcerted by the reality that his story could only be dramatised in so far as it could be commoditised, and struggled with the details of how this could be managed ethically while showing due diligence to business concerns. He summarised his dilemma in comments directed at illegal downloaders:

> What is a fair price for *April Showers* on DVD, iTunes (download or rental), Amazon etc? If that means lowering the price on a certain aspect of the film or doing a special promotion I want to look into it so that I can ensure you're able to see the film without having to turn to questionable means. The fact that the film was on several top downloaded lists was kind of awesome despite how troubling that statement is going to come off to some of my investors and fellow filmmakers. At the end of the day obviously, I want as many people to see the film and get whatever they want/can out of it because that is the intent. I also would like to pay back the good men and women who made it possible for us to make this wonderful film you all like so much. I do believe one good deed deserves another, but understand that in tough economic times one has to be flexible. (*April Showers*, 2011)

April Showers took the raw experience of being under the gun and 'framed' it through a series of negotiations (going to film school, finding investors, recruiting film stars,[3] finding an audience, and telling an entertaining story that is respectful and helpful to fellow survivors) with signifying processes where, in the end, regardless of intention, the ethics of profiting from media violence are unavoidable, and demand the question: At what price?

The idea that message systems encourage media users to make violence for commercial purposes, or purposes that end up having commercial effects, fits school shootings that appear to be driven by social networks. Social networking solidifies the truth that media violence draws crowds in the name of profit. Consequently, the moral choices that face performers like ICP and Eminem as they negotiate art and commerce also confront ordinary media users, who are responsible for how messages are released into the public sphere. Although no one probably intended it to be so, the flurry of online activity around the Finnish cases prompted commercial strategies that confused what had happened, and affected what these events would become in the public mind. This is not an instance to be celebrated as an act of media democracy.

Media violence is not common because young people like it, but its popularity is enhanced by the fact that it is something that more young people are making and sharing. Therefore, making the first point is not to say that young media users are innocent of the moral questions that media violence asks. Studies of school shootings tell us that anxieties about media violence do not necessarily change once violence stops being the property of corporate media. In this case, social media multiply the *means* of interpretation, and the effect has been the transition of a language once deemed to belong to film and television into a popular vernacular. This suggests that digital media have intensified the co-dependence of media industries and their publics (van Dijck, 2010), meaning that media violence remains a question of message systems, as it was in the broadcast era. This intensification is also a factor in other areas where youth and media interact. This brings us to the topic of youth, health and how social media help alcohol manufacturers sell their goods, explored in the next chapter.

CHAPTER SUMMARY

- It is useful to think of media violence as a political message, whose main effect is to shape beliefs about what the world is like.

- School shootings appear so frequently as media events because they encapsulate a number of fears about what it means to live in a world marked by acts of random violence.

- The concepts of cultivation, agenda-setting and myth have been used to explain how media process school shootings into events with political meanings.

- The topic has also seen interesting international comparisons, illustrating how the same sorts of global effects can eventuate from very different national concerns and media practices.

- School shootings invite consideration of how far the commercial logic of media systems has become the prevailing logic of all media culture.

NOTES

1 For further details, see Gerbner, 1969, 1998; Gerbner et al., 1980; Shanahan and Morgan, 1999; Ruddock, 2001, 2011, 2012; Gross, 2009.

2 These interpretations are based on some accounts that claim Harris spoke to Bernal before shooting her, whereas other witnesses claim there was no such conversation.

3 Tom Arnold played the role of Dave Sanders.

7

UNDERSTANDING ADVERTISING AND MARKETING: STUDENTS AND ALCOHOL

Research question.
How do media encourage young people to drink?

Underlying question about media influence.
How do media industries profit from young audiences who participate in the creation of social meanings?

Relevant literature.
Experiments and surveys on advertising effects, policy documents on adjudications on advertising content, trade literature on alcohol marketing after the global financial crisis.

Exemplifying case study.
Students and below-the-line alcohol marketing

Outcomes.
The alcohol industry is adept at using media to establish intimate relationships with different consumer groups and individuals; and always has been

Lessons for understanding media influence.
Ordinary experiences with commercial messages can tell us many things about global marketing trends.

In the early period of media-effects research, the topics of health and advertising were popular research topics; scholars wanted to know how persuasive media messages affected public well-being and patterns of consumption. Global concerns about the effects of advertising on binge drinking, which is mainly seen as a predicament affecting the young in particular, access both of these topics at the same time.

It has always been difficult to find evidence that advertising tangibly encourages alcohol abuse, and things have become harder with the advent of social media. It's difficult to argue that advertising is the problem when so many young people regularly celebrate their drunken escapades on Facebook and the like. Of course, the notion of advertising power conjures up the spectre of direct media effects once again. However, if we look at what research on advertising claims, and indeed if we look at how the alcohol industry sells its wares, this is another topic showing that no one – neither media academics nor media practitioners – believes in direct effects. The topic of drinks marketing is another example of how media work by integrating themselves into the practice of everyday living.

This chapter makes this point by explaining how the alcohol industry has ingratiated itself with university student traditions. On the one hand, this demonstrates the sophistication of media power, but on the other it will also alert you to how easy it is to study how that power works by using evidence that you encounter as part of daily living. At the end of this chapter, you will be able to explain why the power of advertising does not depend on the power to control what people think, and how it is possible to study the effects of marketing by locating commercial messages in the broader world of meaningful objects, identities and places.

ALCOHOL, MEDIA RESEARCH AND UNIVERSITY LIFE

I was about to walk into a lecture hall on a Thursday afternoon in 2006 when something struck me. As I pushed the door open, I noticed something under my hand, at eye level: it was a flyer for a drinks promotion for a local club, advertising ridiculously cheap vodka shots. As an undergraduate, I was no stranger to drinking and student-drinking traditions – in my own experience, alcohol was part of university life. But as the years went by, and as I continued to live my life on campus, it did seem as if invitations to drink were becoming more common and even injunctive. I certainly didn't want my students to be thinking about vodka shots on the way *in* to a lecture. Was I right to think that messages about drinking were becoming a dominant element of the university's symbolic environment? I decided to ask my students, to go and find out. We discovered that advertising is part a social conversation about alcohol, staged in terms of identity and tradition. It was, in other words, another case where small-scale qualitative studies could tell us quite a bit about how media popularise certain ideas.

ALCOHOL AND MEDIA: CORE PRINCIPLES

Turning this into a formal academic focus, this chapter studies how the alcohol industry uses media to promote drinking as a 'natural' cultural pastime. The purpose of doing this is to show how the lessons of the effects debate – and particularly the view that media influence *groups* of young people who are largely 'influenceable' because of their social and historical positions – can be applied to public-health policy. This topic is important, given the efforts of the World Health Organization to impose a global ban on alcohol advertising, especially when that advertising is directed at young people.

To understand what such bans may or may not achieve, it is important to think about what advertising does as an *element* of sophisticated marketing strategies that speak to young consumers in numerous ways. When thinking about advertising, marketing and youth drinking, three things have to be borne in mind. First, although research shows that alcohol advertising doesn't tell young consumers what to think, this is not what that advertising tries to do; advertisers depend on audiences who make their own meanings from what they see, read and hear. Second, policy debates on alcohol regulation benefit from the debate over media effects, explored in Chapter 2. This is especially true when that research is augmented with insights from qualitative studies of how audiences make meaning. Third, alcohol marketing is so ubiquitous that it is relatively easy to gather evidence about how it works, globally. In combination, these elements reinforce the case that alcohol advertising, like all media, was most effective when it targets social groups in the social spaces that those groups find meaningful.

To make these points, this chapter:

- uses Leiss et al.'s (1990) work on advertising as a form of social communication, and recent UK Advertising Standards Authority (ASA) adjudications of offensive alcohol ads, to explain why advertisers count on audiences who can interpret meaning for themselves;

- explains why alcohol marketing does not aspire to control what people think, or to increase general alcohol consumption across total populations, by looking at criticisms of econometric studies of media effects, and examining the changing marketing strategies adopted by marketers during the global financial crisis;

- explains why debates over the meaning of advertising miss the point on how alcohol companies communicate with consumers;

- combines scholarship on advertising as a form of social communication with case studies from British advertising regulation to explain how the belief that audiences *cannot* be persuaded to think or do things they do not want to think or do lends practical support to the alcohol advertisers as they struggle to evade regulation on what they can say;

- presents research about student drinking by student drinkers as an example of *grounded* social research where young people use their own experiences with media to explain the increasing sophistication of global marketing practices.

HOW ADVERTISING WORKS: GOING BEYOND MEANING

The student study is relevant to the topic of global alcohol marketing, as an example of a general trend, where the drinks industry has developed a number of sophisticated strategies to communicate with distinct consumer groups. These strategies suggest two things: first, that advertising is becoming less important as a means of popularising alcohol; second, that knowing media influence young people as socially situated groups helps alcohol companies to address particular consumers in particular ways. These strategies are especially important in global contexts where overall alcohol consumption may be declining. Policy implications follow. In particular, changing ideas about media influence and evolving marketing practices complicate the case for measures such as global advertising bans on alcohol products. The question is, how does this case sit in a world where no one – advertisers, regulatory bodies or young drinkers – thinks that advertising is directly responsible for making young people drink?

Chapter 6 argued that profit-driven message systems have encouraged people to fix a particular meaning to violence: that it is fun, or is at least a useful way of getting attention. However, the genius of message systems is that they also profit from audiences who won't be told what to think or do. This observation has serious public policy implications when it is applied to alcohol advertising. As health professionals, governments and global bodies, like the World Health Organization, struggle to combat alcohol abuse among the young, the drinks industry benefits from the fact that young audiences interpret alcohol advertisements in different ways. Youths often see through cruder persuasion techniques, such as the use of sexist stereotyping (Gunter et al., 2010).

But in many cases, this actually helps advertisers. Moreover, contemporary alcohol marketing provides copious examples of the idea that media messages become most effective when they become a natural part of the cultural environment in which young people live. To put this another way, students' experiences of changing production and marketing practices in the drinks industry underline the point that media content becomes persuasive when it can be delivered in ways that penetrate and indeed create meaningful social spaces. The fact that young audiences can 'play' with media meanings only underlines the capacity of media messages to function as a source of pleasure. The ambiguity of drinking messages helps alcohol companies situate drinking as a seemingly natural part of the leisure world. This is best appreciated by combining insights from effects research and qualitative studies of how audiences interpret media content. The overall lesson here is that the ability to 'decode' clever advertising messages *is not* a defence against alcohol marketing.

TEXTS, AUDIENCES, MEANINGS AND ALCOHOL POLICY

The first step in considering how alcohol marketing works among young consumers is to appreciate the role that audience interpretation plays in making popular culture popular. Early qualitative studies of audiences found that people frequently made sense of media content in surprising ways (e.g. Fiske, 1987, 1992). However, this was never intended to imply that the power of media industries unravelled when unruly audiences disagreed with the implied messages of what they saw, read and heard (Morley, 1992). This is an important lesson to bear in mind when considering alcohol advertising, because if the case for measures such as regulation and prohibition are diminished should we believe that audiences make their own meanings, and why then should alcohol advertising be banned if most young people know that their world will not become instantly better if they buy this or that product?

The significance of audiences' capacities to read media content critically is dampened by the realisation that successful advertising does not depend on telling audiences what to think. Moreover, a focus on interpretation is a dangerous distraction from a full appreciation of the subtleties of alcohol marketing, given the dynamism of strategies that take full advantage of mobile digital media. In 2009, the World Health Organization demanded 'comprehensive prohibitions on advertising and promotions'. With alcohol abuse then accounting for 3.7 per cent of global mortality, increased consumption was particularly sharp 'among youth, females, deprived and rural populations and minorities' (WHO, 2009: 4). Given evidence that early onset drinking led to lifelong abuse, and that advertising made a significant contribution to both (Snyder et al., 2006; Gunter et al., 2010), WHO thought the time was right to treat alcohol like tobacco, and ban all promotions.

Whatever the doubts about how effective bans are, it can be said that media education offers only a partial defence against commercial injunctions to drink: knowing that alcohol advertising makes promises that alcohol will not keep doesn't make that advertising less attention-grabbing and pleasurable (Aitkin, 1989; Gunter et al., 2010). Even though young people know that drinking does not make a person sexier or more popular, they can still appreciate the humour and rebellious air of alcohol commercials, meaning that these advertisements *are* successful in building positive associations with brands, even if this does not immediately lead to purchasing (OFCOM, 2007; Gunter et al., 2010). Regulation debates therefore have to deal with the 'decoding paradox': How do audiences who actively interpret the meaning of media content end up helping people who use media to sell alcohol?

WHY DO ADVERTISERS LIKE AUDIENCES WHO WON'T BE TOLD WHAT TO THINK?

Audiences who make inferences help advertisers subvert the spirit of advertising regulation without breaking the letter. In their seminal *Social Codes of Advertising,* Leiss et al. wrote: 'The problem of modern advertising policy is that the ground upon which the issue of dishonesty first rested has shifted, from the matter of over verbalized deceptions ... to the implied claims ... that a viewer is led to make as a result of the complex language and imagery used in advertising' (1990: 364). Advertising is an object lesson in semiotics, because advertisers quickly learned that it was easier to seduce consumers with lifestyle inferences rather than straight claims about product functionality that could be easily disproved and adjudicated against. Advertising is more transformational than informational (Leiss et al., 1990) because it uses words, images and meanings to associate products with desirable lifestyles.

The trick, however, *depends* on audiences' capacity to read between the lines; if audiences can 'catch the drift', then advertisers can quite literally say one thing while meaning another (Leiss et al., 1990). The briefest glance at the UK Advertising Standards Authority's (ASA) rulings on advertisements that are accused of violating industry codes shows how active audiences[1] are a regulatory headache and an industry boon. UK regulators assume that people can decode what advertisements are really trying to say, but this places an onus on the consumer to complain. Alcohol advertisers benefit in two ways: first, they are spared the trouble of having to justify their work before it becomes public as, say, film and game producers must do when seeking a rating; second, they are furnished with a means of defence when complaints *are* forthcoming. The idea that content has many possible meanings lends advertisers a hand in talking their way out of trouble.

Take, for example, a complaint made about Shepherd Neame's advertisement for Bishops Finger ale. The advertisement in question featured an image of a woman in a low-cut medieval costume sitting provocatively on a bale of hay. Headline text stated 'I love a good session on the Bishops Finger'. In the bottom right corner of the ad, text below an image of a bottle of Bishops Finger Kentish Strong Ale stated 'At 5.4 per cent it's near the knuckle' (ASA, 2006: 29).

A complaint that the advertisement was sexist was successfully appealed against on the grounds that it *could* be read in another way. Shepherd Neame claimed the advertisement intended to reference the 'saucy' humour found in British historical comedies, and that anyone familiar with British popular culture would know that. The ASA agreed. The fact that it could also be interpreted as a vulgar sexual reference, combined with a licentious image, was beside the *regulatory* point.

METHODS FOR STUDYING ALCOHOL AND MEDIA: COPING WITH LIMITED RESOURCES THROUGH GROUNDED THEORY

The second thing to note when considering how advertising affects drinking cultures is that neither academics nor the alcohol industry thinks that these effects work in universal terms. A review of the literature on general effects and a consideration of how drinks marketing changed after the global financial crisis of 2007 show that the question at hand is how different audiences are hailed in different ways by different products and communication strategies.

Therefore, studies that look for how general exposure of general audiences to general messages do not address the processes through which alcohol companies try to sell their products. The 'failure' to find direct general effects of exposure to advertising must be confronted with the possibility that this is, in some ways, the search for an effect that no one is trying to create.

Like the topic of media violence, the search for alcohol-advertising effects has met with limited success, if those effects are understood in terms of the relationship between exposure and immediate behavioural response, unmediated by social factors (Gunter et al., 2010). Econometric studies, for example, that compare overall advertising expenditure with overall consumption in particular markets, have been subjected to extensive criticism. Snyder et al. (2006) found 15–26-year-old Americans who lived where alcohol companies spent a great deal on promotion were more likely to become chronic binge drinkers. These associations stood up to controls for education, gender and ethnicity. However, Schultz (2006) dismissed this conclusion on the grounds that Snyder et al. *assumed*, but did not demonstrate, that spending led to exposure and changed habits. For example, it is just as possible that this spending happened in places where there where alcohol was already easily available to young people (because of the number of retail outlets) and it was this factor that explained consumption. Certainly, many other econometric studies have found either no or weak evidence of advertising effects (Duffy, 1989, 1990; Selvanathan, 1989; Calfee and Scheraga, 1994; Ambler, 1996; Dorsett and Dickerson, 2004; Wilcox and Gangadharbatla, 2006; Broadbent, 2008; Nelson and Young, 2011).

It remains possible that advertising works in other ways beyond the simple ambition to stimulate short-term spending with persuasive messages. Econometric studies look for general consumption patterns, but scholars who favour other research methods have argued, like Comstock, that what really matters is how alcohol abuse has increased within distinct social groups. In a major review of consumption patterns in the UK during the first decade of the twenty-first century, Meier (2010) noted that per capita consumption has fallen, but this general pattern masked the fact that some populations sectors were drinking more, and that this was still having a significant impact on public health. 'Heavy episodic drinking' and the consumption of heavy drinkers have risen, while moderate drinkers have become more moderate. Concerns about drinking and health do not rely on aggregate measures; advertising influence is not necessarily announced by the statistics showing that most people drink more or less, as the case may be, than they did in the past. In fact, drinks marketing in the post-global financial crisis world shows that media matter most when consumption declines, because it is under these circumstances that the alcohol industry becomes most aggressive about using media to find new consumer groups within a shrinking pool of customers.

It is certainly true that the challenging conditions of the global financial crisis did focus the minds of alcohol manufacturers on how they could communicate with customers and associate their products with the lifestyles that drinkers were adopting in straitened times, but often the strategies employed for doing so had little to do with advertising per se. For this reason, obsessing over the meaning of advertisements diverts attention away from the other strategies that the alcohol industry uses to communicate with its customers. During the global financial crisis, alcohol consumption suffered a general decline, but products that sought new markets in new places among new consumers found new success.

According to marketing experts Euromonitor International (2010), the global financial crisis had mostly *changed* spending practices among key publics, who would still pay a lot for drinks as long as they were given a lifestyle reason for doing so. These were not spendthrifts; they were 'frugalistas' and 'recessionistas' (Euromonitor, 2010) who wanted to be thrifty without feeling thrifty. This created a counter-intuitive opportunity for the drinks industry to respond to the global financial crisis by making key products more expensive, then explaining to new consumers how spending more on the right things fitted with cautious consumption. The global financial crisis bifurcated the drinks market, and 'premiumisation' and 'economisation' both emerged as viable strategies. The greater value attached to spending *when* spending meant consumers were perhaps more susceptible to 'hip' and 'cool' appeals, but advertising was less important in marketing strategies that framed drinking across the world of objects that had meanings for potential consumers.

Even packaging was vital in persuading drinkers that alcohol suited their new financial circumstances and identities. For example, changed packaging appealed to eco-friendly consumers, or others who were looking to re-create bar experiences in their own homes. The lesson is that the question of what drinks advertisements mean is but a gateway to the broader questions of how the drinks industry frame the pleasures of drinking by communicating with the customers the industry has, and the customers it wants. These are convoluted processes, where the only way to define what media scholars can say is to return to fundamental issues on researching media influence.

The problems with econometric analyses and the changing tactics brought on by the global financial crisis means that we have to pay attention to basic matters of the strengths and weaknesses of quantitative and qualitative methods when considering how media research can study how advertising and communication may or may not encourage drinking. Statistics are fantastic for describing the dimensions of social conversations about drinking, but are less adept at analysing the processes of these conversations as they become meaningful in groups (Jernigan, 2006). Only statistics can show that under-age drinkers in America are more likely to see alcohol advertisements than adults are. But the outcomes of such realities are harder to determine. This is the leap that needs to be made to prompt policy action.

CASE STUDY: WHY STUDY STUDENT DRINKING?

In the face of marketing campaigns that no longer try to reach a general audience, but are interested in young consumers, studies of student drinkers promise to show how commercial invitations work when they target discrete groups. This was the motivation behind the study reported here.

In 2006, 29 undergraduates studying at a university in Liverpool, England, were asked to keep running diaries of their encounters with alcohol messages, noting the following:

- the type and frequency of alcohol messages;
- the variety of media used;
- the times and places where alcohol messages are encountered;
- the evidence of how often students talk about alcohol and alcohol messages;
- the perceived connections between alcohol messages and student drinking behaviours;
- and suggesting a campaign or activity to promote alcohol awareness among students. What message? Using what medium/media? Did they think it would be better to hold some sort of event, such as a drink-free evening in the Student Union? Was a campaign combining media and face-to-face communication the way forward?

The study aimed to connect the student drinking experience with marketing practice by deploying 'grounded theory'. Grounded theory is an inductive research method that finds general explanations for social behaviours by starting with observations of those behaviours at work (Schatzman and Strauss, 1973). The intention is to prevent researchers forcing observations into theoretical explanations that they already have to hand, because there is no point in research that simply re-creates what the researcher already knows.

Grounded theory is a way of unpacking the positivist baggage often attached to 'method'. Schatzman and Strauss argued that in questions of society and culture, methods are really about 'The working of thought processes' (1973: 109). Method is a strategy for choosing how to gather and analyse evidence, and communicating this procedure to a reading audience so that they may assess the plausibility of results for themselves. A grounded approach accords well with the notions that:

- Studying youth media is itself a cultural process that is actively engaged in politicising youth as an idea.
- Drinking cultures are best viewed as meaningful encounters in social settings (Cherrington et al., 2006).
- The common denominator across both of these conditions is that methods are understood as 'simply ... variation[s] of ... ordinary skills' (Schatzman and Strauss, 1973: 109).

Grounded research sets out to connect ordinary people, places and events with the general dynamics that shape social and cultural life. This is an inevitably interpretative process-more about informed judgement than measurement, where research becomes 'methodical' in so far as it is motivated by a search for a consistent 'story' that is faithful to the evidence before the researcher, where this story guides what evidence ends up being reported (Schatzman and Strauss, 1973).

This was a grounded study because its aim was to combine the students' experience and knowledge to write plausible stories about how drinking became a meaningful part of student life, raising new ways of framing the connections between communication and drinking and knowledge the students could 'use', either as people in search of employment or as members of a university community with responsibilities to that community. Students were asked to write advisory reports on health campaigns directed at their peers based on what they had observed about how messages about alcohol reached and appealed to local students. The student whose ideas best suited the marketers' professional needs won an internship with the social-marketing department.

In the language of grounded research, the purpose of the study was to generate knowledge about 'students' as a particular drinking class, and to develop narratives of 'increasingly dense linkages' between drinking, media and social experience by looking at how students put messages about drinking together in their everyday environment, then to think about other linkages by using this knowledge. These linkages reframed media influence by connecting what the students discovered with recent larger studies of how media affect alcohol consumption. The fascinating thing here was that the participants did make a number of telling observations about the subtleties of alcohol communication. This can be illustrated by contextualising key findings in the reports with regulatory actions on advertising content and recent commercial research on new marketing techniques that the drinks industry can use to offset the effects of the global financial crisis.

THINGS THAT STUDENTS KNOW ABOUT SELLING ALCOHOL

Schatzman and Strauss (1973) recognised that a 'purely' grounded approach is impossible. Research is a matter of 'constant comparison', because 'grounded observations' – what you notice and why you think it matters – is affected by what you are looking for based on what you know about the discipline. Bearing this in mind, by comparing other things the students said with theoretical and empirical developments in scholarly and industry research in drinking and media, the students found three important things that moved beyond the anodyne recognition that young people don't believe the extreme, glamorous promises that alcohol advertisements often make. These three discoveries, detailed below, help explain why active interpretation is not a meaningful defence to drinks marketing. This can be shown in the points where the students' comments intersected the adjudications of the UK ASA (who are tasked with ensuring that alcohol advertising does not claim that drinking leads to social and sexual success) and Euromonitors' professional advice on how to make money from shrinking alcohol markets.

Insight one: Sometimes advertising and marketing can change drinking preferences, even though most of the time it doesn't

Although drinking was usually about taste and affordability, as example of how advertising and marketing could change their habits, students did mention the reinvention of cider as a drink consumed with friends in trendy bars. Irish brand Magners was credited with successfully overcoming their perception that cider was a drink for park-bench alcoholics:

> There's a Magners' advert which shows like a group of four or five friends in the middle of the countryside, right next to this big lake and when I see it, I just like aspire to them so much because it looked like they were having such a good time. They were all like happy and, you know, drinking Magners' together [laughter]. It really works for me that advert, as well ... You're just in awe of them really, aren't you?

> I work in a bar and all of a sudden it's just Magners', Magners' all the time. And where I work, it's in a hotel, they charge £5 a bottle and it still sells. I am even saying to people before I serve them ... because I'll only get it flung back saying I'm not paying that. So I just say that it's a fiver, oh a fiver, right okay. So it's like with a glass of ice and they just sit there all day and drink Magners', must spend a fortune.

Impressionistic or not, these observations were prescient. In 2009, the UK ASA upheld a complaint made against a Magners television advertisement that

> showed a man walking into a pub and a pint of Magners' being poured. The voice-over stated 'Magners' Draught Cider. It's the perfect ice breaker. Making sure the conversation flows, in the time it takes to create a cool, crisp pint. No ice, just pure, premium taste. Magners' Draught Cider, time dedicated to you.' At the end of the ad, the man picked up the pint and turned to talk to a group of friends. (ASA, 2009)

The complaint was upheld because the ASA agreed that Magners' advertising did imply that good times depended on drinking their cider.

Euromonitor agreed that cider had been a trendsetter, so much so that it could save a drinks industry from the worst ravages of the global financial crisis. The company's 2010 report on global consumer conditions verified the students' hunch that cider had achieved the remarkable trick of turning cost into a *benefit* just as drinkers had even less to spend. As one of the few products that thrived despite the global financial crisis and various legislative moves against the industry on price, promotion and content,

> cider/perry could provide an essential escape route for the brewers and manufacturers caught with their backs against the wall due to unfavourable demographics or legislative and taxation hurdles ... And cider has a great track record and a rather summery disposition – ideal for the still gloomy times ahead. (Euromonitor International, 2011: 2)

The newfound global success of cider and perry is an exemplar of the premiumisation enigma, where consumers have been willing to spend more on the right drink although they have less to spend on alcohol. Magners proved that cider could be sold to a more affluent clientele, and the UK government unwittingly contributed to this with its '35 per cent juice' rule. This legislation, introduced in 2008, attempted to act against the lower end of the cider market by stipulating that all cider/perry drinks should contain at least 35 per cent fruit juice (Euromonitor International, 2011). This, in Euromonitor's view, helped cider makers sell their products to richer consumers by fitting into health-conscious consumer lifestyles. Cider was suddenly something worth paying for because it was strangely *healthy*. This showed that the commercial appeal of a drink depends on far more than a simple equation between it and good times; it involves a complex process of meaningful negotiation between drinkers, manufacturers, media-policy regulators and legislative powers. It also showed how the students' early encounters with Magners were a portent of things to come, and how the validity of this observation could be enhanced through connections with other sorts of evidence gathered in different ways.

Insight two: A cheap message in the hand is worth more than an expensive one onscreen

The second observation to emerge from the study was that student drinking was more affected by below-the-line marketing than advertising. The medium most noted in the diaries were flyers. Although flyers were usually an annoyance, a 'campus hazard to be avoided or ignored, the right flyer for the right event was a powerful thing':

> Drinks promotions do ensure *where* that team (JMU Hockey) will be ... The first advertisement I have focused on is LSU's promotion for the new Wednesday Night 'Spank'd' found on the union's webpage, and also on flyers and in the student magazine ... Spank'd hosts *the* cheapest drink offer that the union has seen to date with 99p for a Smirnoff vodka-mixer – The emphasis here not only being on the price but also on the fact that this is not cheap vodka on offer! A factor that will impress many a student.

The ASA also worried about this sort of promotional strategy as numerous drinks outlets battled for the student market in tough times. In 2009, the ASA upheld a complaint against Voodoo Events Ltd, who had distributed flyers for a nightclub evening called 'The Vodka Project', the main advertised appeal being £1 shots all night long. The ASA concluded that the implied message of the flyers promoting vodka at about one-third of the price of a cup of coffee was 'please binge'. This, in fact, was a far more flagrant (and effective) flouting of advertising regulations than anything seen on television, at the cinema or in magazines.

History shows that below-the-line marketing has always been important to sales. When the nineteenth-century UK beer industry sought to win back customers from the gin trade, its main persuasive weapons were the jolly draymen whose affability was seen as a key tool in selling beer to the public; in fact, many brewers thought this to be far more effective than advertising (Reinarz, 2007). Although the industry no longer thinks advertising to be a waste of time, it is still eager to grasp ways of establishing intimate connections with consumers that avoid thorny regulatory challenges, and using 'new' mobile media to manage the 'old' trick of getting the message directly into consumers' hands afford novel methods to create direct, immediate, individualised relationships between brands and consumers. These messages are additionally attractive because, unlike above-the-line advertising, evidence seems to show that it is unnecessary to promise personal transformation to hook the buyer. As an example, Euromonitors cite the American example of MillerCoors' Colorado Native beer:

> Every Colorado Native Label comes with a fixed Snap tag which, if photographed on a mobile device and emailed to a specified phone number, allows the brand to interact with its drinkers. After e-mailing a picture of the logo, a drinker will first get a reply asking for their birthday. After their age is verified, they will be questioned with Coloradocentric trivia about their hobbies and interests, and the database will remember the answers and use them to craft future communications and offers to each individual drinker. With small-scale production, locally sourced ingredients, locally focused, personalised and millennial-embracing offers, MillerCoors is ticking all the right boxes. (Euromonitor International, 2010: 24)

Colorado Native uses newer media to re-create an older, 'tactile' experience that Reinarz (2007) argued was typical of nineteenth-century brewers, who preferred to cultivate interpersonal relations with their clientele. What we see in the Colorado Native example is that digital mobile media let manufacturers do this, achieving relationships with consumers without having to bother going to expensive lengths to appeal to identities in ways that could possibly fall foul of advertising regulators. In this sense, the meaning of advertising truly no longer matters, because digital, mobile technologies let alcohol companies get back to selling their products by using what looks like simple information to foster the impression of a personalised relationship between consumer and product that is grounded in the immediacy of communication rather than narrating identity. Colorado Native shows how complex message systems are effective because they manage the trick of appearing simple – as simple as a flyer in the hand.

Insight three: Alcohol marketing sells products by playing with the meanings of social spaces

The third notable insight from the student study was that alcohol promotion worked on the meanings of social spaces. They felt that if there was a student bingeing problem, and if society needed someone to blame, then that blame should be directed at universities that collaborated by letting their premises be used as drinking space. This, in their view, allowed the drinks industry to subvert student 'traditions'. This began with freshers' week, which was generally seen as little more than an extended festival of intoxication:

> If you look at freshers' week, it's all based around drinking. I mean, if you don't drink, then you're not involved in like meeting new people, making new friends or anything because all you do in freshers week you all go on a pub crawl, go to the restaurants and whatever, meeting new people. For people that don't drink like it just totally excludes them from like the social aspect of things at university, I feel, unless they think that it's cool in society, but even then they go around pub crawls as well so you can't win.

This theme showed why price, availability and marketing are *connected* issues, and is again supported by ASA adjudication case history. In 2011, the ASA rejected a complaint made about a poster for the alcohol retailer Bargain Booze that had been pasted on a payphone near the campus of an English university. The poster featured the legend: 'We love Students! Win a year's worth of free booze.' The complaint alleged that the poster was designed to tempt school children and encourage binge drinking. The retailer responded that the positioning of the advertisement near a university campus clearly indicated the intention to reach consumers of the legal age, and that the 'year's worth of booze' offer in fact amounted to less than one unit of alcohol per day, well within safe drinking limits. On this occasion, the ASA sided with the retailer (Advertising Standards Authority, 2011).

Nevertheless, the student claims and the adjudication issue do identify how commercial messages become persuasive by engaging with and changing the *meaning of social spaces*. Bargain Booze was quite open about its intention to target students, and the economic value of locating its stores near campuses. The idea of messages that worked on the meaning of space in very general ways were important to the students, and particularly telling here was how the infiltration of drinking messages and sponsored events onto campus succeeded because they didn't change anything, but instead complemented (or channelled) drinking traditions. In particular, students observed that the tradition of Wednesday-night drinking, once associated with university sports teams following the traditional Wednesday-afternoon recreational space, had now become a general student drinking night that began on campus, and then dragged students out into local night-time economies *en masse*. Varsity Leisure Group's Carnage UK evenings were identified as a powerful example of this, which made a joke of any suggestion that the drinks industry had any real interest in promoting responsible drinking:

> When it comes to the patterns of student drinking cultures I believe that the huge amount of 'tradition' is the source, especially in terms of sports teams and their drinking habits, and so, due to this, no advertising is required to get people 'out' on a Wednesday night in particular as this 'tradition' remains to be a regularity.

> Even the uni itself doesn't help. Like they put on like these nights like Carnage – it's called 'Carnage' so you can imagine what the night is like.

Carnage is a fascinating example of how the spaces of social media have been used to channel drinking traditions to situate the British university campus as a retail outlet in night-time economies. Explaining how drinking was popularised among the young in the 1990s, Measham and Brain (2005) argued that the drinks industry made itself socially indispensable by infiltrating urban regeneration through its renovation of buildings and use of different products to fit time-shifting architectures that help keep people in cities spending money all day long. Alcopops, for example, were marketed as psychotropic substances designed to appeal to polydrug using clubbers, thereby overcoming the pub/club dichotomy that split the drinking public and discouraged them from city centres. The ASA Bargain Booze controversy illuminated the role of the university as a place which, consciously or not, has relations with local retail outlets, if for no other reason than it congregates recognisable consumer groups who can be easily reached. In the case of Carnage UK, not only can these groups be reached, but literally lead out to retailers. In the words of the company itself, in response to allegations that the company encourages binge drinking:

> The Carnage UK event is a social gathering by a cross social and racial network of students. The object of the event is to bring together the broad cross section of students to encourage social engagement, understanding and friendship, which will assist the individual student to integrate within his/her new community. (Varsity Leisure Group, 2008)

According to one of its customers:

> Carnage UK is a ... fancy dress bar crawl ... you buy a £10 t-shirt which gains you entry to bars and clubs around town ... After half an hour in each bar the students are moved on by the event stewards and this continues until the end venue. (RosieT Online Blogspot, 2008)

With connections to bar chains in all of the UK's major student towns and cities, Carnage UK 'assists integration' by leading students off-campus to show them where to drink locally. Moreover, it avoids awkward questions about its promotional activities by outsourcing its marketing. The company website suspended its own gallery of Carnage UK customers in July 2009, but does carry links to student-maintained Carnage UK Facebook sites in 36 locations where, by late 2009, customers had uploaded over 9000 photographs of young people having fun in drinking establishments. The point here was that social media meant Carnage UK did not have to imply any association between its operations, consuming alcohol and feeling like part of local student communities – because their customers were doing this for them (Ruddock, 2012b).

The Carnage UK story combines the themes of advertising, below-the-line marketing and space. The drinks industry has used below-the-line methods to tap into existing communities, and this strategy is valuable given calls for global action against advertising that is directed at young people. Carnage UK have managed an extraordinary trick; not only have they combined social media with trade relationships with bars and clubs close to university campuses; they have also allowed students to flood Facebook with pictures of young people having fun at their events. Carnage UK doesn't have to insinuate anything about associations between drinking and social success – students are doing it for them, thanks to social media. This is a particularly powerful example of why the construction of alcohol as a pleasurable experience is about far more than adverting content, and another example of how media students could use what they know to make telling comments on how communication shaped drinking among their peers.

CONCLUSION: AND WHAT IS TO BE DONE

As Gordon et al. have recently argued (2010), the case *for* regulation is frequently misunderstood. Here, Gordon et al. made the case that determined regulation can at least move toward levelling the playing field in global media cultures where the evidence is abundantly clear that industries have more power than audiences. In the field of drinking, this insight helps explain a general state of inertia that is out of step with the dynamism of a drinks industry that understands only too well that it does have to work hard to sell its products to consumers through an array of communicative devices.

A look at Euromonitor's advice on using below-the-line methods to break new markets gives lie to the idea that all marketing does is to help people act on decisions they have already made. Media play a larger role in drinking cultures because pricing and availability *are* the main drivers of drinking cultures. The fact that general consumption levels do seem to be about what people can afford forces the drinks industry to seek innovative new ways to associate their products with the shifting socio-political identities that consumers want to have. In a sense, one of the reasons why a semiotic deconstruction of glossy advertising says little about how advertising works is because recent years have seen an expansion of semiotic tactics, right down to kegs that interact with domestic spaces to make staying in feel like the new going out. Semiotic 'counter-insurgency' is carried into the fabric of almost every social occasion one can imagine, public or private. This is a new combination of 'informational' and 'transformational' content, where mobile media make the line between one and the other increasingly difficult to see, thus enhancing the power of alcohol marketing to work as common sense. Understanding the convoluted outcomes of these complex processes will always be controversial, simply because evidence suggests that commercial talk about alcohol has all sorts of consequences, many of which probably have little to do with anything that marketers mean to happen. But none of this can be unravelled simply through savvy readings of media content.

What is clear is that there is lots of evidence to suggest that media do glamorise drinking through a variety strategies and genres, and more to the point the *industry* believes this to be the case, and a survey of recent moves shows that the strategies they follow do far more than simply reinforce the decisions of people who have already decided to drink. Recent market forecasts show that people who already like to drink are doing so in smaller numbers, and in the face of the global financial crisis, drinks companies *are* using new media to find new methods to persuade populations who have not traditionally been core customers that they should be so.

The World Health Organization knows that advertising is but a symptom of how drinking is glamorised in numerous ways:

> While alcohol is marketed through increasingly sophisticated advertising in mainstream media, it is also promoted by linking alcohol brands to sports and cultural activities through sponsorships and product placements, and by direct marketing that uses new technologies such as the Internet, podcasting and mobile. (World Health Organization, 2007: 29)

In this context, the idea that young people are too smart for advertisers helps alcohol companies argue that marketing is a reaction to consumer demand. In Japan and South Korea, new lucrative female markets have, so the story goes, forced distillers to rebrand and refocus on products that appeal to women. But manufacturers have adeptly caught up with youth trend by using social media. In Malaysia, Tiger beer organised a 'blogger party' that sent thousands of images of young Malaysians having fun throughout social networking sites like Facebook, Twitter, flickr and YouTube (Blecken, 2009). Tiger and others in the industry know that advertising is simply one among a range of media measures that brewers and distillers can use to sell their wares; this is why critical interpretations of alcohol advertisements are incomplete defences.

This speaks to the very heart of what the analysis of meaning was supposed to be in media studies. The World Health Organization knows that advertising is just one way that alcohol companies try to reach young consumers, and in this, the topic of advertising, intentionally or not, works as a gateway to reflect on the wider matter of how society communicates about the pleasures and dangers of drinking, and how this total conversation affects drinking habits.

The meaning of drinking is constructed across a variety of 'social texts', even down to the buildings we live around.[2] All of this *means* that the 'meaning of meaning' in media studies needs to be carefully framed if the discipline is to have a say on global health policy on alcohol. The ASA has been more concerned about messages that are not very 'semiotic'; flyers that say 'cheap booze here – and lots of it' because they mean 'cheap booze here – and lots of it'. The 'informational' dimensions of the latter disguises the nature of the problem, which is the ease with which multiple messages make it easy for *audiences* to connect intoxication and fun, and, in this sense, what is at stake is not the lack of importance of meaning, but the multiplication of places where it is made.

This is very significant because is overcomes the false dichotomy between seeing drinking as being driven by price and availability *instead* of media. Messages *about* price and availability are there because of a constant stream of messages about drinking which people encounter in all kinds of places when they are doing something else – like studying. At the very least, what we do know is that Euromonitor's advice is not consistent with the argument that alcohol marketing simply helps people, who have already decided they will drink, to choose what they will consume. Surveying the state of the art in alcohol marketing, it is quite clear that the importance of price and availability have *also* spurred and redoubled efforts to communicate with consumers in new ways to offset the reverses of the global financial crisis. In other words, it is precisely because price is so important that communication is vital among manufacturers who face shrinking and changing markets where traditional, dependable consumers are no longer reliable sources of revenue.

Additionally, there are obvious problems with the self-regulation preferred by most government. In the USA, research has found that compliance with advertising regulations has improved when the alcohol industry has been involved in making the rules; this is hardly surprising, as the same research has also noted that greater latitude has been afforded in what advertising can do. Whatever the limitations of state regulation, its opponents should consider that there is no conclusive evidence that *communication* about alcohol *does not* affect youth drinking. There is evidence of significant effects when a wider evidence base with more variables is considered (Gunter et al., 2010).

However, the solution to this situation is not to regard media as enemies. Instead, the explosion of publicly available devices make it possible to integrate media with community activism, overcoming what is often an unhelpful, and unpractical, distinction between media and other forms of everyday communication; something that the World Health Organization recognises. Media advocacy can educate the public and key stakeholders within the community, resulting in increased attention to alcohol on the political and public agenda. This can lead to reframing the solution to alcohol-related problems in terms of a coordinated approach by relevant sectors, such as health, enforcement, nongovernmental organisations and municipal authorities (World Health Organization, 2006).

The students in the study had a range of activist options open to them, both formal and informal. Another reason why the students blamed the university for encouraging alcohol abuse was because of the way that drinking was celebrated in student publications. As people who could participate in the production of these publications, they were well placed to agitate for change. As people who could get involved in the organisation of events like freshers' week, they could intervene by arranging social occasions where drinking was not central. On a more prosaic level, they could also make more of an effort to include peers who did not drink in their everyday social life. The point is that decoding alcohol advertisements doesn't do anything to stop the infiltration of the alcohol industry into youth as a commercial, urban, *educational* experience, but using knowledge about how heavy drinking is normalised through media can prompt local action, because ultimately commercial messages only work when they connect with material conditions, and because of that there is always something that young audiences can do beyond interpretation.

CHAPTER SUMMARY

- In media-saturated societies, alcohol is 'sold' through a variety of communication strategies; advertising is just one of them, and so it is important to place any conversation about advertising in a broader debate about how young people are involved in the creation of meaning and pleasure around alcohol.

- The debate on how audiences make sense of media content helps explain why it is so difficult to regulate alcohol marketing when we map that debate onto the practices of regulation and below-the-line marketing.

- However, the importance of below-the-line marketing also means that it is easy to find evidence of how the 'big' issues in international alcohol consumption and regulation work in everyday life. Taking a grounded theory approach shows how we can make meaningful comments on these topics, even when faced with limited resources.

NOTES

1 The idea of the 'active audience' is commonly related to the work of John Fiske (1987, 1992). Fiske argued that media content is 'polysemous' (has many meanings) and as a result viewers can interpret the meaning of media content in a number of surprising ways. With the development of editing and sharing practices common to social media, this 'activity' increasingly takes the form of 'rewriting' popular texts; see, for example, Ruddock (2007) on *Top Gun* as a gay film.

2 Consider, for example, Rehab, a bar in the medieval English city of Norwich. Rehab occupies an Elizabethan building, which the company has painted pink. The bar's logo is the yellow smiley face that was a common symbol of the early UK rave scene (1988). The building itself, then, its name and its décor, confronts a number of issues that drive debates on binge culture.

8

UNDERSTANDING POLITICAL COMMUNICATION: BARACK OBAMA, MEDIA CONVERGENCE AND MEDIATED INTIMACY

Research question.
Can social media make young people enthusiastic about voting again?

Underlying question about media influence.
How has media convergence affected the structure of political communication?

Relevant literature.
Bennett et al.'s (2010) study of successful uses of social media by political organisations, Stanyer's (2012) research on the trend towards 'intimate' communication between candidates and voters

Exemplifying case study.
Barack Obama's success in attracting youth voters

Outcomes.
Obama benefitted from a systemic shift toward personalised politics that has been observed throughout the developed world. As President, he has also profited from practices of online 'opinion leading'

Lessons for understanding media influence.
Obama's success was largely about the convergence between media and interpersonal communication. Scholars have been interested in *this* convergence for some time

The topic of how media affect voting decisions is one of the foundational topics of media research. Beneath the deceptively simple question of how news stories, staged media debates, political advertisements and the like either changed or maintained voting preferences, scholars realised that political communication was about more than politicians and journalists debating policies and elections, and political engagement was about much more than voting.

The need for an expansive definition of political communication has been amplified as popular culture and social media have perspicuously come to play an important role in electoral politics. Here again, youth are key, as young voters seemed to be the voting bloc most alienated by traditional politics, and the most enthusiastic adopters of new media politics. This has prompted detailed empirical work on the changing structures of political communication, where scholars like Lance Bennett (2007) and James Stanyer (2012) have set out to gather systematic evidence to show how mediated political discourse has changed in the digital age.

Barack Obama's election as US President energised this project, as a candidate who successfully used new media resources to achieve the goal that the 'older' ones were becoming less and less successful at achieving: getting young people to vote. However, the lesson of new research on digital media and politics is that figures like Obama, who appear to simply exude charisma, are only possible because of changing communication systems that favour personalised politics. The most remarkable thing about these systems is that they seem to have revived much older, interpersonal forms of communication, where young media users play an active role in the circulation of political discourse.

After reading this chapter, you will be able to explain why changing media technologies have enhanced the political importance of popular entertainment. In particular, you should see a connection between ideas about audience participation and performance, introduced in Chapter 4, and research on the role media play in electoral politics.

POLITICS AS ENTERTAINMENT

In 2009, the celebrity gossip magazine *Now* released a survey showing that a majority of its readers thought *American Idol/X-Factor* impresario Simon Cowell would make a great prime minister. Inthorn and Street (2011) followed this up with their own academic research. Why on earth would it make sense to think about a reality talent show judge as a potential national leader? The important thing about Inthorn and Street's study is that it *did not* begin from a judgemental view; it's easy, and boring, to view facts like this as yet more evidence of youthful apathy and ignorance, since celebrity culture is something that seems especially dazzling to the young. Taking pause, Inthorn and Street pointed out that many figures from the music industry have stepped into the political arena with such force, based on their popularity, that 'real' political figures and political processes have to recognise them as real political players. U2's Bono, for example, now sits at the table of international debates on underdevelopment and global poverty, and the matter of how he got there is neither here nor there for the people who now have to talk to him, and listen.

Although from a media studies point of view, it is relevant. When faced with a stark fact, like the idea that many young people think Simon Cowell could run a country, Inthorn and Street point out that the main task is to trace how such a conclusion appears rational. This brings two research questions into play. How do figures from the world of entertainment come to be seen in political terms, as people who embody leadership qualities that elected officials should possess? How do politicians become popular by projecting themselves as entertaining, knowable people? These are perhaps the defining questions in political communication today, and they explain why Barack Obama is fascinating, for the issues he represents vis-à-vis media influence.

POLITICAL COMMUNICATION: ENTER OBAMA

Barack Obama's victory in the 2008 US presidential election was a historical landmark for many reasons; one being that it forced scholars to reconsider some entrenched views they held about how media affect young voters. Scholarly efforts to explain what Obama's election meant, vis-à-vis the history of thought on political communication, centred on youth in two senses. First, 'media malaise' (Zaller, 1994), the global ignorance and ennui television was thought to have cultivated around electoral politics, had been seen as an affliction that preyed on the young in particular (Harrington 2008; Bennett et al., 2011). This was now a thesis that seemed insecure at best, since 2008 had seen the largest voting turnout in the USA since 1960 (Gans and Hussy, 2008), and young people were more or less directly responsible for voting Obama into office. The Pew Research Centre calculated that 66 per cent of voters under the age of 30 voted Democrat in 2008, making for the greatest ever disparity between younger and older voters in electoral history, with the bias in voting preference turning the youth vote into a bloc of unprecedented power (Keeter and Horowitz, 2008). Second, Obama's victory was widely attributed to his youth, his appeal to youth and his gift for using social media to energise young voters. Writing in the *Journal of Visual Culture*, Everett could scarcely have made this case more succinctly:

> Building upon and extending young people's mastery of and full immersion in such online interactive social media forms and technologies as MySpace, Facebook, YouTube, cell phones and short message systems (SMS) ... Obama himself became the essential political change agent that America's digital youth and the young at heart activists decided they could and would believe in – a highly visible and accessible new kind of president with whom they could interact, share their views, and even reinvent America both in the real world and more strategically online. (2009: 195–196).

Popular media sources agreed Obama's game-changing triumph confronted a number of assumptions political commentators had long held to be true about politics, media and young people. Early in his campaign to win the Democratic

Party's nomination as their presidential candidate, Obama showed a flair for mobilising the under-25s in numbers unseen in the post-war period. A political scientist summarised Obama's effect on his profession for *Time* magazine:

> 'Conventional wisdom' – reflected in an article by this reporter earlier this week – 'has a name for candidates who rely on the youth vote: loser,' said Michael McDonald, an expert on voter turnout at George Mason University. 'Clearly, this was different.' (Von Drehle, 2008)

Time further opined it hardly seemed plausible that young Americans who fought wars in Iraq and Afghanistan while being denied decent pensions, health-care and jobs were indifferent to politics; somehow, Obama's campaigning prowess had stirred them into a voting juggernaut (von Drehle, 2008).

From a media studies point of view, Obama's triumph can be explained in reference to a concept called *convergence*. 'Convergence' is a conceptual term with a long history in media studies (Meikle and Young, 2012). This chapter explains why Barack Obama's media strategy was an exercise in convergence by connecting two specific iterations of the idea: the versions offered by Katz and Lazarsfeld in a book called *Personal Influence* (1955), the classic mass-communication study on how people use media to help them make choices in the early broadcast era, and the more recent definitions offered by Henry Jenkins (2006a).

Convergence is an idea that is usually associated with Jenkins (Meikle and Young, 2012), and he used it to describe two processes. First, 'convergence refers to a situation in which multiple media systems coexist and where media content flows across them' (Jenkins, 2006a: 282). Second, convergence is 'a word that describes technological, industrial, cultural and social changes in the ways media circulates within our culture' (2006a: 282). In *Personal Influence*, 'convergence' described how mass and interpersonal communication networks intersected in social occasions when women in the town of Decatur, Illinois, used media information in conversations with their peers about what to buy, what to wear, what movies to see, or what to think about public affairs (Katz and Lazarsfeld, 1955). In this chapter, these definitions are combined to show how convergence connects to the idea presented in Chapter 2, that young audiences actively participate in the production of media effects.

Applied to the topic of political communication, focused on Barack Obama, convergence describes the evolving media practices that political figures and organisations deploy to encourage young people to make personal and emotional connections with political issues. This specifies how media content and technologies were singularly influential in getting young American voters to return to the polls.

As a convergence phenomenon, the Obama campaign was a condensation point for a range of structural changes in both media and the political systems. These changes made it possible for young people to think about and connect with electoral politics in new ways that would not have been possible in the absence of convergent media cultures. This furthers the argument, made in previous chapters, that media influence young people by dictating the terms by which they participate in public life. To make this case, this chapter:

- establishes that Obama's campaign was a landmark in the history of thought on political communication, because it challenged established academic orthodoxies on the relationship between media use and political apathy among young people;

- explains why Obama's victory is best seen as an exercise in convergence;

- defines the 'convergence' question as being about how media structures activate audiences – doing this by connecting early public opinion research with Burgess and Green's (2009) work on YouTube, commercial media and politics;

- uses two studies – Bennett et al.'s (2011) research on social media and changing modes of citizenship, and James Stanyer's (2012) study of the rising importance of 'intimacy' in political communication – to portray Obama as an expression of changing media structures. These new structures encourage intimate relations between politicians and voters by cultivating the intersection between interpersonal and media communication (Bennett et al.) and by capitalising on the flow of political content across media genres (Stanyer).

MEDIA, YOUTH AND POLITICAL APATHY

Bennett et al. (2011), who conducted a major content analysis of the online resources political organisations deployed in the run-up to the 2008 US election, thought that campaign 2008 had brought two different accounts about youth, media and voting into sharp relief. Up until then, there had been a strong tradition in writing on media and politics of blaming mass media, and television in particular, for turning audiences off politics. After Obama, a new body of work on Web 2.0 and the renaissance of political interest among media users appeared. Both positions focused on the young, but Bennett et al. thought neither adequately explained the complexities of mediated politics:

> One story flows from Putnam's (2000) argument that the rise of a passive television culture and declining group memberships has created a 'generational displacement' from politics and public life that is unlikely to be ameliorated by new forms of online civic action. Another narrative depicts young people as 'digital natives' at the forefront of participatory media that may promote new forms of engagement in public life. Both narratives have been challenged: the first by the mobilization of young and first-time voters in Obama's 2008 campaign, the second by research questioning young people's technical proficiency. (2011: 835)

Cautious as they were about celebrating the effects of Web 2.0, the authors were more concerned that the pessimistic view had become the entrenched, global academic default position on media and politics. This clearly needed to be challenged, because it could not explain a major global event such as Obama's victory. Supporting the idea that pessimism had become the global norm, Esser and de Vreese's comparative study on youth, media and voting in the USA and Europe noted: 'The growing reluctance among youth to participate in politics and exercise their right to vote rings alarm bells across the globe' (2007: 1195). In Australia, Harrington further observed that since young people were considered especially susceptible to the distractions offered by media entertainment, youth voters 'represent a looming danger to the future of enlightened, informed public discourse' (2008: 395). Obama's ability to encourage voting by entertaining young audiences had therefore issued a global challenge to research on young people and mediated politics.

Aside from academic questions, the prospect that convergent media might stir dormant youth voters was one that politicians could not afford to ignore. Even if low youth voting is a fact in most parts of the developed world (Esser and de Vreese, 2007), this is a political *conundrum* for politicians that can only be addressed through more sophisticated media strategies. Apathetic or not, particular groups of young people who *might* vote figure highly in the thoughts of campaign strategists. Connaughton and Jarvis (2004) noted that in the USA, the Republican party had spent a decade developing better ways to communicate with young Latino/Latina voters from 1990 to 2000, realising this group would be a powerful force, if mobilised. Other scholars wondered if the 'media problem' was that politician and parties didn't understand how to use media resources. Xenos and Bennett (2007) argued that by 2004 there was much evidence to show young people did want to know more about politics, and did want to use media to learn. This placed an onus on looking at how political organisations used media. In the UK, Gerodimos (2008) argued that when it came to elections, the media problem was the jejune approach that political parties took to Web 2.0 tools. In a content analysis of the web presence of UK political parties and independent interest groups, Gerodimos found a clear distinction between the former and the latter, suggesting that low turnout may be caused by the failure to incentivise voting through using digital resources to their full potential:

> The study found that most top-down youth sites, such as youth parliaments and forums, lacked appealing, relevant content and a clear purpose; their aim was to generically 'involve' young people without a set of specific reasons and benefits that would motivate young users ... NGO sites were much more empowering and strategic in their agenda and reach, with slick, comprehensive and appealing pages. (2008: 964)

In other words, the problem was not young people who used media; it was political campaigners who didn't – at least, not properly.

This is not to say that the role of media in electoral politics has to be reconsidered simply because technologies have changed. There are also grounds for asking if the assumption that media entertainment was bad for politics was ever true. Although television had been cast as the bête noire of the elected official, by the early twenty-first century many politicians were using television entertainment to connect with young voters, and these efforts were paying dividends. Scholars have noted the increasing use of comedy as a vehicle for political communication (Wells and Bull, 2007; Rossing, 2011), the significance of Jon Stewart's youth-friendly *The Daily Show* as a recognised stop on the US campaign trail (Bennett, L.W., 2007), that talk shows have also become a 'must-have' on electioneering schedules (Babcock and Whitehouse, 2005; Stanyer, 2012) and that even reality television has become a resource for reaching people who usually ignore political discourse (Ruddock, 2010).

So when, as thoughts turned to the US presidential election of 2012, Obama chose the occasion of the annual White House Correspondents' Dinner to roast entrepreneur, reality-television star and would-be campaign opponent Donald Trump, he underlined the political value in being able to entertain audiences on television. Contemplating a run in 2012, Trump had endorsed the 'birthers' – a movement of people who, believing that Obama had not been born in the USA, as the US Constitution demands of the President, sought to have the sitting occupant of the Oval Office impeached (Madison, 2011). Said President used the televised dinner to take down the birthers and Trump in one fell swoop. Using a series of jokes based on media clips and pop-culture references, Obama reduced the property tycoon to a laughing stock in a performance that rapidly circled the globe, via YouTube.

Perhaps Arnold Schwarzenegger had inspired Obama's termination of Trump. Schwarzenegger decided to run in the 2003 California gubernatorial election, because he believed incumbent Grey Davis had mismanaged the state's finances. This was a complex case, based on forensic economic analysis that opened itself to equally forensic – and troublesome – investigative journalism. Here, Schwarzenegger met a familiar challenge for public officials; Thornton (2008) pointed out that US presidents have tried to dodge political journalists since Andrew Jackson started his own newspaper in the nineteenth century. The Hollywood action hero, however, had a novel solution to the dilemma: exploiting the media connections he enjoyed as a celebrity, Schwarzenegger ran his campaign through the talk-show circuit, thereby speaking to the public without the intrusion of journalists.

Babcock and Whitehouse saw this as an omen of things to come in media politics. By communicating to voters through entertainment genres, politicians are licensed to state their position at length, without having to give their opponent the right to reply, or subject themselves to the inquisition of political journalists (Babcock and Whitehouse, 2005). Obama certainly enjoyed this freedom when roasting Trump, as he ridiculed the birther movement and Fox News, wondered if 'The Donald' would also turn his attention to other conspiracy theories ('What really happened at Roswell? And where are Biggie and Tupac?'), then asked how making big decisions, like having to choose between firing the actor Gary Busey or the singer Meatloaf from *The Celebrity Apprentice* ('the sorts of decisions that would keep me awake at night') qualified a person for presidential office. Obama's stand-up skill let him take down a potential opponent.

For Obama, YouTube was a cheaper way of pulling off Schwarzenegger's trick: speaking to voters without being interrupted by meddlesome journalistic intermediaries. *The Hollywood Reporter* noted that Obama's speeches were widely posted and shared on YouTube, and that the roasting of Trump had been viewed 7.2 million times by August 2011; more than 2 million more views than the President's announcement of the killing of Osama bin Laden had attracted. This figure dwarfed the attention paid to the videos posted on the White House's official YouTube channel (Hollywood Reporter, 2011).

The roast, then, was another Obama landmark; an instance of what might be called *intimate convergence*. That is, the speech suited media systems with penchants for personal disclosure and self-expression through sharing media content – where this disclosure and expression comes from politicians and voters alike. It is tempting to think of Obama's comedic routine as a triumph for a politician who just happened to be handsome, charming and amusing; Obama simply was an amiable, good-looking, funny guy, and so naturally he could manage a trick that few others could. Yet Obama's capacity for comedy only became an asset because of messages systems that let it be so. These message systems are about *intimate convergence*, for two reasons. In terms of convergence, the mechanics of the speech itself and its circulation among audiences demonstrated, to paraphrase Jenkins (2006a), the flow of media content across different message systems. Obama jokingly presented a clip from Disney's *The Lion King* as his 'birth video' (playing on the birther belief that he had actually been born in Africa), referenced reality television and rap culture, ridiculed Fox News as a particular journalistic genre and enjoyed the fruits of his labours as his performance was shared throughout social media. In terms of intimacy, the speech also showed how Obama turned his personal history into a political asset, in the face of an attack (from Trump and the birther movement) that centred on who he was, not how he had performed in office. As such, Obama's act testified that media have affected political communication by placing a greater onus on personal disclosure, self-actualisation and the cultivation of mediated intimacy between politicians and youth voters (Stanyer, 2012). It also underlined the folly of thinking that media entertainment is a distraction from politics. As such, it was an incident that exemplified how convergence complicates pessimistic views on the political effects of media, but which also demonstrated the need to develop new ways to define these political effects.

CONVERGENCE

'The Trump roast' signalled Obama's appreciation of politics as a form of entertainment that relied on personality and the willingness to reveal the personal. The important thing to note, however, is that the study of convergence suggests that this appreciation was more a matter of compulsion than choice, since his position was clearly one that was preferred by media industries. Obama's capacity to personalise politics was an exercise in media convergence, in the way that Jenkins defined the term, because his 2008 campaign had realised the potential of newer digital resources by combining them with the ongoing strengths of television, political advertising and face-to-face communication. Obama's use of social media was part of a broader communication strategy that also embraced conventional political communication tactics.

Social media were certainly a significant, commented-upon and researched factor in 2008. Writing before the election, American youth activist and communications strategist Rashid Shabazz was clear on the role that social media would play in any victory Obama may win, having secured the Democratic nomination for President:

> New Media (Facebook, YouTube, blogs, etc) … factor in building up Senator Obama's brand and rock star-esque status while simultaneously drawing more youth of legal voting age into the political process. Both youth media practitioners and Obama realize the power of the internet to share stories-key to mobilize (sic) youth and others. On *Facebook* alone there are 18 million young people between the ages of 18–29. (2008: 239)

Wu (2009) found that Facebook was particularly effective in getting young people who visited candidates' pages to communicate with other young people. However, what Wu's study really tells us is that Facebook provided another means for voters to do things that they had been doing for some time.

Returning to Obama's victory in the Democratic primary elections, *Time* magazine's analysis of his communication strategy emphasised its distinctly retro feel. For all his public fretting about living without his BlackBerry if elected, campaign Obama relied on many pre-digital, even pre-mass-media, methods. Studying the impact of elections campaigns on voters in the 1940s, Katz and Lazarsfeld (1955) had found that people were far more likely to be affected by the opinions of the people around them than by anything they heard on the radio or read in newspapers. Apparently, twenty-first-century American politicians had discovered this was still true: according to *Time*'s analysis, Obama's team had absorbed the lessons from recent Republican research on the value of face-to-face communication, where 'they found that having a trusted neighbour or peer make the personal appeal [for a vote on the behalf of the candidate] is a far more effective way to get voters to the polls' (von Drehle, 2008).

The magazine had been investigating this line for some time. As early as 2007, *Time* warned that, given the value of the youth vote, candidates should know social media were no quick-fix to the decades-old puzzle of how to get young people excited about voting again. In that year, *Time* interviewed Heather Smith, then executive director of an organisation called Young Voter Strategies. YVS was an organisation that advised on mobilising young voters. Smith went on to merge the YVS with Rock the Vote, an organisation 'Founded at the intersection of popular culture and politics … to support the tidal wave of young people who want to get involved in elections and seize the power of the youth vote to create political and social change' (Rock the Vote, 2011). According to her biography on the Rock the Vote website, Smith had been involved in several strategies that significantly increased the number of young registered voters across the USA since 2000. As a key figure who has worked to change the impact of the youth vote on US presidential politics, and as president of an organisation that claimed credit for registering 2.2 million young voters in 2008, it is significant that Smith agreed Obama's success was partly due to skilled conventional political techniques – meeting people face to face, and talking about issues:

> 'New technology is certainly helpful in communicating with younger voters, but it shouldn't be the only means of targeting them,' Smith says. Her research shows, in fact, that the same tried-and-true retail politics that works with Iowa retirees – knocking on doors and face-to-face contact – is the most effective way of getting young adults to actually vote for a specific candidate. Also key, not surprisingly, is talking about issues that are most relevant to young adults – namely the Iraq war, college affordability and health care. (Schmidt, 2007)

When it came to conventional media, academic research found that the Obama campaign had made canny use of other traditional techniques. Kaid et al. (2011) noted that Obama had spent a record amount of money of television advertising. The money was well spent. In their experimental study on how 1165 young people judged the spot advertisements used by Obama and McCain, the researchers found that, generally speaking, respondents felt all of the advertisements were useful sources of information, and that this information helped them feel more positive about their power to effect change through voting. At the same time, they thought Obama's advertisements were more effective.

In many cases, Obama's campaign enjoyed substantial synergies between television and social media. Farnsworth and Lichter's content analysis of network news during the campaign showed why television and conventional television journalism were hardly incidental to his ambitions, since 'Barack Obama received the most positive coverage recorded for any major party nominee on network television since the Center for Media and Public Affairs started analysing election news content in 1988' (2011: 354). In this regard, YouTube was attractive as a means of winning young audiences back to the conventional television forums that Obama was using so well. As McKinney and Rill noted, 'the CNN/YouTube debates were designed expressly to engage young media users who are frequent users of YouTube yet not always among the viewing audience for a televised presidential debate' (2009: 392).

Accordingly, Obama's success was about convergence, because his media strategies integrated television, political advertising, social media and good old-fashioned knocking on doors. One goal of this strategy was to activate young voters by changing how media content circulated among them – which is why the political value of Facebook was not especially novel. Because convergence prioritises questions about how messages *circulate* (Jenkins, 2006a), it is an idea that positioned youthful media users as 'active' campaign ingredients, placed to influence the flow of political communication, whether that be through sharing by social media or simply talking to a friend. However, this does not mean that young people *control* political communication. Consider again Everett's point that Obama appealed to youth as 'a highly visible and accessible new kind of president with whom they could interact, share their views, and even reinvent America both in the real world and more strategically online' (2009: 195–196). Obama's success in realising the potential of media convergence suggests his youth appeal was created through media practices that were organised *for* young people, not *by* them. This introduces a model of media power where the onus is on analysing how media content is shared. Katz and Lazarfeld's *Personal Influence* (1955) was one of the first studies to develop this model.

CONVERGENCE AND PERSONAL INFLUENCE

Personal Influence was a landmark study on how media affected society through 'opinion leaders' – the sorts of people that Heather Smith thought would be vital to Obama's success. The study had originated in research on the effects of radio and newspapers on the 1940 US presidential election (Lazarsfeld et al., 1948). That project found voters were most influenced by the opinions of other people they knew and respected. Two things were interesting here. First, the 'influentials' were not necessarily those who one would expect to be influential – they were often spouses, members of social clubs, work colleagues, to name a few. Second, these 'opinion leaders' *did* report paying close attention to media. This led to a 'two-step flow of communication' model, where the central concept was 'that ideas, often, seem to flow *from* radio and print *to* opinion leaders and *from them* to the less active sections of the population' (Katz and Lazarsfeld, 1955: 32).

The two-step flow thesis argued that media power was optimised when people integrated media messages in everyday conversations. *Personal Influence* explained this idea in a chapter titled 'An Essay in Convergence' (1955: 43). Katz and Lazarsfeld used convergence to explain the error of seeing psychological and social audience features as 'factors which intervene between the mass media and their audience and, thus, which modify mass media effects' (1955: 43). Katz and Lazarsfeld hypothesised that beliefs and opinions were grounded in interpersonal relationships, and that these relationships implied their own communication networks; *Personal Influence* set out to examine 'those ingredients of informal primary groups which are, so to speak, the 'active ingredients' as far as the mass communications process is concerned' (1955: 44). Interpersonal communication did not intervene in the mass-communication process – it *completed* that process; in fact, there was no mass communication until people started using media content to communicate with other people in their communities. So, when Katz and Lazarsfeld said 'convergence', they referred to the process where 'opinion leaders' used media content when giving advice to people they knew on what to buy, what to wear, what movies to see and what to think about public affairs. Mass and interpersonal communication were articulated at the point where some people realised that knowing about media content was a way to build friendships, perform civic duties and win kudos among peers.

The concepts of personal influence and two-step flow became extremely controversial in media research.[1] Lang and Lang (2006) blamed Katz and Lazarsfeld for creating the false impression that individual preferences determined the effects of persuasive mass-communicated messages. This, in the Langs' view, led to a tradition of communication studies that focussed on how audiences paid attention to messages they found interesting or useful – usually ones that reinforced things they already believed – and ignored every else. *Personal Influence* (Katz and Lazarsfeld, 1955) was accused of portraying media messages as inert objects, which did nothing until people activated them. This view distracted attention from how media industries cultivated the general social sentiments that guided discrete choices on what to wear, what to buy, or what to think about particular public issues (Lang and Lang, 2006): that is, the criticism goes, the decision not to buy a particular product after seeing an advertisement for that product meant little if advertising in general created the impression that happiness and consumption were the same thing, and Katz and Lazarsfeld discouraged their peers from pursuing this matter.

Nonetheless, the Langs conceded the 'problem' of *Personal Influence* was as much about its appropriation as with anything Katz and Lazarsfeld had actually said about media power. The book's conclusion in fact called for more research on how media content affected opinion leaders. The idea that active audiences completed the mass-communications circuit remained an intriguing possibility, and one that was perhaps better suited to situations where more people act like opinion leaders through social media. Recent work on politics, social media and *personalisation* as a media process demonstrates how the idea of audience as an 'active ingredient' in media influence opened new ways to think about how media industries influence *what* is activated. As an example, Burgess and Green's (2009) YouTube study inherited some of the questions first asked by Katz and Lazarsfeld.

YOUTUBE AND PERSONAL INFLUENCE

Personal Influence (Katz and Lazarsfeld, 1955) is still debated because digital media have made the convergence between media and interpersonal communication a matter of design. Many interpersonal communication networks *are* media networks, YouTube being an example. Indeed, according to Burgess and Green (2009), when it comes to YouTube, there is no need to look for connections between interpersonal and media communication because they are one and the same. The success of Obama's 'Trump roast' demonstrated one of the central observations of their study – that YouTube capitalised on popular media practices that had been in place for some time, and this concentration affected politics because it complemented shifting understandings of what citizenship is. Media use and consumption have become familiar means of building communities based around common interests and identities, particularly among marginalised communities with few other opportunities to develop civic ties.[2] As an example, Burgess and Green mentioned the extensive range of self-help videos created and shared on topics relevant to transgendered people, pointing out that YouTube had become a valuable place for advice, information and support for people for whom face-to-face communication on this topic carried substantial risks. YouTube connected popular media consumption (starting as a place where people shared clips from television and movies) and citizenship (as a place where they also built identities by making and sharing their own content). In this sense, YouTube's political function was a portent of much deeper shifts where 'cultural citizenship' – a process where people use media to form communities and interests that do not necessarily correspond to the mechanics of the nation state – becomes the primary vehicle through which people connect with public affairs:

> Beyond the very obvious and much-hyped role YouTube videos and audiences played in the 2008 US Presidential Election, the ordinary activities of its users, in theory, could constitute practices of cultural citizenship; if they encounter one another under the right conditions, the website is an enabler of encounters with cultural differences and the development of political 'listening' across belief systems and identities. (Burgess and Green, 2009: 77)

The tricky thing here is to conceive what being an 'enabler' means vis-à-vis media power, and it is here that Burgess and Green addressed the query at the end of *Personal Influence*: How are opinion leaders affected by media (Katz and Lazarsfeld, 1955: 316)? This question becomes more pressing when considering social media, where millions of people are trying to lead opinions by drawing attention to the media content they share. Burgess and Green pointed out that YouTube's commercial success capitalised on groups and individuals who felt powerless. Burgess and Green conceded that any analysis of YouTube had to begin from the simple fact that the medium's rationale was to let individuals create and share media content in order to attract advertising revenue. The fear, in this sense, is that YouTube has eclipsed alternative and community media by seeming to offer the same functions, while tying those functions to corporate rather than community interest. If this is true, then YouTube users are much like the 1960s youths that Thompson wrote about – people who wanted to live in societies where more people can speak in public, but can only articulate this aspiration by sharing content which, in the main, comes from the institutions that monopolise public attention. That said, Burgess and Green thought YouTube complicated the relationship between media business and democracy as 'a site of similar opportunities as those offered by community media, not in spite of, but *because* of its mainstream commerciality' (2009: 76). Surveying the evidence on how communities used YouTube, and responded to its operation as a commercial endeavour, the authors concluded two things. First, the medium had a particular appeal for communities with few other chances to establish a public presence, the popularity of YouTube help videos among transgendered users being a case in point. Second, if users had become increasingly frustrated at how events such as the CNN/YouTube debate signalled how mainstream media operations were monopolising the medium, at least the medium itself became a vehicle where knowledge about the commercialisation of public culture could be seen and discussed. Nevertheless, the wealth of material on the presidential campaign 2008 created and shared via YouTube ultimately raised more questions than answers. As the authors put it:

> The presence of such material could be taken as an indication of a significant degree of engagement in US politics by the YouTube community, and on popular rather than official terms. But arguably, the forms of political engagement hinted at in these videos could have just as much to do with celebrity culture. (Burgess and Green, 2009: 50)

What we can say is that media like YouTube have converged the two convergences detailed by Jenkins (2006a) and Katz and Lazarsfeld (1955), since the flow of content between platforms has integrated interpersonal and media communication networks. Had *Personal Influence* been written today, it might have ended with this question instead: How do commercially structured media networks encourage young media users to incorporate convergent media resources in specific ways? That is to say, the question of how media affect people who are interested in politics, and who seek to lead their peers, is even more important given the range of leadership opportunities afforded by digital media practices.

INTIMACY: DIGITAL MEDIA AND THE INSTITUTIONAL EXPLOITATION OF THE PERSONAL

Burgess and Greens' (2009) research offers one explanation for how powerful media institutions remain powerful institutions thanks to users who act like opinion leaders: sharing not only the interpretation of media content, but the content itself.

In the tradition of the personal influence project, we might say that YouTube has facilitated the exercise of personal influence by also accelerating the personalisation of political communication – the tailoring of widely distributed media content, made for a mass audience, to suit the needs of particular groups and people. Burgess and Green were open to the possibility that YouTube is simply a commercial site that has helped powerful media and political organisations create the impression that phenomena like celebrity culture are things that the public want, instead of things that media industries create. Their study therefore begs a larger narrative, where the trends and possibilities hinted at in YouTube can be explained in relation to other dynamics in political communication across a wider range of media platforms. Post-Obama studies suggested that modern political communication industries have found two ways to incorporate citizens: incentivising cultural citizenship by connecting it to everyday identity practices, and multiplying the ways that audiences can experience intimate connections with politicians. Both of these possibilities describe how structured message systems cultivate the conditions that activate audiences, and determine the effects that activation will have.

Bennett et al. (2011) conducted a systematic content analysis of 348 political websites with vested interests in the 2008 presidential election. The organisations behind these sites crossed the political spectrum, from recognised political parties, to community service organisations, to single-issue activist groups. Ultimately, the authors felt the most successful ones were those that converged mass and interpersonal communication by letting users develop knowledge by making identities and connecting with other people. The analysis of these sites revealed two approaches to using online resources. The first, and less successful approach, used sites as vehicles for transmitting information about the offline world: for example, political parties who simply repeated information about who they were, what they believed and what they planned to do, that was already available in other media. Such sites, it seemed, simply hoped to 'capture' young voters who were not paying attention to things like televised debates. Implicitly, the assumption here was that politics remains an 'offline' affair, and that voting is a duty. This is based on the notion of 'dutiful citizenship':

> The core characteristic of the DC style is that individuals participate in civic life through organized groups, from civic clubs to political parties, while becoming informed via the news, and generally engaging in public life out of a sense of personal duty. (Bennett et al., 2011: 838)

Bennett et al. observed this 'transmission' approach to online resources mistakenly tried to revive a flagging citizenship model that its target audience were not interested in.

On the other hand, 'online only' organisations that existed first and foremost as a digital presence attracted more attention by prioritising features encouraging users to express themselves and seek out new connections with other people. These features were in tune with the model of 'actualizing citizenship':

> This citizenship typology enables us to think about a generational shift away from taking cues as members of groups or out of regard for public authorities (opinion leaders, public officials, and journalists), and toward looser personal engagement with peer networks that pool (crowd source) information and organize civic action using social technologies that maximize individual expression. (Bennett et al., 2011: 839)

In 2008, the Obama campaign's online resources had made more use of tools that let potential voters share rather than receive knowledge, build their own blogs, and even create their own groups. In the context of 'personal interest', we might say that Obama's media team helped people to become online opinion leaders, more so than his Republican opponents. Having created this network, Obama could be confident that his comedic attack on Trump would be widely circulated by supporters who were well accustomed to using social media to affect the opinions of other people. So, Bennett et al. provided a message system explanation for Obama's popularity, premised on Katz and Lazarsfeld's (1955) understanding of convergence. The most effective online political resources used in 2008 were those that blended media and interpersonal communication by allowing potential voters to express opinions, construct online identities as opinion leaders and create their own political communities. Obama's team understood this better than John McCain's did.

James Stanyer's (2012) study of 'intimate' political communication built a similar argument; Obama's success was about structured media practices, because he was uniquely positioned to generate positive news attention, since his personal characteristics suited media systems that increasingly focussed on the personal qualities of those who run for public office. This tactic capitalised on the flow of political communication content between media genres. Stanyer used international comparative data on political media content from several Organisation for Economic Co-operation and Development (OECD) countries to argue that Obama's success testified to significant global shifts in the nature of political communication, as that communication is produced through the intersections between changing media and political systems. In essence, the convergence in media content, where it is very difficult to tell where news and campaigning ends and entertainment begins, has accelerated a trend where political communication pays more attention to who a candidate is as a person than it does to what that candidate stands for as a would-be public servant.

Before considering Stanyer's analysis in detail, the changes that he set out to explain were encapsulated in a unique electoral moment: the YouTube hit video 'I got a crush on Obama'.[3] Viewed over 17 million times (Webley, 2010), the video, made by an entertainment site called Barelypolitical.com, featured a young woman singing a song laced with sexual innuendoes in the form of political puns where, in various states of undress, the singer confessed to being in love with the would-be president. The video is far less of a transgression than it first appeared to be. Voting publics and Europe, North America and Australia had become accustomed to hearing about the sex lives of their leaders (Stanyer, 2012). When 'Obama Girl' predicted 'up in the Oval Office, you'll get your Head of State', she sang to an audience who knew such things happened, thanks to the Monica Lewinsky scandal that almost had Bill Clinton impeached. In the UK, Tony Blair went out of the way to describe his sexual prowess during his time as Prime Minister, revealing in interviews that he was usually 'up for it five times a night' (Stanyer, 2012: 2). The publicised sex lives of presidents and prime ministers were symptoms of a deeper truth – that the period since 1995 had seen a dramatic increase in media attention to the personal lives of politicians across OECD countries. Stanyer saw this as a process of 'intimization', involving 'exposure of information and imagery about the politician as a person; the public scrutiny of personal relationships and family life; and the opening up of personal living spaces or spaces a politician might reasonably expect to be private from the public gaze' (Stanyer, 2012: 15). Some of this was caused by political change, such as the need to use personality to overcome weakening party loyalties. Other media-related factors included the risks and opportunities created by the growing number of media genres that took interest in political affairs: reality media, talk shows and social media.

Stanyer combined media content analysis with analysis of political systems to identify the conditions under which 'intimization' flourished. One of his research questions examined factors that allowed leaders to attract 'benign' media coverage. Although a great deal of attention has been paid to the proliferation of news about political scandal and sleaze, Stanyer also pointed out a common trend across OECD countries where the news and entertainment media give extensive coverage to aspects of leaders' personal lives that create positive images: birthdays, families and holidays. Stanyer gathered evidence on media coverage of these items, as well as political biographies, for 27 leaders across nine countries. When the results were tabulated, he discovered Barack Obama led the table on benign coverage by some distance. On average, leaders in his sample attracted 101 benign media references. Obama had 368, and his closest competitor, France's Nikolas Sarkozy, was some distance behind, with 262.

Seeking an explanation for this phenomenon, Stanyer argued that a close analysis of his data revealed 'recipes' that blended certain political systems with particular media institutions to maximise the likelihood of benign coverage for a leader. Although the trend towards personalisation was observed across the nine nations, the scale of that personalisation was not uniform. Using statistical correlation procedures, Stanyer found that benign exposure was highest in presidential democracies 'with low party membership, and the leader needs to personally bond with voters, and is young, part of the so-called baby boomer generation, there will be a high level of personal exposure' (2012: 68). Extending Stanyer's 'recipe' metaphor for media effects, Obama's looks, wit and charisma were the icing on the cake for a baby-boomer candidate in a presidential democracy who could not count on party loyalists.

CONCLUSION

Taking Katz and Lazarsfeld (1955), Burgess and Green (2009), Bennett et al. (2011) and Stanyer (2012) in combination, Obama's success in mobilising the youth vote probably had much to do with the transformation of personal influence into an entirely mediated phenomenon, and the personalisation of campaign massages. In either case, while it is true that young voters were the active ingredients that made his media strategy a success, in many ways their activity was a reaction to the changing structures of messages systems that often made the distinction between interpersonal and media communication impossible to make.

The first chapter argued that the study of how young people use and are affected by media has been central to the broader investigation of media influence as a political phenomenon. This chapter has applied this argument to electoral politics, using the Obama presidency as a case study. Obama's election as America's first African-American President was widely identified with young voters and the potential of social media. These aspects of the Obama presidency were a gateway to reflecting on how social media fit into a history of thought on the personalisation of electoral politics. Obama's YouTube success, for example, reflects the possibility that the figure of the opinion leader, first introduced in political communication research during the 1940s, was an idea ahead of its time. Certainly, Burgess and Green's reflection on the politics of YouTube provides one answer to Katz and Lazarsfeld's conundrum: How do media affect people who actively seek out information in self-directed ways, for the purpose of exercising leadership among peers? Burgess and Green framed YouTube as an exemplar of how media and interpersonal communication networks can be one and the same, since YouTube's business plan depends on providing the capacity to make communities by making and sharing media content. This making and sharing affords personal, emotional connections with political issues, and this ethic is well tuned to more general shifts in political communication that incentivise voting in two ways: encouraging voters to think the political world is something they can make, and promising audiences unprecedented access to politicians as people. All of this is further evidence of the message systems view of media influence, introduced in the chapters on binge drinking and school shootings. It clearly matters that Obama was a whip-smart, funny, handsome candidate, but the only reason why this mattered is because of media systems that allowed these characteristics to be shared with the public in ways they could re-share, hence creating the impression that politics is something that people do, not something they watch. In this sense, Obama's success in appealing to young voters created the opportunity to think about media influence in terms of both content and technology, using the concept of convergence. As we shall see in the concluding chapter, this connects the topic of youth, media and voting to cardinal debates on the role young media users play in determining the nature of media power.

CHAPTER SUMMARY

- Barack Obama's presidency challenged the common assumption that media were the cause of political apathy among young people.

- Obama's media strategy was an exercise in convergence – an important academic term that describes how media practices blend content from a variety of genres and platforms, in a way that integrates media content and technology with interpersonal communication networks.

- Obama's YouTube presence identifies a continuum in writing on political communication – in particular suggesting that mid twentieth-century work on opinion leaders established a number of ideas that were ironically more relevant to the analysis of social media.

- Obama's success, as a youth media phenomenon, represented a historical break that gestures towards new ways of conceiving centralised media power.

NOTES

1 Space prohibits a detailed exploration of these critiques. Suffice to say that Gitlin's (1978) sustained criticism of the project was highly influential in defining ideological approaches to media power in the 1980s. Current writing emphasises that, for all its flaws, *Personal Influence* (Katz and Lazarsfeld, 1955) was a complex study whose lessons are still being interpreted. For more on this, see the 2006 special edition of Annals of the American Academy of Political and Social Science, vol. 608.

2 Henry Jenkins' *Textual Poachers* (1992), for example, detailed how sharing and editing media content in fan communities, through practices like annual conventions and writing and sharing fan fiction, had become popular among *Star Trek* fans in the 1980s. Will Brooker (2003) similarly detailed how the sharing of *Star Wars* content had helped fans of the genre survive as communities despite the quarter-century gap between films.

3 Go to www.youtube.com/watch?v=wKsoXHYICqU.

9

UNDERSTANDING CELEBRITY: BAM MARGERA AND THE ROLE OF SPORT IN MEDIA CONVERGENCE

Research question.
Why do young people find celebrities so enthralling?

Underlying question about media influence.
What does the prevalence of celebrity culture say about changing structures in global media industries?

Relevant literature.
Graeme Turner on 'ordinary' celebrities, Ellis Cashmore on sporting celebrity, David Rowe on media sport

Exemplifying case study.
Pro-skateboarder turned *Jackass* star Bam Margera

Outcomes.
Margera is a celebrity because he is unique as a sports star who is good at looking ordinary on television. This is hugely attractive to a variety of media platforms

Lessons for understanding media influence.
The convergence between media and interpersonal communication is accentuated by a celebrity industry that voraciously uses ordinary life and ordinary people as its raw material

Barack Obama's success indicates that a common question – Why do young people find celebrities so enthralling? – hints at some complicated changes in media industries, and the ways that audiences engage with them. Indeed, some very important media scholars believe that young people's apparent obsession with celebrity is a compelling reason why it's important to hang on to the idea that global media industries exercise control over how we understand, discuss and live in the world. All of this is to say that a serious study of celebrity culture is worthwhile, and it needs to get beyond clichés about 15 minutes of fame, which really say very little about why celebrity features so forcefully in young people's imagination.

In fact, research on celebrity culture summarises perhaps *the* basic question in media studies: How do media process social reality, in ways that transform that which they represent? We know we live in a world where things really happen, we know we access many parts of that world through the media, and so we know we are vulnerable to manipulation from industries that, even with the best will in the world, do not show us things exactly as they are. If this is the core of media influence, then researching how real people are represented *as* real through media narratives that serve commercial ends is a useful way to explain this media effect. At the same time, the *growth* of celebrity culture asks interesting questions about why media's 'reality effects', which have always been present, now focus so much on the production of fame and celebrities with whom young people strike up relationships of unprecedented intensity.

This chapter answers this question by considering sporting celebrity. It does this for two reasons. First, media sport has been the vanguard for changes in global media industries, as competition for audiences has intensified between digital platforms. Second, the sporting celebrity – the athlete who really does have a skill, regardless of the attention he or she gets – is an ideal figure to illustrate why talent needs media industries to achieve fame, and how celebrity depends on the ability to suit the needs of particular industries at particular times. As such, the sporting celebrity reinforces some of the lessons from studies of school shootings: that commercial media process *aspects* of social reality with *strategic goals* in mind.

As a case study, the chapter considers the radio career of American extreme-sport and reality-television star Bam Margera. The story of how Margera ended up becoming a radio personality demonstrates the celebrity industry's 'reality effect' in action, showing how a particular aspect of his private life – his love of hanging out with friends from his youth – became a tool for attracting a global audience of listeners.

At the conclusion of this chapter, you will be able to understand why celebrity is a useful concept in explaining how global media practices bring social reality to life. You will also understand why research on media sport – a topic that rarely features in research on youth and media – provides a valuable forum for considering general media effects.

CELEBRITY CULTURE: THE ENDGAME OF MEDIATISATION

Early in 2008, the parents of 18-year-old Corey Delaney left their son home alone in the Melbourne suburb of Narre Warren. Departing for a vacation on Australia's

Gold Coast, they left strict instructions: 'no parties'. Naturally, their orders were ignored, and chaos ensued as gatecrashers descended on the family home. Less predictably, events got so out of hand that police dogs and even a helicopter had to be called in to restore order, and Melbourne Police Commissioner Christine Nixon threatened to charge the family $20,000 for all the trouble.

A few days later, it seemed Corey had found a way to pay. Interviewed about what had happened on the news magazine show *A Current Affair*, Delaney incensed host Leila McKinnon by refusing to remove a pair of yellow-rimmed sunglasses he was wearing. The sunglasses, he explained, were famous – part of his image as an emerging celebrity. Indeed, within days, the apprentice carpenter had an agent and a series of public appearances lined up. Within months, he was on Australia's *Big Brother*. He *was* a celebrity.

It doesn't matter that he soon disappeared from public view. Despite the rapid demise of his fame, Delaney wasn't a victim, in any simple sense. In the end, he'd been right about the glasses, and if Australia's celebrity industry used him, he was happy enough to play along. Delaney's story reminds us that the lesson of celebrity culture is not about 15 minutes of fame; it is that real people and real events, many of them mundane, are a vital resource for global media industries under constant pressure to fill space and time. Moreover, his instinctive pursuit of fame gestured to another possible effects of celebrity culture: the sense that the only things – and people – that really matter are those who fit into media narratives.

WHY CELEBRITY?

In the field of political communication, Barack Obama was able to convert his gift for comedy into political capital because this skill suited media entertainment industries, and capitalised on the common practice of sharing entertainment through social media. Obama symbolised a change where, for good or ill, with the right combination of conditions, politics is an exercise in mediated personality (Stanyer, 2012). In this, Obama was as much a celebrity as he was a politician (Burgess and Green, 2009) and was, as such, an index of a far broader range of media influences.

Writers like Graeme Turner (2004) think 'celebrity' has had profound cultural effects. Celebrity is a major tool for gathering audiences, and media professionals spend a great deal of their time producing celebrity content. Turner believed that the concentration on celebrity, from industries and audiences, may have effected a profound change in what people generally expect from life. For this reason, he also saw celebrity as a fulcrum in the battle for the soul of media studies. Turner believed celebrity defines a general model of media influence that avoids problems endemic in the more simplistic behaviourist approaches mentioned in Chapter 1. Bam Margera helps illustrate how this model works, as a figure whose celebrity has been constructed by selling a narrative about youth to a global audience by engaging with newly emerging media platforms.

Margera's success dramatises the allure of celebrity culture for young people, clarifying why there is something really quite logical beneath the apparently widespread desire for fame, no matter how fleeting. Margera is a professional skateboarder, reality-television, film and radio personality. He is a sports star[1] who has converted bad behaviour, drawing on the familiar narrative of the home-alone teen having fun (think movies such as *Risky Business* and *Ferris Bueller's Day Off*), into a media career spanning multiple platforms. Margera successfully made fun his living because his celebrity image is highly attractive to different media businesses. His success is down to talent, imagination and the industrial production of celebrity, and indicates why many young people apparently regard celebrity as an attainable thing. The celebrity industry creates the impression that anyone can be discovered as a celebrity, when the truth is a little different: anyone who can be *processed* by media industries can become a celebrity.

To understand this point, it is important to understand why talent and skill do not guarantee fame. Margera is significant in this respect, because although his fame is grounded in a skateboarding prowess that cannot be disputed, this ability is tangential to his presence as a transmedia celebrity. Margera's athletic prowess may well have been a natural talent that was discovered, but celebriti-sation depends on the selective cultivation of talents suiting the particular needs of particular media industries at particular moments in their history. Margera's career as a satellite-radio personality is especially telling on this point.

Summarising the rationale for this chapter: celebrity is an important indica-tor of how global media might influence social expectations, its influence seems to affect young people in particular, and Bam Margera is a vivid case study, as someone who performs a youthful identity whose authenticity is anchored in his status as an extreme-sport star who has capitalised on (and been commod-itised by) requirements of emerging media platforms. There are three stages to this argument:

- explaining who Margera is, and describing how publicity around him builds a convincing vision of authenticity that blends his lives, in and out of media, into an organic whole – this synthesis turns on his love of skateboarding, and his ongoing loyalty to the group of friends he made as a teenager;

- relating Margera's success to the literature on celebrity and media sport, paying particular attention to the work of Graeme Turner (2004), David Rowe (2004a, 2004b) and Ellis Cashmore (1999);

- interpreting Margera's radio career as indicative of the particular value of sporting celebrity within the 'media sport cultural complex' (Rowe, 2004a) that has become central to global, convergent media industries.

WHY BAM MARGERA?

Chapter 1 introduced a young man called Terry who, in the glare of a national moral panic, simply wanted to have fun with his friends. Bam Margera has turned this youthful desire into a media career, metamorphosing from a teen skate-boarder into a celebrity and even a media industry in his own right. Margera became a professional skateboarder at just 13. Lucrative commercial endorse-ments followed, and soon Margera was able to buy his parents a house and become the family breadwinner – all before reaching the legal age of majority. The seeds for Margera's reality-media career were sown around the same time, as he began filming the pranks that he and his friends played around the town of Westchester, in Pennsylvania, USA. These videos, known as the *CKY* (Camp Kill Yourself) series, came to the attention of Johnny Knoxville, then a journalist working in California's extreme-sports scene. Eventually, the *CKY* concept became the MTV hit *Jackass*, a compendium of skating tricks, slapstick, stunts and practical jokes. *Jackass* was so popular that it became a film franchise that surely exceeded even the wildest of the *CKY* team's dreams. According to the IMDB database, 2010's *Jackass 3* cost $20m to make, earned $50m on its opening weekend in the USA and by January of 2011 had a turnover of almost $120m worldwide.

During the same period, Margera became a popular reality-television figure, playing the role of the rebellious 'home alone' youth. *Viva La Bam* ran for five seasons between 2003 and 2006. Centring on life at 'Castle Bam', the gothic mansion that Margera had bought for his family and friends to share, *VLB*'s punchline was that Bam's parents had to tolerate incessant pranks and stunts because pranks and stunts had paid for the house. So, when Margera built a skate ramp in the living room, painted his sleeping father blue, hosted death-metal concerts and demolition derbies, laid waste to the backyard by re-enacting the American Civil War (helped by an especially destructive potato cannon), built a tree house that was really a bar and even blew up the house his early skating cheques had paid for, his parents could do nothing.

The lesson was summarised at the end of the show's opening credits. Margera skates to the top of a half-pipe while a voiceover asks 'Bam Margera – what's he gonna do next?' Margera effortlessly flips the board into his hand, looks at the camera and answers, 'Whatever the fuck I want'. Margera appeared to have mellowed little in his next MTV venture, *Bam's Unholy Union*. Chronicling the months leading to Margera's wedding to childhood sweetheart Missy Rothstein, *BUU* depicted a man bent on still doing as he pleased, even as the world of adult responsibility beckoned. When his bride picked a dress he didn't like, he shot it with paint pellets. On the day of the wedding, his best man arrived in a wheelchair, having broken both ankles in a near-suicidal skateboarding stunt at Castle Bam.

For all the feigned chaos in his shows,[2] Margera presents as a particularly *authentic* figure. His fame is grounded in an undoubtable talent for extreme sports, and his film, television and radio ventures are all about having fun with friends from his youth. The impression that Bam's media ventures are but a mirror for who he is has been underlined in interviews where journalists have set out to discover the man behind the mayhem. These stories *about* the celebrity business are also, of course, *part* of the celebrity business. From an analytical perspective, they are as valuable for what they do not say as what they reveal.

PRODUCING CELEBRITY

Magazine journalism on Margera presents his off- and on-screen existence as one. As contrived as *Viva La Bam* was – Margera could only set about wrecking and remodelling his family homes because MTV was paying him to do so – it nevertheless represented a truth because this was the life that Margera continued to lead. Margera loves skating, his friends and making media. His fame springs from these passions. In a 2008 interview with the skateboarding magazine *Huck*, reporter Jay Riggio journeyed to Castle Bam to find a man who really does live there, really does use the death-defying skate ramp that MTV built on a daily basis and really does literally bleed for his art:

> Bam is an impressive skater and exciting to watch. After dropping in on the massive two-storey steep-ass roll-in, Bam carves around the giant gap that bridges a good eight-foot drop. It's insane. After doing it, he tells how his friend Brandon Novak broke both legs trying the very same thing, bailing in mid-carve and smashing into the corner of the coming transition. Did I mention that Bam pretty much just woke up? (Riggio, 2008)

Discussing *Jackass 2*, Margera described wounds sustained in stunts where he had rubber bullets fired at him and was branded on the buttocks with the image of a penis. When Riggio asked why a multi-millionaire would subject himself to such pain and indignity, Margera responded, 'Cause I want to one-up *Jackass* one and I want to make my friends laugh and my fans laugh as well'. For Margera, doing as he pleased and making media were one and the same. As a young skater, he had been as interested in filming his stunts as in doing them. To celebrate the completion of *Bam's Unholy Union* for MTV, Margera 'rewarded' himself with three months editing and completing his film *Minghags*, a comedy loosely based on the experiences of his childhood friend and fellow *Jackass* Ryan Dunn. Margera paid for the whole movie, featuring a cast gathered from his hometown, and made it using his own production equipment.

Speaking to *Rolling Stone* magazine, Margera described how his media career beyond *Jackass* was mostly about being a good friend. *Viva La Bam* was an apology, of sorts. Margera explained that the series was his effort to make amends to his friends whom the *Jackass* franchise had exploited:

> The whole first season of *Jackass* is my *CKY* videos, and everyone in California took the credit. Now Knoxville is sitting pretty on the royalties … and my friends are digging in the dumpster for a peach pit. (Grigoriadis, 2004)

Margera's sense of injustice at this state of affairs drove his solo engagement with MTV: '*Viva La Bam*, then, is Margera's chance to make his friends whole: Of the forty-odd people working on *Viva* twenty-five are friends' (Grigoriadis, 2004). Perhaps this was unsurprising, given that loyalty to his youth had been an enduring theme of Margera's career. As a teenager, he had left school in solidarity with classmate Chris Raab, who had been expelled. Raab was cast in *Viva La Bam*, assuming a central role in the series' finale. Margera also expended considerable media energy on rehabilitating fellow teen skating prodigy and future best man Brandon Novak. Novak's professional career had been derailed by a drug addiction. To focus Novak's attention in a positive direction, Margera made *Dreamseller*, a film about Novak's life. When Ryan Dunn was killed in a car accident on the way home from a night's socialising in Westchester, film critic Roger Ebert alleged via Twitter that Dunn had been drunk at the wheel. Determined to defend his friend, Margera took a local television news crew to the crash site and publicly broke down while describing his grief. However much he has attracted the accoutrements of celebrity – the regular attention of Perez Hilton, the dalliance with Jessica Simpson and even the celebrity sex tape – he remains, in public, a simple young man who just loves to skate, have fun and keep the good times rolling by inviting a paying audience to watch. In Margera's own worlds:

> I just want to make funny movies and keep skating and do music videos for bands. I would prefer it without the fanfare, but I'll deal with it, 'cause at the end of the day, I get to do what I want to do. (Grigoriadis, 2004)

RADIO BAM

Margera's radio career ostensibly extended his chance to have fun with friends. In 2004, US satellite radio station Sirius announced:

> The premium satellite radio provider known for delivering the very best in commercial-free music and sports programming to cars and homes across the country, welcomes skateboarder and TV personality Bam Margera as the latest celebrity athlete to host his own show exclusively on Sirius FACTION, the innovative new music channel created especially for action sports enthusiasts. (Sirius Investor Relations, 2004)

The show is produced from Margera's home. Its staple is a chaotic mix of music and chat as the star and his friends regale listeners with their latest gossip and adventures. The show seems to be another example of Margera being paid to do as he pleases, but the prosaic realities of global media business lie behind this impression. Margera was part of Sirius' broader strategy to attract audiences with a line-up of extreme-sport-star DJs. The station already featured surfer Kelly Slater and fellow skateboarder Tony Hawk. Margera starred in the *Tony Hawk's Underground* video game. The Margera deal was further proof that Sirius was willing to pin its commercial gamble; the conviction that new satellite radios would encourage audiences to pay for content that it was easy enough to find via other platforms – especially internet radio – on the allure of the sports celebrity. The Sirius deal underlined, perhaps more clearly than any other aspect of his career, that Margera's celebrity was the product of his ability to fulfil the needs of changing media platforms in lucrative but also highly competitive global markets.

The most powerful celebrities are those who persuade us that for all our awareness of how media manipulate the reality we see, he or she really is as he or she is. Margera fits the bill in this respect. At face value, Bam is paid to be Bam. He does this in shows where he continues to do the things that he has always done with his high-school friends. And he does this with great honesty; he is perfectly open about the fact that doing as he pleases requires deals to be struck with global media operations who are, in some respects, more controlling and tiresome than his parents (Gregoriadis, 2004). As the publicity around Margera demonstrates, he is happy to tell audiences how his celebrity it made. But, like Obama, the question is: What else needs to be present such that his talent for pranks, skating, bonhomie and media critique become the stuff of global media content? It's not that Margera isn't a talented person whose tenacity has turned a hobby into a media industry in its own right, and who isn't afraid to bite the hand that feeds; it's that it is an incomplete account of why he is famous. To fully appreciate why the radio show is one of the most interesting aspects of his career, in contrast to the films and television shows that are more obvious sources of his fame, it is necessary to turn to studies of celebrity as an industry, and sport as the vanguard for global consumer culture.

BAM MARGERA, CELEBRITY STUDIES AND MEDIA SPORT

Celebrity has deepened the place of media in daily life in two ways. First, celebrity occupies more and more of the leisure time of media audiences (Couldry, 2002; Ruddock, 2007). Second, the celebrity industry thrives on the ordinary: it either subjects ordinary members of the public to intense public scrutiny (in shows like *Big Brother*), or else it presents entertainment superstars going about ordinary life, albeit in fabulous settings (Tolson, 2001; Turner, 2004). Either way, celebrity is another media phenomenon whose influence seems to grip young audiences in particular. Graeme Turner (2010) notes that surveys from around the world routinely find young people whose main ambition is to be famous. Celebrity seems to have had the deep effect of determining what young people expect from their lives, creating the impression that media celebrity is a viable path to self-affirmation. Many young people, it seems, think a life in media is the only one worth living.

Celebrities, as Turner put it, 'are becoming embedded in our culture's repertoire of understandings of what it is to be a subject, what constitutes identity and what kinds of performance of identity might be desirable' (2010: 18). This is an enormously significant statement, in the context of the general debate on the nature of media influence. Turner's position on celebrity takes conventional effects questions – like whether reality-television contestants, and their bad behaviour, affect what young audiences think are acceptable ways of acting – and applies them to deeper questions of cultural identities. It is not simply that bad behaviour is seen as fun, it is that it is seen as constitutive of particular forms of identity that may garner public validation; nothing less than affirmation of the self (Turner, 2004). When we consider the idea, it becomes clear that while parents may worry that *Viva La Bam* might give their teenagers ideas about how to create mischief in the home, it is also worth asking how these narratives contribute to a sense of being in the world.

It isn't strange that Sirius would be interested in a radio show that centres on Margera and his friends doing what they would be doing anyway, given the ubiquity of ordinary people doing ordinary things across media content. According to Turner (2004), the allure of celebrity, and its success in helping global media to penetrate deeper into the foundations of social life, is closely allied with the industrial function of reality media. Reality media realises the commercial value of media content that features people and places which are, in many respects, ordinary. This value has encouraged media industries to encourage the public to collaborate in the spectacularisation and commoditisation of everyday life. Consequently, celebrity is a media reality that everyone contemplates, since the ubiquity of reality media has created the impression that celebrity is now far more 'democratic' than it has ever been. This is not an illusion. According to some estimates, UK television, for example, offers over 20,000 speaking parts to ordinary people every year (Turner, 2004).

However, this fact has other outcomes. Intentionally or not, the cumulative presence of ordinary people affects perceptions of reality by articulating consumption, identity and personal validation as all part of the same process (Turner, 2004). If people wish to appear in media to win approval, this is a relatively tangible goal, but media industries profit most from this state of affairs. At any rate, the simple desire for fame noted in surveys of the young is far less vacuous than appears at first blush; it is, in some respects, recognition of media reality.

Turner believed the production of celebrity from ordinariness had widespread social effects because it differed in kind from the production of stardom. When Hollywood turned ordinary, modestly talented people into stars, the process was about delivering them from 'ordinariness'. In contrast, the transformations we see on reality television involve no transformation at all:

> The trend is for contestants to be 'ordinary' people without professional self-presentation skills or theatrical training or media background. If it were not for the fact that they have agreed to be on camera twenty-four hours a day, seven days a week for several months, they could plausibly stand in for the ordinary viewer. (Turner, 2004: 60)

Where the aspiring movie star desired change, the reality celebrity seeks affirmation. Reality media tells people it is okay to be who they are, but this creates a particular form of media dependency that enhances the power of the media centre. 'Although an ordinary person can use *Big Brother* to take a shot at fame … they are still at the mercy of the system that creates them and within which they have a limited future' (Turner, 2004: 54). Overall, Turner's point is that the ordinary has entered into an extraordinarily complex deal with media industries who invest enormous energies in reproducing what already exist as it already exists. Celebrity differs from stardom because it is a transformation that appears to effect no transformation at all, except that the ordinary person becomes a media person. However, this is an especially powerful version of the 'media as mirror' myth disguising *the* fundamental change in media systems where the celebrity becomes 'a means of advancing transnational branding across a wide range of industries, not just media or entertainment' (2004: 16).

SPORTING CELEBRITY

Studies of media sport depict the process with unrivalled lucidity. Sports stars are especially useful for disguising the structural truth about celebrity production, because the space between their real existence and media presence is closer than for others. Sports stars seem to be famous because their talent has earned it, but for the sporting celebrity, talent is a necessary but not sufficient condition for fame. Sports stars prove they are the best at what they do through fair and open competition (Turner, 2004). Sports celebrities, on the other hand, are, like reality-media figures, subjected to a processing that has little to do with their playing abilities. The fact that their undeniable skills are an unimpeachable precondition for celebrity makes them ideal for disguising the celebrity trick (Turner, 2004).

Ellis Cashmore's (1999) analysis of David Beckham explains these ideas with admirable clarity. Beckham marked a genuine departure in sporting fame as a football star who was especially popular among young audiences who were otherwise uninterested in the sport, and whose value *as an athlete* came to paradoxically rely less and less on his playing ability. This situation came about because sport had become a media spectacle, and audiences consumed sporting stars across a variety of media genres to the point where an athlete's performances had become but a sliver of their public profile.

Beckham's playing talent was a sort of insurance policy that guaranteed a return for processes of celebrity that turned him into something other than a football player. Yet, ironically, the marketability of his talent made his ability as a player secondary to his value to his team. Cashmore argued that Beckham became the first real football celebrity: that is, someone who became popular among young audiences with little interest in the sport, and who came to accept this fame as part of his career. In many ways, he had no choice in this matter, since his talent first blossomed while playing for a club that was just beginning to think of itself as a global brand in a sport that had become highly valued by global media interests. That club, Manchester United, quite literally needed a face on a T-shirt, as merchandising became more important to revenue streams and playing success.

This quickly led to an unprecedented situation, where Beckham's value off the field was even important to the clubs for whom he played (Cashmore, 1999). When Beckham was transferred from Real Madrid to LA Galaxy in 2007, his departure was principally felt off the field, with some estimates suggesting the move cost the Spanish club up to $30m in lost shirt sales per annum (Sky News, 2003). The LA Galaxy deal was a dizzying blend of commercial inducements that revealed how important Beckham had become as a media industry in his own right. As reported by the BBC, Beckham was offered around US$250m, a figure comprising salary, commercial endorsements, a percentage of merchandising profits and share in the club itself. In return, Beckham was to bring a global media audience. Timothy Leiweke, president of the AEG entertainment company who owned the team, put it like this: 'David is truly the only individual that can build the "bridge" between soccer in America and the rest of the world' (BBC News, 2007a). As the same report noted, AEG was a sponsor of an LA-based soccer school – founded by David Beckham.

His years in LA revealed that his presence at the club and presence on the field were different things. Anxious to remain in the England team, Beckham engineered a series of loan moves to European teams. By 2011, he had appeared in just 48 of the 106 games that the Galaxy played during his spell at the club. However, the frustration at a player who seemed to have signed for a club that he didn't really want to play for only peaked when his larger presence as a Galaxy personality failed to translate into the attention the club had craved, since neither live match attendances nor viewing figures had changed appreciably in that time (Donegan, 2011). Even so, a handsome world-class footballer with a particular appeal to young audiences, Beckham retained a value with a tenuous connection with his playing talent. He also symbolised why celebritisation had become central to cultural economies (Cashmore, 1999).

CELEBRITY AND MEDIA SPORT

The Beckham phenomenon reflected the changing formations of media sport. According to David Rowe, media sport powerfully condenses the question of how media have moved to the centre of cultural life. Fundamentally, sport

> occupies vast tracts of electronic, print and cyber media space; directly and indirectly generates a diverse range of goods and services produced by large numbers of companies and workers; absorbs substantial public resources in the form of programmes, subsidies and tax exemptions, and is strategically used by the political apparatus in the name of the people. (2004b: 3)

Sport, athletes and the media now exist in a co-dependent 'media sports cultural complex', which describes 'all the media and sports organizations, processes, personnel, services, products and texts which combine in the creation of the broad and dynamic field of contemporary sports culture' (Rowe, 2004a: XX). Media help sport, and athletes matter deeply within cultural, political and economic life, even for audiences who are not particularly interested in either. Rowe's crucial point is that sport is not a media spectacle because events such as football's World Cup are already objects of intense public interest – media spectacularisation makes it so. This became all the more true as media cultures became implicated in processes of globalisation: 'the enhanced flows of people, capital, ideas and technologies around the world' (Rowe, 2004b: 11). Like celebrity, global media make sport a phenomenon that orchestrates the popular imagination and everyday life. Clearly, then, the sporting *celebrity* is a powerful figure, all the more so given aggressive battles over sports contents rights brought on by the condition of what Hutchins and Rowe (2009) called 'digital plenitude'.

Hutchins and Rowe point out that sport has always attracted media interests because it guarantees audiences and revenue, and this capacity has become all the more important within digital networked media cultures characterised by the intense competition afforded by the capacity of digital technologies to host more content. This capacity has amplified struggles between media interests who now have to compete in a much broader field for audiences. Changing media technologies have moved media sport further into the centre of cultural life because it now affords a wider range of business opportunities:

> Significantly lower barriers of access and cost have multiplied the number of media companies, sports organizations, clubs, and even individual athletes who can produce and distribute content for online consumption and allowed large numbers of users to appropriate, modify, and share digital sports footage through web sites. (Hutchins and Rowe, 2009: 356)

Within these struggles, the athlete's image is a priceless asset, if it can be harnessed:

> These developments are representative of an emerging 'convergence culture' in which content flows across several media platforms ... and the burgeoning value of individuals as commodities and cultural signs in late modernity, as demonstrated by the growth of celebrity culture in both sport and the wider entertainment industries. (Hutchins and Rowe, 2009: 365)

It is no coincidence that Bam Margera managed his own transition from skateboarder to transmedia celebrity by becoming a media producer, because he emerged just as the multiplication of media technologies and business interests encouraged athletes to take as much interest in their image rights as they do in diets and training schedules, building and controlling these rights vital to career longevity. Hutchins and Rowe noted that mobile media and practices such as blogging let athletes construct themselves as public figures, often to the chagrin of sports governing bodies (witness the numerous English Premier League football players who have found themselves in conflict with their clubs and the English Football Association over ill-considered tweets). Further, the authors noted that these practices were pioneered in extreme sports. Although they did not mention Margera, it is apparent that the *CKY* videos were an embryonic exercise in athletic 'authorship', now a de rigueur element in the globalised, digitised media sports cultural complex.

When viewed through the lens of literature on celebrity, sporting celebrity and media sport, it isn't surprising at all that Sirius should pay for a radio show that simply featured Margera and his friends goofing around at home. Margera's desire to validate his friends in *Viva La Bam* reflects two things. First, the sort of celebrity that is produced by international media's voracious commoditisation of ordinary people doing ordinary things in ordinary settings, and the way that these production trends have made the general desire for fame among young people really quite sensible, in so far as this desire is really about the need for personal validation. Second, Margera had the added appeal, as a sports star, of a celebrity with a particular purchase on authenticity, grounded in his undoubted physical skill.

In this regard, Margera is a vehicle to apply Ellis Cashmore's (1999) analysis on the nature of media sport stardom, developed in his work on David Beckham, to a changed media environment where athletes routinely produce their own image through business transactions with media organisations. Margera's skilled manipulation of his media career where, like Beckham, his status as a star skateboarder rapidly became almost irrelevant, speaks to the machinations of the 'media sport cultural complex' (Rowe, 2004a), a phrase denoting the central role sport plays in convergent global media cultures that seek audiences through 'content streaming' (Murray, 2003), making the same material available across different media. Margera's Sirius show demonstrates how sporting celebrity has become a vital resource as the competition for global audiences intensifies under conditions of 'digital plenitude' (Hutchins and Rowe, 2009). To appreciate this still further, consider the history of SiriusXM satellite radio, and the way this history explains the value the station placed on celebrity.

MARGERA, CELEBRITY, SATELLITE RADIO AND MEDIA SPORT

Few events better demonstrated the economic and legal complexities of convergent media cultures than Sirius' efforts to establish the market for satellite radio, then dominate that market by finding the right combination of technology and content to attract the right subscribers to its pay services. From its inception, sport and celebrity were the key content ingredients intended to pull listeners away from rivals.

In 2001 Sirius became the first company to launch its satellites, based on little more than a hunch that there were enough people willing to pay to listen to make the operation a going concern (Beardi, 2001). From its inception, Sirius knew the case for satellite radio had to be based on much more than the self-evident appeals of crystal-clear, commercial-free content. Sirius has to demonstrate the viability of a new venture within changing media consumption patterns characterised by the growing power of niche markets. Sirius was a pioneer in grasping the nettle of digital plenitude, inspired by the potential market in media sport. In 2006 senior Sirius executive Sam Benrubi outlined the reason for his company's optimism:

> Just because the audience is small doesn't mean it doesn't have value for an advertiser. Both traditional radio and cable have built a good business around niche programming. Take sports stations, for example. Often mediocre performers in the ratings, the stations are lucrative revenue generators. (Bachman, 2006: 22)

Benrubi referenced MTV as an exemplar of the global capacity for niche market-ing. Hence it is clear why Margera, as a sport and MTV star, would appeal to the emerging station.

In July 2008, Sirius took its global footprint a step further by merging with rival XFM. The merger provoked fears of monopoly power in an emerging field (Bachman and Yorke, 2007; Eggerton, 2007; Rehr, 2007), which threat-ened significant cultural effects. Canadians worried that SiriusXM, as it came to be known, threatened the integrity of traditional media regulations designed to protect their musicians (Chiasson and Dougherty, 2005). How-ever, proving the risks at play in global media operations that are part and parcel of global consumer culture, the value of Sirius stocks actually dropped by over 40 per cent in the space between the two companies agreeing to merge in 2007 and the Federal Communications Commission (FCC) approv-ing the deal in 2008 (Kharif, 2008). Investors regarded satellite radio as a high-risk venture, vulnerable to the vagaries of the competition engendered by 'digital plenitude' and, indeed, the broader consumer market. From its inception, Sirius gambled on the unproven premise that there were enough people in the USA and Canada who were willing to pay for subscription radio to make a satellite service a viable economic concern (Beardi, 2001). Their optimism was partly based on potential profits from tie-ins with the automo-bile industry, as the latter started to offer satellite radios as standard fea-tures. Merging Sirius and XFM just after the global financial crisis, and the significant reversals suffered by the auto industry, was hardly likely to enthuse investors, with General Motors predicting a 12 per cent fall in auto-mobile sales in 2008 (Kharif, 2008).

Much as the Sirius/XM merger had been resisted on the grounds that it would create an anti-competitive media juggernaut, in fact the 2008 merger could also be seen as a defensive mood designed to help satellite radio sur-vive, not thrive. Even after the merger, SiriusXM's fortunes remained rocky. By 2010, the station had managed to turn significant 2009 losses ($52.7m) into profit, but not before Nasdaq had threatened to delist the company from the stock exchange due to poor performances (Kharif, 2010). The company's future remained precarious, partly because they had failed to secure its prize asset: shock jock Howard Stern, whose contract with the company was due to expire.

Stern's importance to Sirius underlined the value of celebrity as a 'guaran-tee' in volatile markets where success depended on so many variables beyond the company's control. Sirius lured Stern from CBS radio with a staggering deal: stock options worth $220m, dependent on his ability to achieve target ratings – which he did within a year (Bachman, 2006). Yet this was probably money well spent. The story of Stern's migration from CBS to Sirius underlined how powerful celebrities had become as commodities in digital markets. After agreeing the switch to Sirius from the CBS-owned Infinity Radio, Stern was sur-prised to find Infinity insisting that he work out his notice. Stern reacted by spending the ensuing three months deriding CBS on air, imploring listeners to buy satellite radios and follow him to Sirius, and generally giving his new employers millions of dollars worth of free advertising. For all the humiliation, Infinity kept Stern on air because his rants ensured a large audience and advertising revenue (Klaassen, 2005).

CBS were willing to tolerate this, and Sirius were willing to wait, because Stern could drag audiences from one radio station, and radio platform, to another. He was, simply, such a popular DJ that people would pay to hear from him. When it comes to Margera, although his role in the Sirius strategy was less central, it was also more complex because, unlike Stern, he had added value as a source of 'content streaming' (S. Murray, 2003). He may not have been able to command an instant audience of millions of confirmed radio fans, but he could complement the drift by attracting people who enjoyed *Jackass*, *Viva La Bam*, *Bam's Unholy Union*, video gamers who played *Tony Hawk's Underground*, fans of the Finnish band *Him* (who Margera, a lover of Finnish rock music, had expended considerable energy on breaking in the USA), and even people who remembered him for his once famed ability as a professional skateboarder. Vital as Stern was to Sirius, it was Margera who encapsulated the station's take on the sort of content that made niche media work. Paying for a small portion of his 'fun' lifestyle was a small price to pay, in comparison.

CONCLUSION: BAM MARGERA, CELEBRITY, AND A 'DEEP' MODEL OF MEDIA INFLUENCE

At face value, there doesn't seem to be much to say about Bam Margera; he simply uses film and reality media to prolong his adolescent obsessions with skateboarding and playing elaborate pranks on and with his childhood friends. The Sirius show was, on one level, an extension of this career – most episodes feature Margera and his friends sitting around in his home studio, drinking and recounting stories of their (often drink-related) misadventures. However, it is the very 'ordinariness' of the 'Margera format' that secures him as an ideal figure to explain how celebrity works in 'the media sports cultural complex'.

The impression of authenticity, projected through media, is the key 'trick' that makes celebrity work as a particular form of media influence. According to Chris Rojek, 'Celebrity is a culture of faux ecstasy, since the passions it generates derive from staged authenticity rather than genuine forms of recognitions and belonging' (2001: 90), and further, 'The search for authenticity is a gesture to a submerged moral world engulfed by the incessant commercialism and artificial titillation of consumer culture' (2001: 161). What Rojek was suggesting was that, beneath the patina of authenticity, celebrities grab the imagination of young people because they are condensation points for diverse media and commercial interests. Celebrities are pivotal to commercial success in convergent media cultures, due to their power to draw the same audiences (and the revenues those audiences bring) across platforms and genres in ways that reach into the ordinary lives of young people (Turner et al., 2000; Turner, 2004), often by creating the impression that they, too, are ordinary people (Tolson, 2001; Turner, 2004).

Sporting celebrities are especially important in this regard, because media sport has always been a valuable resource for attracting global audiences (Rowe, 2004a), and because of the unique capacity that sports celebrities have for embodying 'authenticity', creating the impression that carefully constructed media personae capture something that is true. The industrial import of sporting celebrity has grown, since today's sports stars are much more aggressive about producing, controlling and monetising their media personae, thanks to changing media environments marked by aggressive struggles over contents rights (Hutchins and Rowe, 2009). Bam Margera is notable in this sense as someone who has taken a far greater hand in the production, editing and distribution of his image under conditions of digital plenitude.

All of this matters because, according to Graeme Turner (2010), celebrity is a media phenomenon that demands a fundamental rethink on the nature of media power, and again, young people are central in this rethinking. Turner defines celebrity as *the* 'content motor' that drives the media convergence described in the last chapter (Turner et al., 2000; Turner, 2004, 2010). This 'content motor' is particularly suited to media societies because it manipulates distinctions around the 'ordinary' – celebrity culture appeals to ordinary people by promising to close the space between stars and the public – either by offering ordinary people easy access to stardom or by reducing the space between stars and the public by emphasising the extent to which fabulous stars are ordinary people too (see also Tolson, 2001). Turner also identified celebrity as a topic around which it may be possible to find distinct 'reality effects' brought about by media alone, and visited on the young in particular.

At the same time, this is a topic where it seems that we can think of powerful effects as *cultural* phenomena that don't trick or corrupt young people, in the way envisaged by people like David Grossman, mentioned in the first chapter. What Turner does is take the apparently facile desire for fame for fame's sake, deemed to be endemic in the youth cultures created by media societies, and describe why this desire, injurious to society as it might be, in fact makes sense in the context of the role that media play in organising social life and, therefore, the social imagination. From this vantage, Bam Margera's efforts to validate his friends and his lifestyle – to claim the right to do whatever the fuck he wants to – through media practice is a spectacular example of a bargaining process that many young people enter into when living media lives. Another way to put this is to say that Margera is a public 'text', and understanding how that text is made also tells us about the way that society works. This is the point that Rowe makes about media sport:

> By gaining a better knowledge and understanding of how media sports texts are produced and what they might mean, it is possible to learn more about the societies in which 'grounded' and 'mediated' experience intermesh in ever more insidious and seemingly seamless ways. (2004a: 35)

Celebrity defines a particular independent reality effect that media have through the notion of talent as a necessary but insufficient condition for fame. Ingeniously, by showing that talent alone is not enough to secure celebrity, media create the impression that celebrity is a democratic phenomenon which can be visited upon anyone. This is only a partial truth, since fame *is* visited on those who can be processed in ways that attract audiences, and the qualities that attract audiences change according to the media businesses in question. This is why Turner argues that the analysis of celebrity demands close attention to the very specific conditions of the production of distinct celebrities.

Hence Bam Margera *radio* personality is valuable in explaining how celebrity works, and how it appeals to the young in particular. Thinking about it again, as rich and successful as he is, Margera's media tactics have been another sort of 'defensive tactic' employed to defend a youthful space for fun that he enjoys with his friends. Yet his success in doing this on the radio clearly depended on the convergence between his social life, his identity as an extreme-sport star who marches audiences across multiple platforms, and the unique needs of a risky venture into satellite radio. His media adventures suggest that ambitions and attitudes to media practice that are common in youth cultures have become raw materials that media industries can commoditise, and then project back into the youth social imagination – deepening the sense that it is almost impossible to think, act or *be* socially without access to media resources. This is why scholars like Turner believe the time is right to revisit the idea of media influence, and why the topic of youth and celebrity raises fundamental questions about the very nature of critical media research. In the concluding chapter, we turn to these questions.

CHAPTER SUMMARY

- Celebrity culture is a genre that seems to have merged media and interpersonal communication; the desire for fame, common among young people, could be about the desire for validation. This is a rational response to media-saturated societies.

- Celebrity culture turns ordinary life into a media event. Sports celebrities are especially valuable commodities in global media cultures. The impression that their fame is a natural outcome of their talent disguises the media processing at play in the production of celebrity. For the sports celebrity, talent is incidental to fame.

- Bam Margera has become a sports celebrity who can be relied on to attract an audience in shows that are basically about hanging out with old school friends, living out youthful fantasies about doing as you please. He is unique as an example of an ordinary sporting celebrity who trades in youthful narratives. Moreover, his career as a satellite radio DJ indicates the commercial value of sporting celebrity in competitive global media markets.

NOTES

1 The fact that Margera is not conventionally thought of as a sports star, thanks to his success as a media personality, is exactly the point. The biography on his own website proudly boasts that a teen poll in 2005 voted him 'Favourite athlete turned TV star', he was ranked as one of America's best-known athletes in 2007 and he was also lauded as 'the most influential/powerful person under 30 by *Stuff* magazine' (Margera, 2012).

2 In the opening credits of each show, viewers are warned they are about to see a series of stunts performed by trained and supervised professionals, and they are not to re-enact what they witness. Indeed, anticipating hosts of young people who may try to repeat Margera's essential trick-converting home videos into an international film franchise, *Jackass* warned that the producers would refuse to watch any media clips sent to them by fans.

10

UNDERSTANDING CRITICAL MEDIA STUDIES: CHILD SOLDIERS, MEDIA BUSINESS AND MEDIA EDUCATION

Research question.
Considering all the case studies, what is the best way to conceive media influence?

Lessons for understanding media influence.
Critical media research should be 'problem' focussed. Young people need access to media, therefore there is an inherent problem in the fact that their well-being depends on media industries whose main job is not to look after them. This is different from arguing that media are 'bad' for the young

Underlying question about media influence.
What defines critical media research?

Outcomes.
Instances where access to media resources have helped young victims of war also shed light on how difficult it is to get media resources to the young people who need them most. We must therefore be careful about basing media education on the assumption that young people are willing and able to express themselves through media

Relevant literature.
Liz Bird's criticisms of research on youth, media and creativity. David Gauntlett, Henry Jenkins and Jean Burgess on media education and popular creativity

Exemplifying case study.
Child soldiers in Africa and South America: How can media help them, and what are the risks involved in using media to address this form of systematic exploitation?

Youth and Media has argued that if we study how young people are represented in media, and look at how youths engage with media resources, we end up discovering a lot about fundamental concepts and methods in media studies – particularly around the issue of how media help give shape to social reality. Having challenged many traditional orthodoxies – especially around the topic of media effects – it makes sense to end by asking: What is critical media research?

The question is aimed at getting beyond the impression that, when it comes to young people, scholars must either regard media culture as a predatory danger for youths who simply do not understand the symbolic worlds in which they live, or celebrate the capacities of young media users who, history tells us, have always been able to figure media out for themselves. Looking at what well-known media scholars have written about the creativity of young media users, we can see two things: first, it is relatively easy to find evidence that supports positive and negative views of media influence, but second, even the most optimistic of writers about young people and media are alert to the inherent risks posed by global media industries.

Instead of thinking about media as either 'good' or 'bad', media scholars look at the risks inherent in a world where the democratic *potential* of media culture is difficult to realise. To explain what this observation means, and why it matters, this chapter looks at case studies of how child soldiers can be helped by gaining access to media, and the dangers and obstacles that lay in the path of helping them heal through media creativity. The purpose of doing this is to show the difference between 'risk' and 'danger' as critical concepts. Media culture is 'risky' because the self-evident capacities of mobile media to improve communication and enhance social inclusivity are frequently beset by practical obstacles. This established, you will be able to explain why it makes sense to look for inherent problems in situations where access to media resources is important to well-being.

MEDIA IN A DANGEROUS WORLD

In 2007, the world met Madeline, a 15-year-old girl from the Congo who came to the United Nations (UN) in New York to testify to her experiences as a child soldier. Outside the UN, the people who met Madeline did so through a documentary that was shared via YouTube (Ferrero, 2007). The tens of thousands of people who watched the 10-minute clip heard that in 2007 there were an estimated 300,000 child soldiers in the world. Chillingly, viewers discovered that child soldiers are valuable because they are fearless and quick to train; apparently, the average African child could master an AK47 assault rifle in 45 minutes.

This terrifying fact is worth remembering in debates about youth, media and creativity. We know about Madeline because she got the chance to speak to the world through YouTube. But her story tells us that she came from a world where it is easier to channel creativity and ingenuity into weapons training than media production, and we don't know the names of the 299,999 other children who are thought to have taken up arms in that year. Madeline asks media scholars two questions: How easy is it for young people to realise the potential of mediatisation, and how is media use affected by the other demands that societies place on young people?

YOUTH AND MEDIA: WHAT'S THE PROBLEM?

These questions make the question of media influence a matter of access, not exposure, and so it's worth thinking about how Madeleine's story fits into the one that this book has told about media and power. *Youth and Media* began by distinguishing between *direct* and *powerful* media influence. The founding argument of the book is that defining media effects as the direct, observable outcomes of exposure to dangerous content is not the best way to explain how media influence young people. Nevertheless, holistic accounts of media cultures, analysing the consumption and use of media in social, historical, political and economic contexts, find many instances where media do direct the habits, tastes, attention and ambitions of young people in directions that principally serve other people's interests. Furthermore, given the indubitable centrality of media in social life, this represents a major political challenge to any society that aspires to inclusivity.

But why should the study of youth and media begin from the assumption that media exert an influence *over* young people? To do so implies there are inherent risks in media cultures; that there is, in essence, a 'problem'. Some scholars think this assumption to be the death of media studies (Gauntlett, 2011). To conclude the book, this chapter argues that the 'problem' is worth retaining as a legitimate foundation for media studies, for two reasons. First, globally speaking, the young people who need access to media and media education the most – people like Madeline – are those who have the least access to it. When it comes to access, there is indeed a problem. Second, there is an inherent tension in media-saturated societies because media have become integral to the social well-being of young people, but the economic viability of media resources always precedes their public value.

This redefines the 'dangers' posed by media cultures. Where public debates customarily frame 'harm' as a function of exposure, commercial media cultures do just as much damage by creating barriers to access; in other words, the problem isn't exposure, but *lack* of exposure. To illustrate this alternative view on how media create problems in young people's lives, this chapter considers the plight of child soldiers in Africa and South America. These young people are forced into violence by the adults who are supposed to care for them. In these settings, access to media resources has been offered as a *solution* to social violence. Yet, even so, the process of engaging child soldiers with media resources creates many very real dangers for them. Because of this, their experiences are highly pertinent to international controversies over media education and the scale and significance of popular creativity among young people – what Bruns (2007) called 'produsage'. By looking at how child soldiers, paramilitaries and victims of political violence use media – or in fact, don't – it is also possible to take a position on critical media research that focuses on the risks presented by the indubitable marriage of creativity and commerce in participatory media cultures. The child-soldier case study suggests that young victims of political violence in Africa and South America stand at the cusp of critical media analysis that engages with important debates on the nature and purpose of media education and the emerging interest in popular creativity afforded by widening access to the means of media production.

There are four parts to this chapter:

- summarising what the book says about media influence;

- exploring current debates on young media users, popular creativity and media education;

- applying the lessons of these debates to studies of 'media poor' – young people in Nigeria, Sierra Leone and Colombia;

- defining a research agenda for critical studies of youth media.

YOUTH AND MEDIA: SUMMARISING THE CASE FOR INFLUENCE

It is legitimate to start studying young people and media by assuming the presence of a problem because, in a world where many of the self-evident benefits of media-saturated societies are widely championed (i.e. an iPhone 4S advertisement featuring a soldier on active duty seeing his new baby for the first time via the 'Facetime' feature, which makes the point that new technologies really do make it easier to keep in touch with the people we love, and this is obviously a great thing), it is important to recognise the many instances where young media users express unease about their media experiences, or else where those experiences are handily appropriated by other interests.

A 'problem' angle does not imply that media influences are direct, intentional or unidirectional, but it does assume they are powerful. The topic of celebrity culture, covered in the last chapter, encapsulates key differences between behaviourist and cultural understandings of media power. Academic studies of celebrity show the complexities of media cultures and the sophistication of young media users can be appreciated without dismissing the case that media industries have a major impact on how young people see the world. Turner (2010) thought celebrity culture probably has agitated an incremental shift in the expectations young people have about life, and this is one instance of the inevitably profound effects that media saturation brings to perceptions of, and more importantly, expectation about social reality. When it comes to scholars such as Turner, then, the point of objecting to people like David Grossman (see Chapter 1) is that the latter's concerns are a distraction from the limitations media cultures impose on the majority of ordinary young people who do not transgress legal, moral or social norms in any obvious way. If wanting fame is really about yearning for validation, then celebrity culture raises the general question of how it is that a perfectly understandable human aspirations comes to be tied to the interests of media businesses. This is one central question in critical media studies.

Fundamentally, it is increasingly difficult to describe social reality without considering the role media play in making that reality as it is. Although Twitter or Facebook clearly didn't cause the Arab Spring, events in Egypt, for example, unfolded as they did because of social-media businesses. Would Wael Ghomin have emerged as a political leader if he hadn't worked for Google? Perhaps, but the fact that he did gave him access to resources that shaped the history of the event in particular ways. That said, the organisational power of the media becomes really effective when it evolves into a less noticeable feature of everyday life.

According to the studies covered in this book, young people have learnt to live with the commercial basis of media operations across a range of experiences, including the organisation of the self. We saw that E. P. Thompson was disturbed by the fact that already, by the 1960s, although there was widespread dissatisfaction with commercial media among young people, the effects of this dissatisfaction were limited by the fact that the young didn't seem to be able to imagine a different mode of organisation, and this ultimately secured the corporate power. In numerous instances, this remains true: in Florida, student rage at injustice was converted into a handy solution for the woes of regional media; in China, desires for more of a public say was channelled into texting practices that turned a profit and ameliorated the state; in Palestine, desires for autonomy and community between young women was tied to phone contracts. The positioning of the university as a retail space makes it easy for students to run their traditions through drinking, with alcohol marketing oiling the wheels. On school shootings, whether trying to come to terms with tragedies or engaging in mindless voyeuristic fantasies online, young media users have to deal with the economies of attention – in the Finnish experience, this inadvertently deepened the commitment to commercial interest as a journalistic bottom line. Apparently spontaneous examples of youth media activism mask innovative and potentially sinister ways that media companies work their ways into business, government and everyday life all at the same time.

More importantly, when researchers ask young people about how and why they use media, these young people frequently express unease at the fact that they are obliged to use media and engage with media businesses as a matter of course. Accounts of having to listen to raps that you hate in order to get through the horrific business of soldiering are powerful testaments to this position. Even those who make content for youth markets are unhappy at the compromises required to access that market – we saw this in Andrew Robinson's insights on the deals needed to make *April Showers* and in the ICP's comments on rap violence. In both cases, we see how Thompson's claim that the main effect of media cultures is to limit the social imagination to the parameters of commercial cultures was remarkably prescient.

There are many instances, then, when media industries limit human creativity within the bounds of things that can be monetised. There is nothing new about this; artists have always had to eat, and have always relied on people who would pay for the art they liked. However, perhaps this commercial drive matters more when media practice is the 'hub' of social life, and media and interpersonal communication are difficult to separate. Media practices direct social life. The directions themselves are open to conflict, but increasingly the idea that business interests will drive those outcomes is assured. This isn't necessarily a bad thing, but in a world where the benefits of media plenitude are obvious (my grandfather could have used an iPhone 4S when he too was at war during my mother's birth, but as it was he didn't get to see her until she was almost 4 years old; it's obviously a good thing that soldiers today don't have to endure such delays), it is important to do research on those who can only dip a toe into a media saturated world. This is crucial consideration in debates on media education, as they developed around the notion of popular creativity.

CURRENT DEBATES ON YOUNG MEDIA USERS, POPULAR CREATIVITY AND MEDIA EDUCATION

In 2011, media anthropologist Liz Bird cautioned that Brun's concept of 'pro-dusage' was the endgame in a troubling tendency among media researchers to seek out and celebrate young people who used media resources in highly creative ways. Bird thought research on popular creativity committed the same validity error that had been observed in effects studies. Chapter 2 mentioned Comstock's observation that the claims for effects research were weakened by over-reliance on student samples. In similar fashion, Bird warned the undoubted spread of resources and access to resources for popular creativity have had more of an effect on academics than the public, because it has made it easier than ever to find examples of young media users doing all manner of creative things with media that do not reflect corporate interests in any obvious ways. The attraction of studying the many people who do interact with media in rich and empowering ways made it easy to ignore the many others who do not.

In illustration, Bird mentioned her research among young Nigerian school pupils, whose only exposure to the internet was the occasional glimpse of their high-school principal using it in his office. For Bird, the shift to digital, networked cultures, and the emerging interest in popular creativity afforded by these platforms, exacerbated a long trend in critical audience research of ignoring young people with sparse access to media resources, or else those who have little to say about how they use media, when they can. The question of access, as we shall see, is crucial to understanding the practice of critical media education.

David Gauntlett is a media scholar whose outlook on media influence mirrors the perspective that concerned Bird. Gauntlett's call for a 'Media Studies 2.0' (2011) was an attempt to redefine media studies as the study of popular creativity. Gauntlett believed the case for strong media effects is intellectually bankrupt. Further, he also thought the call for stronger protection against commercial media was unrealistic, since governments are unlikely to act in an effective way to meet community needs, and in any case stronger regulation is unnecessary since ordinary people are well versed in making do with the media they can get to do the identity work needed for a life that feels worth living.

Gauntlett presented the prevalence of popular creativity as a 'fact' that is just as important as the power of commercial and political interests in media industries, and there was no reason why media scholars should not begin from the former assumption. This, he believed, had a major impact on the practice of media education. Rather than have students write essays about the insidious effects of global media industries, based on studies using theories and examples that are simply not relevant to the media world in which students live, those students should have the opportunity to be assessed through creative media work where they express themselves, not the outmoded ideas of the people they have been forced to read.

Gauntlett's advice to take widespread creativity as the starting point for media education has implications for the sorts of young people who show up in media studies. We can see this by looking at two quotes from Gauntlett's 'Media studies 2.0 and other battles around the future of media research' (2011). First, Gauntlett challenged scholars to dispense with

> outmoded notions of 'receiver' audiences and elite 'producers', to enable a new project where 'conventional concerns with power and politics are reworked ... so that the notion of super-powerful media industries invading the minds of a relatively passive population is compelled to recognise and address the context of more widespread creation and participation. (2011, location 223)

By taking this perspective, and by getting students to make sense of media cultures by making things rather than writing essays, using other people's ideas 'to make pretentious statements about trivial aspects of unimportant media' (2011, location 1091), media studies would be in a better place to help society, tying media creativity to making identities that afforded meaningful engagements with the world. Gauntlett argued that this was actually a Victorian idea that came from John Ruskin:

> Ruskin argued that human creativity should be unleashed, and must dare to risk failure and shame, so that the richness of humanity can be properly expressed. Today we have the tools to easily experiment, and to share our haphazard innovations with others. We should push ourselves in the direction of diverse and unusual experimentation, rather than the risk-averse version of 'professionalism' which prefers bland competence. (2011, location 1073)

What we learn from Gauntlett is about the importance of approaching media education from a public/social good point of view. What we don't learn about is how this matches concerns about media influence, or how the ideas apply to people who aren't free to express themselves since they either don't have access to resources or else because using them would be dangerous.

Gauntlett's 'Media studies 2.0' was a project about popular creativity. Aside from those who had directly criticised his work, the thousands of scholars who still study media influence simply did not exist in Gauntlett's paradigm. By dismissing the case for media influence, Gauntlett also dismissed the publics who worry about or suffer from social problems that media are involved in. Consider again the quote about what creative media students should be doing. It is curiously asocial. What about people who suffer social risks because they live in societies where it is not safe to express oneself? Or what about situations where the young people who do make creative use of scant resources, that are now more widely available than ever before, simply remind us of others who can't?

With these reservations in mind, Henry Jenkins' *Fans, Bloggers, and Gamers* (2006b) is notable as a study on popular creativity that took a far more conciliatory position on media effects. Jenkins agreed that the public have every right to be concerned and angry about media violence, especially the graphic sort found in games like *Grand Theft Auto 3*, which lets young gamers – or anybody, for that matter – gain pleasure from murdering sex workers. Jenkins believed the main impediment to effective action on problematic media content was that the parameters of public debates on the issue prevented constructive dialogue between pro-censorship and pro-education interests. Ultimately this dialogue would matter because Jenkins also had his own version of 'deep' media influence caused by the commercial imperatives of media production:

> What is bad about a lot of games isn't that they are violent but that they trivialize violence. They tell us little about our inner demons because they fall back too quickly on tried and true formulas. (2006b: 203–204)

Here, Jenkins was not rejecting the notion of influence; he was instead urging a different model of social learning than that offered by David Grossman (whose work came in for sustained criticism in the book). Jenkins believed that properly designed games could help young people to think about the causes and outcomes of real violence, connecting them to the topic of social inequality. His position was that this was what games could do, but that most of the time, because of commercial injunctions against formula breaking and risk taking, this happened all too rarely. The only solution, then, was for academics to become involved in the production of new games.

Ultimately, Jenkins believed that he and pro-censorship campaigners shared the same 'concern for American youth', but the real trouble was that

> [t]his debate always gets presented as if there were only two sides – mothers battling to protect their kids and the cigar-chomping entertainment bosses who prey on American Youth. This formulation allows no space to defend popular culture from any position other than self interest. (2006b: 205)

Setting aside the inference that critical media scholars are tasked with defending popular culture, Jenkins, unlike Gauntlett, did not dismiss the case for significant media influence – quite the reverse – and nor did he think that American youth lived in worlds of abundant creative opportunities created by media systems. While committing himself to work inside media industries as a vehicle for introducing the cultural concerns that drive critical media studies, and people who worry about the social influence of the media, Jenkins clearly regretted the absence of a space where he could address the effects case.

The idea of engaging with media industries to encourage them to pay more attention to the social issues of their work was clearly a good one, but in this Jenkins chose to focus on shaping the materials that young people would end up using, rather than looking at the users themselves. In this regard, Jean Burgess' (2006) Australian-based work on digital storytelling is a useful perspective in how to address inequality when studying the practices through which people used social media to tell the world about themselves. Burgess combined Gauntlett's commitment to the study of ordinary creativity as a social practice with Bird's concern that it is far to easy for researchers to overestimate the impact of popular creativity by focusing on the high end. Burgess recognised how vital it is to place any media research in the context of the everyday practices that people use to make sense of themselves and the things that happen to them: 'if ordinary people have the opportunity to create content for public consumption for the first time, they choose to use this opportunity to talk about the serious business of the human experience – life, loss, belonging, hope for the future, friendship and love–mean to them' (2006b: 211–212). She also noted how easily popular creativity is shackled to commercial concerns, citing Turner's celebrity work as a case in point. Like Bird, Burgess urged researchers to resist the allure of popular creative forms that quite obviously set out to resist the power of media industries and other institutions. Researchers should also avoid the trap of making these voices fit into pre-existing narratives: 'Neither anti-populist critique nor the unreflexive celebration of the fan-producer of computer games do anything to make the voices of the less culturally and technologically privileged citizen more audible' (2006b: 211).

Jenkins and Burgess represent a strand of research on popular creativity that is concerned with attending to the interfaces between social and media inequality by seeking out the voices of young people with limited media choices. As an example of one such person, consider the following comment from 'Adela', a 15-year-old Colombian girl who had spent four years serving as a child soldier in a paramilitary group, prior to being rescued by social workers:

> The social welfare system only preoccupies itself with whether we helped clean or that we studied, but never worried about what we, who had been part of the armed conflict, felt. I believe that it is very important. It is so important for the children who have been involved in armed conflict to have someone who will listen to them, who will allow us to freely express ourselves, and to have someone who understands us. The social welfare system doesn't do that. They don't give us psychological assistance. I believe most of my fellow child soldiers feel the same way. (Cited in Duarte and Caruso, 2009: 365).

Adela was a participant in Taller de Vida, a community media initiative designed to help Colombian child soldiers recover from their ordeal by making short films on their experiences. In this account, Adela presented the chance to express herself as being as important to survival as food, clothes and shelter. Certainly, media helped an outrageously abused child. But, thinking about Burgess' argument, what do we hear in this account? Hearing Adela means not only paying attention to her words, but also asking how it is she came to speak, and how her voice came to be heard. That is, we need to pay attention to the relations of production and distribution that made Taller de Vida available as a resource. What does it say about places where activists use media to help young people at risk from violence? What risks do such activities take, and what do these situations tell us about new directions in critical media research that looks at the effects media businesses have on young people, and their social opportunities? To answer these questions, the next section considers the experiences of young soldiers and paramilitaries in Nigeria, Sierra Leone and Colombia.

YOUTH AND POLITICAL VIOLENCE: THE RISKS OF USING MEDIA TO END POLITICAL VIOLENCE

In Nigeria, organised political violence carried out by young people has been a major national issue since 1993. Adebanwi's (2005) study of the youth wing of Nigeria's Oodua People's Congress (OPC) implied that access to digital storytelling would help young Nigerians who are driven to arms and partisan vigilantism by older politicians, because as things stand violence is the only medium those young people have to write themselves into Nigerian history. The OPC was formed among Yoruba youths in 1993, following a decision by the ruling military regime, led by General Ibrahim Babangida, to annul free elections, just as voting appeared to be heading in the direction of a Yoruban candidate, Moshood Abiola. By 2000, levels of violence among OPC youth had become so extreme that police in Lagos were ordered to shoot any OPC members it encountered without question. Like so many youth groups in other parts of the world, young OPC members became the symbol of the tensions resulting from years of military rule (Adebanwi, 2005). The missing ingredient is, of course, the media, in so far as no one thought this violence was caused by watching too many action adventure movies.

The OPC youth wing were useful to older, non-violent politicians, 'as elders mobilise and instrumentalise youth violence from which they can keep a safe distance' (Adebanwi, 2005: 351). Their violence was also symbolic, seen as a device to reclaim the 'warlord' tradition of the nineteenth-century Yoruba people, and to overcome the perception among other Nigerians that, by the 1993 dissolution, 'the Yoruba had come to acquire the image of easy-going and partying people at best ... and cowards at worst' (2005: 357). Without validating it, Adebanwis' research established that violence enacted by the youth wing of the OPC was an organised political attempt to write a particular version of Nigerian history where the Yoruba were the true champions of national interests. OPC violence fell into distinct genres: struggles between OPC factions, struggles with non-Yoruba over economic and political territory and vigilante activities, as the OPC sought to police its own territory. This 'symbolic' violence was real enough – involving things like crucifying robbers in Yoruba districts. But it was also a political action, with political dividends. Against an image of a continent gone mad in the face of intractable ethic conflicts, Adebanwi's study instead sought to point out that the apparent orgy of OPC youth violence was comprehensible as the outcome of a complex political history where youth was a cultural driver, working in combinations with ethnic, religious and regional identities.

None of which, of course, detracts from the truth that political violence has become a significant risk for young Nigerians, either as victims of violence or people who are induced to behave violently to serve the political ends of others. In this respect, and given the notion that youth violence in Nigeria is a narrative act, some have advocated media as the *solution* to social violence in the country. In their review of the role that journalists have played in Nigerian political violence, Omenugha and Adum (2008) argued that better journalism training could improve political stability. Peace journalism, for example with a commitment to explaining the causes of violence, and also tracking how the justice system caught and punished criminals, would be far more constructive than the existing tendency to report violence crime in sensationalistic ways – a tendency that contributed to the 'shoot on site' policy directed at young OPC members. At any rate, although existing journalism practices, enacted in newsrooms that tended to re-create the political divisions within Nigerian society, were part of the problem in the 'cycle of violence', they were also potentially part of the solution.

If David Gauntlett were to look at this solution he would probably – and quite correctly – point out that it would require costly and time-consuming structural changes to Nigerian journalism, and in the meantime young people would continue to suffer. So what about quicker solutions where young people work with things that are already in place? What if Yoruba youth could express their view of where they belong in Nigerian politics and Nigerian history through media instead of vigilantism?

Such initiatives have been established in Sierra Leone. In 2008, Banker White and Zach Niles, two American documentary makers, won a grant to establish WeOwnTV, a three-year project designed to give young people in Sierra Leone the equipment and the training to tell other people about their experiences in the war-ravaged nation (Cavagnaro et al., 2011). More than this, WeOwnTV set out to train a new generation of media professionals who would be committed to peace journalism. White and Niles' experiences making a film about young people in Sierra Leone inspired the project. The film featured Black Nature, a young rapper who shared the story of the hardships he had suffered through political violence. Much as WeOwnTV was proud of its achievement, it was also keen to point out that these achievements were hard won in a nation where the 'youth voice' is often used by established political parties towards their own end. There is much talk about the youth voice in Sierra Leone, but relatively few young people get to speak in ways that the public hear. As in Nigeria, the established media were another obstacle. However, this was not simply because political powers in Sierra Leone were interested in creating a situation where young people were spoken about, but remained silent; it was also significantly because of the absence of media space – with only one state broadcaster and a media sphere that was otherwise awash with pirated material, a sea in which independent alternative media were all too easily lost (Cavagnaro et al., 2011). The crucial thing about this is that where Gauntlett seems to suggest that the matter of the general effects that the flow of commercial media had on society was a different question from the matter of how popular creativity contributed to a sense of well-being, WeOwnTV, for all the pride its operators take in its achievements, sees alternative voices and commercial media as being part of the same cultural economy where the prevalence of one affects the extent to which the other can survive. Valuable as it was, WeOwnTV was clearly a precarious project, reliant on the generosity of private funding, and vulnerable to the effects of a media system where entertainment was mostly pirated.

The stakes are even higher in Colombia. Duarte and Caruso (2009) explained how Taller de Vida operated under intensely dangerous conditions. By Colombian government estimates, in 2008 up to 8000 children were at arms in paramilitary units. Children were easily recruited in a country where poverty was rife. In Adela's case, the violence she faced as a soldier was preferable to the abuse she had received at home. At any rate, child soldiers had become a major fighting resource in a nation effectively locked in a civil war, so efforts to 'rescue' them were highly risky (Duarte and Caruso, 2009). This was precisely the sort of situation that Gauntlett's take on common creativity did not imagine. True, Adela valued freedom of expression, but that freedom was hard won, and took courage to claim. Efforts to keep child soldiers out of a life of violence, using art therapy and the like, provoked the anger of the paramilitaries – and bloody reprisals (Duarte and Caruso, 2009).

These stories from Nigeria, Sierra Leone and Colombia are about the necessity for self-expression, the role that media can play in supporting this need and the barriers to making this potential a reality. It's depressing to contemplate that it is easier for OPC members to express their cultural identity by crucifying their enemies than it is for an abused Colombian girl to explain what has happened to her on a DVD. In the wider field of youth media work, two things are clear. First, access to creative resources is a major boon for young people at risk. Second, access to these opportunities is frequently hard to come by, and requires skilled media management, not only in producing media training but also in negotiation the far trickier waters of funding.

The fascinating thing about the African and South American studies is that they are places where the desire to be seen in media, to have one's existence validated by media, is a matter of survival, not vanity. Turner wasn't interested in celebrity for celebrity's sake, but in reflecting on what celebrity says about tendencies in media societies. The case of child soldiers shows that media education may matter most in situations where access to media is scarce. The difficulty of granting child soldiers access to media resources as they try to heal from their ordeals, teaches the lesson that the main social 'harm' caused by media is to divide youth world into 'media youth' and 'non-media youth'. These case studies are important empirical evidence in current debates over how free young people are to use media resources to become the people that they want to be.

Placing these examples against other research on media activism among disadvantaged young people, Bird's (2011) warning about focusing on those who can freely express themselves is apposite given studies of how access to effective media resources is shackled by the challenges of providing funding (Gonzalez, 2009), training, media education that focuses on distribution as well as production (Kitaef, 2008; Brunner et al., 2009; Burton, 2009; Rael, 2009; Squires and Schriner, 2009), and the political challenges of coordinating with official government programmes and policies that sometimes don't have the best interests of young people at heart (Peckover et al., 2008). In fact, it is not possible to understand how brave and imaginative Adela and Taller De Vida are without accounting for the multiple technological, educational, political and economic factors that make silence an easier option for young Colombian victims of violence. To not begin from the examination of the barriers to participation in participatory media cultures is to do a disservice to people like Adela.

CONCLUSION: YOUNG PEOPLE AND DEFINING CRITICAL MEDIA RESEARCH

Adela, then, is another young person whose experiences symbolised the political dimensions of media cultures. Thinking about her, and the other case studies covered in the book, *Youth Media* ultimately identifies four aspects of critical media analysis:

Critical media research pays close attention to evidence

Beginning research by recognising an endemic tension in media cultures does not mean assuming that all media experiences are 'bad' or work in the same way. In this regard, we would do well to attend to E. P. Thompson's view on cultural history – particularly the way he gathered evidence from over a long time period showing how forms of culture that were supposed to 'contain' popular politics ended up having the opposite effect. The lesson here is that the ability to carefully research and describe how a media practice comes to life is a valuable academic skill that involves no judgement as to whether media are 'good' or 'bad'. Critical media research is most interested in ordinary media users.

Respecting evidence means paying attention to things that are ordinary –understanding that these things might, at first blush, seem trivial or unimportant

If we think about the Sierra Leone case, we see that Gauntlett is right to say that the problem here is not the spectacular actions of powerful Western media industries, but rather the more mundane practices of people who sell pirated material in street markets and the like – and this example leads to the third point.

Critical media research is interested in media businesses and changing business practices in media cultures

Critical media research demands an interest in how media businesses operate. Gauntlett argued that the creative opportunities offered by easily available media could be explored in isolation from the commercial interests that make those resources available. His view was that the study of popular creativity does not need to engage with the fact that most media resources are there to make money. This is an untenable position because creativity and commerce are indivisible. Fêted film director Spike Lee said the biggest creative challenge in making his first film, *She's Gotta Have It*, was funding it; this required almost as much ingenuity and imagination as anything else (Babelgum Film, 2011). The film, which grossed $8.5m having cost just $175k to make, had been completed with two film rolls paid for with the money that Lee and the crew had saved from collecting empty soda cans, which could be redeemed for 5c a piece, on the New York set (Babelgum Film, 2010). *She's Gotta Have It* launched Lee's career, and he went on to become one of the finest storytellers of his generation. *Do the Right Thing*, Lee's 1989 movie about racial tension in New York, was widely proclaimed as one of the finest political films of its time. It's ironic to think that without the soda-can idea, Lee may never have gotten the chance to tell his tales. The ongoing search for funding in WeOwnTV shows that this sort of entrepreneurship is also a condition of participatory media cultures, and it is meaningless to speak of creativity without commerce in a situation where the ability to have your voice heard is about distributing products in a competitive market dominated by pirated material. Recent research on media piracy suggests that this is an observation that is likely to become more important to understanding media cultures. In fact, the problems of WeOwnTV show how a media business angle is vital to reframing important debates on popular creativity. Considering Karaganis' analysis of media piracy, WeOwnTV and the pirates who make their life difficult are both making creative responses to the same conditions: 'high prices for media goods, low incomes and cheap digital technologies are the main ingredients of global media piracy' (2011: 1). Karaganis argued that piracy is a little understood term. Thus far, the proprietary interests of established global media conglomerates have defined it as when piracy can also be viewed as a predictable and even defensible response to the inequalities of global pricing. Although media pirates simply seek profit with no political goal in mind, the practice of piracy 'has also disrupted this bad market equilibrium and created opportunities in emerging economies for price and service innovations that leverage new technologies' (2011: 1). The piracy issue shows how a focus on media business is no longer about studying the global power of global media operations. Sierra Leone and Finland tell us that commercial drives don't just come from media businesses. On the other hand, as we saw in Chapters 3, 7 and 8, participatory cultures do create attractive opportunities for media businesses and governments to appropriate popular creativity among young people for political and commercial purposes. In either case, now is a spectacularly bad time to argue that popular creativity can be studied in isolation from the machinations of global media economies.

Young people are central to understanding the essential elements of critical media research

If we were forced to pick a person who best represents why *and how* media matter, socially, culturally, politically and historically, Adela would be a good choice. Media violence didn't make her take up arms; the crumbling economy of a war-torn nation, and the adults who failed to protect her from it, were to blame. Any analysis of the place of media in Adela's life has to start from this basis. Adela had to fight. But she also had to fight to get to use media creatively. The fact that even such a dispossessed young person still felt compelled to make herself in media shows how deeply media have colonised the global youth imagination, and why the matter of access to media is a defining political question, and challenge. Adela's story exemplifies an understanding of media power where media don't independently cause anything, but are key ingredients in the production of social outcomes, as public resources that aren't publicly owned. When it comes to critical media research, then, youth isn't wasted on the young.

EPILOGUE:
DOING YOUTH AND MEDIA

Chances are, you're reading this book because you have to. It's a set text on an undergraduate unit, somewhere in the world. So what are you supposed to do with it? In these last few pages, I'm going to explain how the four criteria in critical media research translate into practical steps you can take to start doing media research. But first, let's review why media research on young people matters.

PUTTING IT ALL INTO PRACTICE: YOUTH, MEDIA, DEMOCRACY

When Lord Justice Leveson opened his inquiry into the ethics of the UK press in November 2011, he started with a simple assumption: media are perspicuously integral to the health of society. The hearings were prompted by revelations about British tabloid journalists hacking into the mobile-phone conversations of politicians, celebrities and even members of the public in their search for sensationalistic stories. Leveson set to discover if the hacking scandal was symptomatic of a culture of collusion between the press, politicians and the police, which worked against the public interest. The reason why this mattered was clear: 'The press provides an essential check on all aspects of public life. That is why any failure within the media affects all of us' (Leveson Inquiry).

The Inquiry invited submissions from anyone worried about the media's public accountability. In response, 73 youth-oriented organisations endorsed 'Fair Press and Accessible PCC for Children and Young People' (Giner and Jones, 2012), a report on the systematic misrepresentation of young people in the news. The report weaved together evidence from content analyses, excerpts from press reports and editorials, interviews with young people and comments from others who were concerned about representations of youth in the media. It concluded that news stories about young criminals were so common in Britain that conventional journalistic practices amounted to a form of anti-youth discrimination, as devastatingly offensive as racism or sexism. The submission argued that journalists offered few positive images of young people, and the prevalence of negative youth images alienated young audiences. This was all the more so since young people had no idea how to complain about hostile media. Nineteen-year-old Rachel Aston summarised the case:

> I didn't even know that you could complain about the press. I really think it is important that the issues here are taken into account, young people do so many amazing things but only the minority involved in anti social behaviour ever get in the news. (Giner and Jones, 2012: 1)

Anti-youth discrimination in the British press mattered because it exemplified the profound damage which unscrupulous and unregulated media industries could inflict on society as a whole. The press's treatment of youths was, the report suggested, a troubling index of their attitude to any social group who lacked power. As go young people, so goes the world.

Were these accusations fair? Much of the evidence was damning indeed. It included quotes from teenagers who claimed journalists had goaded them into furnishing lurid fantasies of urban decay, replete with knives, guns and violence. Were these typical experiences? Were the excerpts where *some* journalists clearly did demonise the young in vicious ways really representative of what *most* journalists did most of the time, when writing on youth? Had the authors of the submission been so keen to make their point that they only reported evidence fitting their case? Clearly, the persuasiveness of the submission depended on how systematically its data had been gathered and interrogated. Nevertheless, the Leveson Inquiry, and the submission on youth and media, made three things clear: it is now accepted that the media exercise a major influence over public life; the experiences of young people with media are highly instructive as to how this social influence comes about; and although on a common-sense level we know that media really matter, showing how they matter involves tricky questions about how evidence of media influence can be collected and studied.

Of course, doing this properly is a time-consuming and expensive business. But as societies become more mediatised, so do the prospects that these societies will need people who know how to research the effects of mediatisation. This research will begin from knowing how to ask the right questions, knowing that the matter of media influence can be conceived and studied in numerous ways. Here are some observations on how understanding the lessons of this book can help you to become one of those people.

IF YOU'RE NOT THAT INTERESTED IN YOUNG PEOPLE, DON'T WORRY – YOU'RE REALLY DOING MEDIA RESEARCH

This is the main lesson to be drawn from the observation that 'young people are central to understanding the essential elements of critical media research'. This book has made extensive use of case studies to make the point that media research involves figuring out how media matter in identifiable ways for identifiable groups of people. When academics do this, they very often turn to young media users. The trick, for you, is to get past the specifics of the case studies to recognise the research process underneath. What you've encountered are a number of strategies for looking at how media are created, circulated and used. You've read about the distinctions between quantitative and qualitative methods, and learnt that good media research fits the right method to the right question. I'll explain more about what this means at the end of the chapter.

THINK ABOUT WAYS OF RESEARCHING MEDIA ORGANISATION

That's organisation, not organisations. Media cultures can't be understood without discussing the global reach of sophisticated media industries that reach right into everyday life. But, somewhat perversely, the scale of mediatisation also makes this power tangible and thus *researchable*. Chapter 7, on students and drinking, showed strategies for gathering evidence from your local environment to make valid comments about the specifics of media power. The specificity of media influence – the fact that it always works somewhere for someone – means you can say interesting things about media, even with limited resources, because media are at work where you are. That's what the student drinking research showed. Doing research therefore becomes a matter of learning to find research questions that match your resources – and goals.

Consider the chapter on social media and dissent. One of the learning outcomes was that local activism around local issues provide valuable insights on how media organisations connect with community grievances. You could try finding an example near you of how a media has facilitated activism around a particular issue. Your research might be structured by answering questions like this:

- What events or conditions motivated the movement?
- Who organised it? How did leadership develop?
- What social media does the movement use?
- How do the social-media platforms develop relationships between businesses, government organisations and other media?
- Who are the stakeholders in the movement, and do they share the same interests?
- What resources would you need to do a larger project on the topic?

MEDIA STUDIES: LEARNING IS DOING

I once asked a group of undergraduates what *they* thought the main lesson of a class I was teaching on youth and media was. One replied: 'To teach us why all the stuff we like is all bad.' I think the response was somewhat tongue-in-cheek;

the comment came from a high-achieving student, and it's hard to imagine that anyone can do well in a subject from which they feel so alienated. At the same time, it was a telling response, in so far as it reflected unease from experienced media academics about what has happened to media teaching.

Respected media-education expert David Buckingham (2006) argued that academics often don't teach how media contribute to the social risks young people face as well as they should, because it's easy to slip into the teaching mode the student criticised; when teaching media influence, all too often the things students know about media are defined as a problem rather than a resource. This is a problem for teachers too. Graeme Turner (2012), whose work has been explored in Chapter 9, lamented that the excitement of teaching about popular culture that he felt in the 1970s and 1980s has largely evaporated. This is because, in his view, that earlier period of media research was characterised by a conscious feeling, shared by lecturers and students alike, that they were engaged in a cooperative research project aimed at establishing the value of studying popular culture as a mode of social inquiry.

I don't think the picture is this bleak for media academics, be they lecturers or undergraduates. It is easy to overcome these problems, but only if students *do* research. Students are in a great position to gather information about how media cultures work, and bring new practices to the attention of those instructing them. In my own experience, for example, the student-drinking project reported in Chapter 6 was a fantastic time spent working *with* students to figure out how the ideas they had learnt during their media degrees could explain drinking culture. Their analysis of how that culture worked changed many of my ideas on media and power. Students should remember that academics want to learn about changing media practices. So, evidence that existing knowledge doesn't explain how media 'work', in your experience, is tremendously exciting.

A lot of valuable media research gets done in the conversation between lecturers and students. One impediment to this conversation is that students are often understandably unsure as to how their personal experiences as media users have a place in scholarly analysis. One way to get over this is to biographise your studies. Why are you interested in media? Does this interest stem from the things you've enjoyed reading, watching, listening to or doing? What is your media biography? As your life has changed, how have your media tastes and habits done the same thing, have these changes had anything to do with the social climates you have lived in, and when you put this story together, does this have anything to do with your interest in media as an academic subject?

This exercise isn't as esoteric as it might seem. Niall Ferguson is one of the most successful historians in the world today. Ferguson holds a Professorial Chair at Harvard University, and his work has achieved that rare feat of winning acclaim from both his peers and the public. Much of his status came from the success of his provocative book about the Great War, *The Pity of War* (1998). That book, aimed at dispelling what Ferguson thought were a series of myths about World War I, began with a tremendously personal account. Here, Ferguson explained how his historical interests were inspired by wanting to know more about his grandfather, who had fought in the trenches.

Ferguson's story tells us you can go a long way in academia by following your nose; pursuing research problems that are, on one level, really quite personal. Use the biography exercise to find out if this approach can work for you.[1] At the end of the exercise you might discover that your ordinary experiences as an ordinary media user are a valuable foundation for interesting research.

So I've invited you into a conversation. We can carry this on via http://andyrud dockmediaresearch.wordpress.com. At this site, you'll find learning exercises relating to each of the chapters, and new case studies which also reflect the theme of the book. My importantly, from my point of view, you'll be able to tell me about things happening in your part of the world, expanding the people and issues connected to the topic of youth and media.

NOTE

1 You can see my version at http://andyruddockmediaresearch.wordpress. com/2012/06/06/learning-activities-understanding-media-content-thinking-about-social-and-cultural-approaches-to-media-effects-using-autoethnography.

REFERENCES

Abercrombie, N., & Longhurst, B. (1998). *Audiences: A Sociological Theory or Performance and Imagination*. London: Sage.

Adebanwi, W. (2005). The carpenter's revolt: youth, violence and the reinvention of culture in Nigeria. *Journal of Modern African Studies*, 43(3), 339–365.

Advertising Standards Authority (2006). Compliance report. Available from www.asa.org.uk/Resource-Centre/~/media/Files/ASA/Reports/AlcoholSurvey Report2006Final.ashx.

Advertising Standards Authority (2009). ASA adjudication on Wm Magners Ltd. Advertising Standards Authority. Retrieved from www.asa.org.uk/ASA-action/ Adjudications/2009/2/Wm-Magners-Ltd/TF_ADJ_45841.aspx.

Advertising Standards Authority (2011). Adjudication on Bargain Booze Ltd. Retrieved October 27 2011 from http://www.asa.org.uk/Rulings/Adjudications /2011/2/Bargain-Booze-Ltd/TF_ADJ_49752.aspx.

Aguado, J. M. & I. J. Martinez (2007). The construction of the mobile experience: the role of advertising campaigns in the appropriation of mobile phone technologies. *Continuum: Journal of Media and Cultural Studies*, 21(2), 137–148.

Aitkin, P. (1989). Television alcohol commercials and under-age drinking. *Journal of Advertising*, 8(1), 133–150.

Altheide, D. (2009). The Columbine shootings and the discourse of fear. *American Behavioral Scientist*, 52(10), 1354–1370.

Ambler, T. (1996). Can alcohol misuse be reduced by banning advertising? *International Journal of Advertising*, 15(2), 167–174.

Anderson, C., & Murphy, C. (2003). Violent video games and aggressive behavior in young women. *Aggressive Behavior*, 29, 423–429.

Anderson, C., Shibuya, A., Ihori, N., Swing, E., Bushman, B., Sakamoto, A., Rothstein, H.R., & Saleem, M. (2010). Violent video game effects on aggression, empathy, and prosocial behavior in Eastern and Western countries: a meta-analytic review. *Psychological Bulletin*, 136(2), 151–173.

Anderson, J. (2008). The production of media violence and aggression research: a cultural analysis. *American Behavioral Scientist*, 51(8), 1260–1279.

April Showers (no date). To steal or not to steal … with some questions. Retrieved 4 December 2011 from www.aprilshowersmovie.com/2009/07/03/to-steal-or-not-to-stealwith-some-questions/.

Aslama, M., Hellman, H., & Sauri, T. (2004). Digitalizing diversity: public service strategies and television program supply in Finland in 2002. *JMM: The International Journal on Media Management*, 6(3–4), 152–161.

Asthana, S. (2008). Teaching about media, media education, learning and literacy: sketching a dialogic process. In S. T. U. Carlsson, G. Jacquinot-Delaunay, & J. Tornero (eds), *Empowerment Through Media Education: An Intercultural Dialogue* (pp. 251–258). Goteborg: Nordicom.

Babcock, W., & Whitehouse, V. (2005). Celebrity as postmodern phenomenon, ethical crisis for democracy and media nightmare. *Journal of Mass Media Ethics*, 20(2), 176–191.

Babelgum Film (2011). Interview with Spike Lee: financing his first film. Podcast, retrieved 15 February 2012, from www.babelgum.com/130710/interview-with-spike-lee-financing-his-first-film.html.

Bachman, K. (2006). Defying gravity. *Mediaweek*, 16(5), 18–22.

Bachman, K., & Yorke, J. (2007). FCC's Martin hints at nixing a Sirius, XM merger. *Mediaweek*, 17(4), 4–6.

Balaji, M. (2009). Owning black masculinity: the intersection of cultural commodification and self-construction in rap music videos. *Communication, Culture & Critique*, 2(1), 21–38.

Bandura, A. (2009). Social cognitive theory of mass communication. In J. Bryant & M. B. Oliver (eds), *Media Effects: Advances in Theory and Research* (3rd edn, pp. 94–124). New York: Lawrence Earlbaum.

Banks, J. (1997). MTV and the globalization of popular culture. *Gazette*, 59(1), 43–60.

Barker, M. (2005). Loving and hating Straw Dogs: the meanings of audience responses to a controversial film. Particip@tions, 1(2). Retrieved 10 January 2011 from www.participations.org/volume%202/2_02_barker.htm.

Barthes, R. (1977). *Image, Music, Text*. New York: Noonday Press.

Barthes, R. (1993). Myth today. In *Mythologies*. New York: Noonday Press.

Batson-Savage, T. (2007). 'Hol' awn mek a answer mi cellular': sex, sexuality and the cellular phone in urban Jamaica. *Continuum: Journal of Media and Cultural Studies*, 21(2), 239–251.

Bazalgette, C. (2008). Transforming literacy. In S. T. U. Carlsson, G. Jacquinot-Delaunay, & J. Tornero (eds), *Empowerment Through Media Education: An Intercultural Dialogue* (pp. 245–250). Goteborg: Nordicom.

BBC News (2005). 'Bad boy' Cameron keeps it real. 25 October. Retrieved March 3 2007 from http://news.bbc.co.uk/2/hi/uk_news/politics/4363818.stm.

BBC News (2007a). Beckham agrees LA Galaxy move. Retrieved 10 October 2011 from http://news.bbc.co.uk/sport2/hi/football/6248835.stm.

BBC News (2007b). Gun salute hoodie criticises MPs. Retrieved 3 March 2007 from http://news.bbc.co.uk/2/hi/uk_news/england/manchester/6389703.stm.

BBC News Africa (2012). Joseph Kony: profile of the LRA leader. Retrieved 10 July 2012 from www.bbc.co.uk/news/world-africa-17299084.

Beardi, C. (2001). Sirius XM heat up satellite radio race. *Advertising Age*, 72(2), 4–26.

Bennett, A. (2007). 'As young as you feel': youth as cultural discourse. In P. Hodkinson & W. Dieke (eds), *Youth Culture: Scenes, Subcultures and Tribes*. London: Routledge.

Bennett, W. L. (2007). Relief in hard times: a defense of Jon Stewart's comedy in an age of cynicism. *Critical Studies in Media Communication*, 24(3), 278–283.

Bennett, W. L., Wells, C., & Freelon, D. (2011). Communicating civic engagement: contrasting models of citizenship in the youth web sphere. *Journal of Communication*, 61, 835–856.

Beresin, E. (1999). Media violence and youth. *American Psychiatry*, 23, 111–114.

Beveridge, Sir William (1948). *The Beveridge Report* (Cmnd 6404.). London: HMSO.

Bird, S. E. (2011). Are we all producers now? *Cultural Studies*, 25(4–5), 502–516.

Blecken, D. (2009). Building a beer brand in the blogosphere. Campaign Asia-Pacific. Retrieved 6 June 2012 from www.campaignasia.com/Article/211612, case-study-building-a-beer-brand-in-the-blogosphere.aspx.

Blumer, H. (1933). *Movies and Conduct*. New York: Macmillan.

Bratich, J. (2011). Kyber-revolts: Egypt, state-friended media, and secret sovereign networks. The New Everyday: A Media Commons Project. Retrieved 20 August 2011 from http://mediacommons.futureofthebook.org/tne/pieces/kyber-revolts-egypt-state-friended-media-and-secret-sovereign-networks.

Bristow, M. (2011). China takes popular TV talent show Super Girl off air. *BBC News Asia-Pacific*. Retrieved 7 July 2011 from www.bbc.co.uk/news/world-asia-pacific-14972480.

Broadbent, T. (2008). Does advertising grow markets? *International Journal of Advertising*, 27(5), 745–770.

Brooker, W. (2003). *Using the Force: Creativity, Community and Star Wars Fans*. New York: Continuum.

Brown, K., & Hamilton-Giachristis, C. (2005). The influence of violent media on children and adolescents: a public-health approach. *The Lancet*, 365(9460), 702–710.

Brunner, A., Kirschmann, P., Pumphrey, M., & Vu, O. (2009). Integrating Web 2.0 into youth programming. *Youth Media Reporter*, 3, 137–140.

Bruns, A. (2007). Produsage.org: From Production to Produsage: Research into User-Led Content Creation. Retrieved 15 October 2011 from http://produsage.org/node/9.

Bryant, J., & Oliver, M. B. (2009). *Media Effects: Advances in theory and research* (3rd ed.). New York: Routledge.

Buckingham, David. (2006). *Media Education: Literacy, Learning and Contemporary Culture* (4th edn). Cambridge: Polity.

Burgess, J. (2006). Hearing ordinary voices: cultural studies, vernacular creativity and digital storytelling. *Continuum: Journal of Media and Cultural Studies*, 20(2), 201–214.

Burgess, J., & Green, J. (2009). *YouTube*. Cambridge: Polity Press.

Burton, P. (2009). Roots & Branches-Rural Youth Arts in Northern England. *Youth Media Reporter*, 3, 56–61.

Cahn, S. (1998). Spirited youth or fiends incarnate: the Samarcand arson case and female adolescence in the American South. *Journal of Women's History*, 9(4), 152–180.

Calfee, J., & Scheraga, C. (1994). The influence of advertising on alcohol consumption: a literature review and an econometric analysis of four European nations. *International Journal of Advertising*, 13(4), 287–310.

Carlsson, U., Tayie, S., Jacquinot-Delaunay, G., & Tornero, J. M. P. (2008). *Empowerment through Media Education*. Goteborg: International Clearinghouse on Children, Youth and Media.

Carragee, K., & Roefs, W. (2004). The neglect of power in recent framing research. *Journal of Communication*, 54, 214–233

Cashmore, E. (1999). *Beckham*. Cambridge: Polity Press.

Cavagnaro, P., Niles, Z., Reiser, E., & White, B. (2011). This is our generation: Sierra Leonean youth views through film. *Youth Media Reporter*. Retrieved 4 December 2011 from www.youthmediareporter.org/2011/02/this_is_our_generation_sierra.html.

CBC News Canada (2009). Montreal student sounds alert over planned UK school attack. Retrieved 20 April 2009 from www.cbc.ca/news/canada/story/2009/03/20/concordia-student-forum-norfolk.html.

CCCS Women's Studies Group (1978). *Women Take Issue*. London: Hutchinson.

Charters, W. W. (1932). A technique for studying a social problem. *Journal of Educational Sociology*, 6, 196–203.

Cherrington, J., Chamberlain, K., & Grixti, J. (2006). Relocating alcohol advertising research: examining socially mediated relationships with alcohol. *Journal of Health Psychology*, 11(2), 209–222.

Chiasson, G., & Dougherty, S. (2005). Canada groups try to block Sirius, XM. *Advertising Age*, 76(29), 16.

Chomsky, N. (1997). *Media Control: The Spectacular Achievements of Propaganda*. New York: Seven Stories Press.

Chyi, H., & McCombs, M. (2004). Media salience and the process of framing: coverage of the Columbine school shootings. *Journalism & Mass Communication Quarterly*, 81(1), 22–35.

Clarke, J., Hall, S., Jefferson, T., & Roberts, B. (1978). Subcultures, cultures and class. In S. Hall & T. Jefferson (eds), *Resistance through Rituals* (pp. 9–74). London: Hutchinson.

Cohen, S. (1972). *Folk Devils and Moral Panics: The Creation of the Mods and Rockers*. London: MacGibbon & Kee.

Coleman, R. (2008). The becoming of bodies. *Feminist Media Studies*, 8(2), 163–179.

Coleman, S., & Dyer-Witheford, N. (2007). Playing on the digital commons: collectivities, capital and contestation in videogame culture. *Media, Culture & Society*, 29(6), 934–953.

Collier, J., Liddell Jr., P., & Liddell, G. (2008). Exposure of violent video games to children and public policy implications. *Journal of Public Policy & Marketing*, 27(1), 107–112.

Comstock, G. (2008). A sociological perspective on television violence and aggression. *American Behavioral Scientist*, 51, 1184–1211.

Coninck-Smith, N. (1999). 'Danger is looming here': moral panic and urban children's and youth culture in Denmark, 1890–1914. *Paedagogica Historica*, 35(3), 643–664.

Connaughton, S., & Jarvis, S. (2004). Apolitical politics: GOP efforts to foster identification from Latinos, 1984–2000. *Communication Studies*, 55(3), 464–480.

Conrad, K., Dixon, T. L., & Zhang, Y. (2009). Controversial rap themes, gender portrayals and skin tone distortion: a content analysis of rap music videos. *Journal of Broadcasting & Electronic Media*, 53(1), 134–156.

Consalvo, M. (2003). The monsters next door: media constructions of boys and masculinity. *Feminist Media Studies*, 3(1), 27.

Cooks, L. (2003). 'Pedagogy, performance, and positionality: teaching about whiteness in interracial communication'. *Communication Education*, 52, 245–257.

Couldry, N. (2002). Playing for celebrity: Big Brother as ritual event. *Television & New Media*, 3, 283–293.

Couldry, N. (2004). Theorising media as practice. *Social Semiotics*, 12(2), 115–132.

Curran, J. (2002). *Media and Power*. London: Routledge.

Curtis, P. (2012). Kony 2012: the reaction. *Guardian*. Retrieved 20 July 2012 from www.guardian.co.uk/politics/reality-check-with-polly-curtis/2012/mar/13/reality-check-kony-2012-reaction.

David Cameron: The fightback is under way. (2011). *Independent*. Retrieved 20 March 2012 from www.independent.co.uk website:http://www.independent.co.uk/news/uk/crime/david cameron-the-fightback-is-under-way-2335193.html.

de Gregorio, F., & Sung, Y. (2009). Giving a shout out to Seagram's gin: extent of and attitudes towards brands in popular songs. *Journal of Brand Management*, 17(3), 218-235

DeFleur, M., & Ball-Rokeach, S. (1989). *Theories of Mass Communication*. New York: Longman.

Denora, T. (2000). *Music in Everyday Life*. Cambridge: Cambridge University Press.

Dixon, T., Zhang, Y., & Conrad, K. (2009). Self-esteem, misogyny and afrocentricity: an examination of the relationship between rap music consumption and African American perceptions. *Group Processes and Intergroup Relations*, 12(3), 345–360.

Donald, S. H. (2011). Chinese media studies: a belated introduction? *Media International Australia*, 138, 57–65.

Donegan, L. (2011). David Beckham rides roughshod over LA Galaxy to get his own way. *Guardian*, 4 January. Retrieved from www.guardian.co.uk/football/blog/2011/jan/04/david-beckham-la-galaxy-tottenham-hotspur.

Dorfman, A., & Mattelart, A. (1984). *How to Read Donald Duck: Imperialist Ideology in the Disney Comic* (2nd edn). Santiago, CA: International General.

Dorsett, J., & Dickerson, S. (2004). Advertising and alcohol consumption in the UK. *International Journal of Advertising*, 23(2), 149–171.

Duarte, D., & Caruso, N. (2009). Youth media as a tool for human rights advocacy in Peru, Colombia and Iraq. *Youth Media Reporter*, 3, 62–67.

Duffy, M. (1989). The effect of advertising on the total consumption of alcoholic drinks in the United Kingdom: some econometric estimates. *International Journal of Advertising*, 1(2), 105–117.

Duffy, M. (1990). Advertising and alcoholic drink demand in the UK: some further Rotterdam model estimates. *International Journal of Advertising*, 9(3), 247–257.

Eck, B. (2001). Nudity and framing: classifying art, pornography, information and ambiguity. *Sociological Forum*, 16, 603–632.

Eggerton, J. (2007). XM-Sirius deal faces serious hurdles in D.C. *Broadcasting and Cable*, 137(9), 43.

Egypt Independent (2011). Protesters give army deadline to choose sides. Retrieved 10 March 2012 from www.egyptindependent.com/node/307834.

Elbaradei, M. (2011). Wael Ghonim. *Time*. Retrieved 20 November 2011 from www.time.com/time/specials/packages/article/0,28804,2066367_2066369_2066437,00.html.

Endres, F. (1978). The pit-muckraking days of McClure's magazine, 1893–1901. *Journalism Quarterly*, 55(1), 154–157.

Esser, F., & de Vreese, C. D. (2007). Comparing young voters' political engagement in the United States and Europe. *American Behavioral Scientist*, 50(9), 1195–1213.

Euromonitor International (2010). Beyond the crisis – the new consumer and the alcoholic drinks industry. Retrieved 5 July 2011 from www.euromonitor.com/beyond-the-crisis-the-new-consumer-and-the-alcoholic-drinks-industry/report.

Euromonitor International (2011). Cider/perry: apples, pears and ignoring the laws of gravity. *Euromonitor International*.

Everett, A. (2009). The Afrogeek-in-Chief: Obama and our new media ecology. *Journal of Visual Culture*, 8(2), 193–196.

Eyal, K., Metzger, M., Lingsweiler, R., Mahood, C., & Yao, M. (2006). Aggressive political opinions and exposure to violent media. *Mass Communication and Society*, 9(4), 399–428.

Farnsworth, S., & Lichter, R. (2011). Network television's coverage of the 2008 Presidential Election. *American Behavioral Scientist*, 55(4), 354–370.

Fee, J. (2005). Reconnecting with the body politic: toward disconnecting muckrakers and public journalists. *American Journalism*, 22(3), 77–102.

Feldstein, M. (2006). A muckraking model: investigative reporting cycles in American history. *Harvard International Journal of Press/Politics*, 11(2), 105–120.

Ferguson, N. (1998). *The Pity of War*. New York: Basic Books.

Ferrero, D. (2007). Child soldier. Retrieved 22 July 2012 from www.youtube.com/watch?v=_6IMjnwztTo&feature=player_embedded.

Fiske, J. (1987). *Television Culture*. London: Routledge.

Fiske, J. (1992). *Power Plays, Power Works*. London: Verso.

Forman, M. (2004). Freaks, aliens, and the social other: representations of student stratification in US television's first post-Columbine season. *Velvet Light Trap: A Critical Journal of Film & Television*, 53, 66–82.

Frau-Meigs, D. (2008). Media education, crossing a mental rubicon. In U. Carlsson, S. Tayie, G. Jacquinot-Delaunay, & J. M. P. Tornero (eds), *Empowerment through Media Education: An Intercultural Dialogue* (pp. 169–180). Goteborg: Nordicom.

freeflowingwind (Producer). (2008). Super girl Yang Lei. Retrieved 7 July 2012 from www.youtube.com/watch?v=arXbkBWdki4.

Fung, A. (2006). Think globally, act locally: China's rendezvous with MTV. *Global Media and Communication*, 2(1), 71–88.

Gans, J., & Hussey, C. (2008). African-Americans, anger, fear and youth propel turnout to highest level since 1960. Retrieved 4 December 2011 from www.american.edu/loader.cfm?csModule=security/getfile&pageid=23907.

Gatrell, V. (1994). *The Hanging Tree*. Oxford: Oxford University Press.

Gauntlett, D. (2011). Media studies 2.0, and other battles around the future of audience research. Retrieved 15 January 2012 from www.theory.org.uk/david/kindle.htm.

Gerbner, G. (1969). Toward 'cultural indicators': the analysis of mass mediated public message. *AV Communication Review*, 17(2), 137–148.

Gerbner, G. (1998). Cultivation analysis: an overview. *Mass Communication and Society*, 1(3–4), 175–195.

Gerbner, G., Gross, L., Morgan, M., & Signorelli, N. (1980). The mainstreaming of America: violence profile #11. *Journal of Communication*, 30, 10–29.

Gerodimos, R. (2008). Mobilising young citizens in the UK: a content analysis of youth and issue websites. *Information, Communication and Society*, 11(7), 964–988.

Giner, S. and Jones, R. (2012). Fair press and accessible PCC for children and young people. Available at www.ncb.org.uk/media/537409/_presschange4youth_recommendations_to_leveson.pdf.

Giroux, H. (2003). Youth, higher education, and the crisis of public time: educated hope and the possibility of a democratic future. *Social Identities*, 9(2), 141–168.

Gitlin, T. (1978). Media sociology: the dominant paradigm. *Theory and Society*, 6(2), 205–25.

Glasgow University Media Group (1976). *Bad News*. London: Routledge & Kegan Paul.

Gonzalez, T. (2009). Funding the nascent field of youth media. *Youth Media Reporter*, 3, 33–36.

Gordon, R., Hastings, G., & Moodie, C. (2010). Alcohol marketing and young people's drinking: what the evidence base suggests for policy. *Journal of Public Affairs*, 10, 88–101.

Götz, M. (2008). Reception studies of girls methodological pitfalls to avoid. *Journal of Children and Media*, 2(1), 81–2.

Gray, A. (2003). *Research Practice for Cultural Studies*. London: Sage.

Grigoriadis, V. (2004). The notorious Bam. *Rolling Stone*. Retrieved 4 January 2012 from www.vanessagrigoriadis.com/bam.html.

Gross, L. (2009). My media studies: cultivation to participation. *Television & New Media*, 10(1), 66–68.

Grossman, D., & DeGaetano, G. (1999). *Stop Teaching Our Kids to Kill: A Call to Action against TV, Movie and Video Game Violence*. New York: Crown.

Gunter, B. (2008). Media violence: is there a case for causality? *American Behavioral Scientist*, 51(8), 1061–1122.

Gunter, B., Hansen, A., & Touri, M. (2010). *Alcohol Advertising and Young People's Drinking*. London: Palgrave Macmillan.

Haahti, A., & Yavas, U. (1983). Tourists' perceptions of Finland and selected European countries as travel destinations. *European Journal of Marketing*, 17(2), 34.

Hall, S. (1980). Encoding/decoding. In S. Hall, D. Hobson, A. Lowe, & P. Willis (eds), *Culture, Media, Language: Working Papers in Cultural Studies, 1972–79* (pp. 128–138). London: Hutchinson.

Hall, S., & Jefferson, T. (1978) *Resistance through Rituals*. London: Hutchinson.

Halliday, J., & Garside, J. (2011). Rioting leads to Cameron call for social media clampdown. *Guardian*. Retrieved 30 August 2011 from www.guardian.co.uk website: http://www.guardian.co.uk/uk/2011/aug/11/cameron-call-social-media-clampdown

Harrington, S. (2008). Future-proofing journalism: youthful tastes and the challenge for the academy. *Continuum: Journal of Media and Cultural Studies*, 22(3), 395–407.

Harris, A. (2004). Introduction. In A. Harris (ed.), *All About the Girl: Power, Culture and Identity* (pp. xxii–2). London: Routledge.

Hebdige, D. (1979). *Subculture: The Meaning of Style*. London: Methuen.

Herman, E., & Chomsky, N. (1988). *Manufacturing Consent*. New York: Pantheon.

Hijazi-Omari, H., & Ribak, R. (2008). Playing with fire: on the domestication of the mobile phone among Palestinian teenage girls in Israel. *Information, Communication & Society*, 11(2), 149–166.

Hobson, D. (1980). Housewives and the mass media. In S. Hall, D. Hobson, A. Lowe, & P. Willis (eds), *Culture, Media, Language: Working Papers in Cultural Studies, 1972–79* (pp. 93–103). London: Routledge.

Hogeveen, B. (2007). Youth (and) violence. *Sociology Compass*, 1(2), 463–484.

Hollywood Reporter (2011) Donald Trump roast is Obama's most watched speech on YouTube. Retrieved 4 December 2011 from www.hollywoodreporter.com/news/donald-trump-roast-is-obamas-186466.

Hoodie pic 'proves Cameron point'. (2007). Retrieved 20 March 2007 from www.news.bbc.co.uk website: http://news.bbc.co.uk/2/hi/uk_news/politics/638 9277.stm.

hooks, b. (1994). *Outlaw Culture*. London: Routledge.

Hope, D. (2010). Library of Congress to house Twitter archive. Retrieved 25 January 2011 from www.msnbc.msn.com/id/36525336/ns/technology_and_science-tech_and_gadgets/t/library-congress-house-twitter-archive/.

Hovland, C. (1948). Social communication. *Proceedings of the American Philosophical Society*, 92(5), 371–375.

Huang, K., & Chitty, N. (2009). Selling Participation to Audiences in China. *Global Media Journal*, 2(1), 123–147.

Hujanen, J. (2009). Informing, entertaining, empowering. *Journalism Practice*, 3(1), 30–45.

Hunan TV (2007). *Super Girls*. Retrieved from 20 May 2011 http://news.hunantv.com/English/Activity/200712/t20071226_24927.html.

Hutchins, B., & Rowe, D. (2009). From broadcasting rationing to digital plenitude: the changing dynamics of the media sport content economy. *Television & New Media*, 10(4), 354–370.

Innis, H. (1947). *Minerva's Owl*. Retrieved 7 June 2012 from www.gutenberg.ca website: http://gutenberg.ca/ebooks/innis-minerva/innis-minerva-00-h.html.

Insane Clown Posse (2010a). About ICP: biography. Retrieved 20 March 2011 from www.insaneclownposse.com/icp2010/?page_id=2.

Insane Clown Posse (2010b). Fresh news: featuring ICP and the psychopathic family. Retrieved 20 March 2011 from www.insaneclownposse.com/icp2010/?page_id=3 .

Interview with Marilyn Manson, Dramatic new scenes for celebritarian needs (2005). *Manson Wiki*. Retrieved 28 September 2012 from www.mansonwiki.com/wiki/Interview2005/11/03_Dramatic_New_Scenes_for_Celebritarian_Needs.

Inthorn, S., & Street, J. (2011). 'Simon Cowell for prime minister'? Young citizens' attitudes towards celebrity politics. *Media, Culture & Society*, 33(3), 479–489.

Sirius Investor Relations (2004). Professional skateboarder and 'Viva La Bam' host Bam Margera to host show on Sirius satellite radio. Retrieved 20 November 2011 from http://investor.sirius.com/releasedetail.cfm?releaseid=152164.

Isotalus, P. (2001). Presidential campaigning in Finland and Americanization. *World Communication*, 30(2), 5.

Jenkins, H. (1992). *Textual Poachers*. London: Routledge.

Jenkins, H. (2006a). *Convergence Culture: Where Old and New Media Collide*. New York: New York University Press.

Jenkins, H. (2006b) *Fans, Bloggers, and Gamers*. New York: New York University Press.

Jernigan, D. (2006). Importance of reducing youth exposure to alcohol advertising. *Archives of Pediatric and Adolescent Medicine*, 160(1), 100–102.

Johnston, A. (2011). World views: Egypt's tensions. Retrieved 10 February 2011 from www.bbc.co.uk/blogs/seealso/2011/02/world_views_egypts_tensions_2.html.

Jones, K. (1997). Are rap videos more violent? Style difference and the prevalence of sex and violence in the age of MTV. *Howard Journal of Communication*, 8(4), 343–356.

Kaid, L., Fernandes, J., & Painter, D. (2011). Effects of political advertising in the 2008 presidential campaign. *American Behavioral Scientist*, 55(4), 437–456.

Karaganis, J. (ed.). (2011). *Media Piracy in Emerging Economies*. Columbia, SC: Social Science Research Council.

Katz, E., & Lazarsfeld, P. (1955). *Personal Influence: The Part Played by People in the Flow of Mass Communication*. Glencoe, IL: Free Press.

Kearney, M. (2005). Birds on the wire: troping teenage girlhood through telephoney in mid-20th century US media culture. *Cultural Studies*, 19(5), 568–600.

Keeter, S., & Horowitz, J. (2008). Young voters in the 2008 election. Retrieved 14 November 2011 from http://pewresearch.org/pubs/1031/young-voters-in-the-2008-election.

Khan, A. (2008). Media education, a crucial issue in the building of an inclusive knowledge society. In S. T. U. Carlsson, G. Jacquinot-Delaunay, & J. Tornero (eds), *Empowerment through Media Education: An Intercultural Dialogue* (pp. 15–18). Gothenburg: Nordicom.

Kharif, O. (2008). Sirius XM's dual concerns: debt, delisting. Retrieved 10 December 2011 from www.businessweek.com/technology/content/dec2008/tc20081212_917411.htm.

Kharif, O. (2010). Sirius XM shines a little brighter. Retrieved 10 December 2011 from www.businessweek.com/technology/content/may2010/tc2010054_384765.htm.

Khoo, O. (2011). Chinese media studies from an inter-Asian perspective. *Media International Australia*, 138, 128–136.

Kirkpatrick, D.D., & Slackman, M. (2011). Egyptian youths drive the revolt against Mubarak. Retrieved 4 February 2011 from www.nytimes.com/2011/01/27/world/middleeast/27opposition.html?_r=1.

Kirsh, S. (2007). *Children, Adolescents and Media Violence*. London: Sage.

Kistler, M. E., & Lee, M. J. (2010). Does exposure to sexual hip-hop music videos influence the sexual attitudes of college students? *Mass Communication & Society*, 13(1), 67–86.

Kitzinger, J. (2004). *Framing Sex Abuse*. London: Pluto Press.

Klaassen, A. (2005). Sirius asking top dollar for spots on Stern show. *Advertising Age*, 76(34), 6.

Kurkela, V., & Uimonen, H. (2009). De-monopolizing Finland: the changing contents of Finnish commercial and public radio stations, 1980–2005. *Radio Journal: International Studies in Broadcast & Audio Media*, 7(2), 135–154.

Lang, K., & Lang, G. (2006). Personal influence and the new paradigm: some inadvertent consequence. *The Annals of the American Academy of Political and Social Science*, 608, 233–250.

Larkin, R. (2009). The Columbine legacy: rampage shootings as political acts. *American Behavioral Scientist*, 52, 1309–1326.

Lasswell, H. D. (1971). *Propaganda Technique in World War I*. Cambridge, MA: MIT Press.

Lazarsfeld, P., Berelson, B., & Gaudet, H. (1948). *The People's Choice: How the Voter Makes Up His Mind in a Presidential Campaign*. New York: Columbia University Press.

Leiss, W., Kline, S., & Jhally, S. (1990). *Social Communication in Advertising* (2nd edn). London: Routledge.

Leveson, Lord Justice (2011) Leveson Inquiry: Culture, Practice and Ethics of the Press. Available at www.levesoninquiry.org.uk.

Levine, M., & Harrison, K. (2009). Effects of media on eating disorders and body image. In J. Bryant & M. B. Oliver (eds), *Media Effects: Advances in Theory and Method* (3rd edn, pp. 490–516). New York: Routledge.

Lin, A., & Tong, A. (2007). Text-messaging cultures of college girls in Hong Kong: SMS as resources for achieving intimacy and gift-exchange with multiple functions. *Continuum: Journal of Media & Cultural Studies*, 21(2), 303–315.

Lincoln, S. (2005). Feeling the noise: teenagers, bedrooms and music. *Leisure Studies*, 24(4), 399–414.

Livingstone, S. (2009). On the mediation of everything: ICA Presidential Address 2008. *Journal of Communication*, 59, 1–18.

Livingstone, S. (2012). Exciting moments in audience research: past, present and future. In H. Bilandzic, G. Patriarche, & P. J. Traudt (eds), *The Social Use of Media: Cultural and Social Scientific Perspectives on Audience Research* (pp. 257–274). Chicago: Intellect.

Madison, L. (2011). Trump/O'Reilly spar over birther issue. Retrieved 4 December 2011 from www.cbsnews.com/8301-503544_162-20049229-503544.html.

Maras, S. (2007). Communicating criticality. *International Journal of Communication*, 1(1), 167–206.

Margera, B. (2012). Bam BIO. Retrieved 14 January 2012 from www.bamargera.com/bio.html.

Martin-Barbero, J. (2006). A Latin American perspective on communication/cultural mediation. *Global Media and Communication*, 2(3), 279–297.

Mazzarella, S. (2007). *20 Questions about Youth and the Media*. New York: Peter Lang.

McCombs, M. (2005). A look at agenda-setting: past, present and future. *Journalism Studies*, 6, 543–557.

McCombs, M., & Shaw, D. (1972). The agenda-setting function of mass media. *Public Opinion Quarterly*, 36, 136–187.

McIntyre, J. (2003). Media violence in the news. *American Behavioral Scientist*, 46(12), 1617.

Mckee, A. (2006). Censorship of sexually explicit materials in Australia: what do consumers of pornography have to say about it. *Media International Australia Incorporating Culture & Policy*, 120, 35–50.

McKinney, M. S., & Rill, L. A. (2009). Not your parents' presidential debates: examining the effects of the CNN/YouTube debates on young citizens' civic engagement. *Communication Studies*, 60(4), 392–406.

McLaughlin, L. (1995). Feminist communication scholarship and 'the woman question' in the academy. *Communication Theory*, 5, 144–161.

McRobbie, A. (2007). Top girls. *Cultural Studies*, 21(4), 718–737.

McRobbie, A. (2008). Young women and consumer culture. *Cultural Studies*, 22(5), 531–550.

McRobbie, A., & Garber, J. (1978). Girls and subcultures. In S. Hall & T. Jefferson (eds), *Resistance through Rituals* (pp. 209–222). London: Hutchinson.

Measham, F., & Brain, K. (2005). 'Binge' drinking, British alcohol policy and the new culture of intoxication. *Crime, Media and Culture*, 1, 263–284.

Meier, P. (2010). Polarized drinking patterns and alcohol deregulation. *NAT Nordic Studies on Alcohol and Drugs*, 25(5), 383–408.

Meikle, G., & Young, S. (2012). *Media Convergence: Networked Digital Media and Everyday Life*. London: Palgrave Macmillan.

Michelle, C. (2007). Modes of reception: a consolidated analytical framework. *Communication Review*, 10(3), 181–222.

Molloy, M. (2012). Kony 2012 YouTube video hits 50m views as Obama hails online campaign *Metro*. Retrieved from www.metro.co.uk website: www.metro.co.uk/news/world/892657-kony-2012-youtube-video-hits-50mviews-as-obama-hails-invisible-children-campaign.

Morley, D. (1980). *The Nationwide Audience*. London: British Film Institute.

Morley, D. (1992). *Television Audiences*. London: Routledge.

Morozov, E. (2009). Iran: downside to the 'Twitter revolution'. *Dissent*, 56(4), 10.

Mungiu-Pippidi, A., & Munteanu, I. (2009). Moldova's 'Twitter revolution'. *Journal of Democracy*, 20(3), 136–142.

Murray, J. (2007). Historically, how have researchers studied the effects if media violence on youth? In S. R. Mazzarella (ed.), *20 Questions about Youth and the Media* (pp. 135–152). New York: Peter Lang.

Murray, J. (2008). Media violence: the effects are both real and strong. *American Behavioral Scientist*, 51(8), 1212–1230.

Murray, S. (2003). Media convergence's third-wave content streaming. *Convergence*, 9(1), 8–18.

Muschert, G. (2007). The Columbine victims and the myth of the juvenile super-predator. *Youth Violence & Juvenile Justice*, 5(4), 351–366.

Muschert, G. (2009). Frame-changing in the media coverage of a school shooting: the rise of Columbine as a national concern. *Social Science Journal*, 46(1), 164–170.

Muschert, G., & Carr, D. (2006). Media salience and frame changing across events: coverage of nine school shootings, 1997–2001. *Journalism & Mass Communication Quarterly*, 83(4), 747–766.

Muschert, G., & Peguero, A. (2010). The Columbine effect and school anti violence policy. In S. Burns & M. Peyrot (eds), *Research in Social Problems and Public Policy: New Approaches to Social Problems Treatment* (pp. 117–148). Bingley: Emerald.

Napoli, P. M. (2010). Revisiting 'mass communication' and the 'work' of the audience in the new media environment. *Media, Culture & Society*, 32(3), 505–516.

NBC News (2007). 'When the time came, I did it': Virginia Tech gunman sends multimedia confession to NBC. Retrieved 3 April 2008 from www.msnbc.msn.com/id/18183995/.

Nelson, J., & Young, D. (2011). Do advertising bans work? An international comparison. *International Journal of Advertising*, 20(3), 273–296.

Nikken, P., Jansz, J., & Schouwstra, S. (2007). Parents' interest in videogame ratings and content descriptors in relation to game mediation. *European Journal of Communication*, 22(3), 315–336.

Now Daily (2009). Simon Cowell tops Prime Minister survey. Retrieved 20 May 2012 from www.nowmagazine.co.uk/celebrity-news/342449/simon-cowell-tops-prime-minister-survey.

Nylund, M. (2009). Mega-sporting events and the media in attention economies. *Nordicom Review*, 30(2), 125–140.

O'Malley, T. (2002). Media history and media studies: aspects of the development of the study of media history in the UK 1945–2000. *Media History*, 8(2), 155–173.

OFCOM (2007). Young people and alcohol advertising: an investigation of alcohol advertising following changes to the Advertising Code. Retrieved 30 March 2009 from www.asa.org.uk/Resource-Centre/~/media/Files/ASA/Reports/Youngpeo plealcoholadvertising_20071116.ashx.

Oliver, M. B., & Krakowiak, M. (2009). Individual differences in media effects. In J. Bryant & M. B. Oliver (eds), *Media Effects: Advances in Theory and Research* (pp. 517–531). New York: Lawrence Earlbaum.

Omenugha, K., & Adum, A. (2008). Nigeria's spiral of violence: can the media build a culture of peace? *Media Development*, 55(1), 50–54.

Osgerby, B. (2004). *Youth Media*. London: Routledge.

Pascoe-Watson, G. (2007). Cameron's call-up for teenagers. Retrieved from www.thesun.co.uk/sol/homepage/news/article262776.ece.

Patrick, G. (2007). Teenage 'pistol' hoodie gloats. Retrieved 30 March 2007 from www.thesun.co.uk/sol/homepage/news/article19390.ece.

Peckover, S., White, S., & Hall, C. (2008). Making and managing electronic children: e-assessment in child welfare. *Information, Communication & Society*, 11(3), 375–394.

Penny, L. (2010). How Twitter changed the face of dissent. Retrieved 20 January 2011 from www.newstatesman.com/blogs/laurie-penny/2010/12/informa tion-solidarity.

Peterkin, T. (2008). Teenager cautioned for wiping snot on David Cameron's back. Retrieved 16 April 2008 from www.telegraph.co.uk/news/uknews/1895773/ Teenager-cautioned-for-wiping-snot-on-David-Camerons-back.html.

Peterson, R., & Thurstone, L. (1932). *The Effect of Motion Pictures on the Social Attitudes of High School Children*. Ann Arbor, MI: Edwards Brothers.

Petty, R., Brinol, P., & Priester, J. (2009). Mass media attitude change: implications of the elaboration likelihood model of persuasion. In J. Bryant & M. B. Oliver (eds), *Media Effects: Advances in Theory and Research* (pp. 125–164). New York: Routledge.

Phillips, D., & Carstensen, L. (1986). Clustering of teenage suicides after television news stories about suicide. *New England Journal of Medicine*, 315(11), 685–689.

Pieslak, J. R. (2007). Sound targets: music and the war in Iraq. *Journal of Musicological Research*, 26(2), 123–149.

Pieslak, J. (2009). *Sound Targets*. Bloomington, IN: Indiana University Press.

Pietilä, V. (2005). *On the Highway of Mass Communication Studies*. New York: Hampton Press.

Rachel Hoffman Case (2009a). Retrieved 5 May 2011 from www.tallahassee. com/section/hoffman01.

Rachel Hoffman Case (2009b). Uncovering the truth. Retrieved 5 May 2011 from www.facebook.com/group.php?gid=47350501912.

Rachel Hoffman Case (2009c). Retrieved 5 May 2011 from http://twitter.com/#!/HoffmanCase.

RachelHoffmancase's Channel (2009d). Retrieved 5 May 2011 from www.youtube.com/RachelHoffmancase.

Rael, R. (2009). Social justice radio: a strategy for long-term change. *Youth Media Reporter*, 3, 167–170.

Reading, A. (2005). Professing porn or obscene browsing? On proper distance in the university classroom. *Media, Culture & Society*, 27, 123–130.

Reaves, S. (1984). How radical were the muckrakers? Socialist press views, 1902–1906. *Journalism Quarterly*, 61(4), 763–770.

Rehr, D. (2007). XM-Sirius merger? NAB won't hear of it. *Broadcasting and Cable*, 137(10), 28.

Reinarz, J. (2007). Promoting the pint: ale and advertising in late Victorian and Edwardian England. *Social History of Alcohol Review*, 22(1), 26–44.

Riggio, J. (2008). Bam Margera: skating's king of mischief. Retrieved 1 February 2012 from www.huckmagazine.com/features/bam-margera/.

Roberts, B., & Groenendijk, L. (2005). Moral panic and Holland's libertine youth of the 1650s and 1660s. *Journal of Family History*, 30(4), 327–346.

Rock the Vote (2012). Retrieved 30 September 2012 from www.rockthevote.com/about/.

Rodman, G. B. (2006). Race ... and other four letter words: Eminem and the cultural politics of authenticity. *Popular Communication*, 4(2), 95–121.

Rojek, C. (2001). *Celebrity*. London: Reaktion.

Rossing, J. (2011). Comic provocations in racial culture: Barack Obama and the 'politics of fear'. *Communication Studies*, 62(4), 422–438.

Rowe, D. (2004a). *Sport, Culture and the Media: The Unruly Trinity* (2nd edn). Maidenhead: Open University Press.

Rowe, D. (2004b). Mapping the media sports cultural complex. In D. Rowe (ed.), *Critical Readings: Sport, Culture and the Media* (pp. 1–23). Maidenhead: Open University Press.

Ruddock, A. (2001). *Understanding Audiences*. London: Sage.

Ruddock, A. (2007). *Investigating Audiences*. London: Sage.

Ruddock, A. (2008). Media studies on fire: audiences, reception, and the experience of antisocial behavior. *Popular Communication*, 6(4), 248–261.

Ruddock, A. (2010). 'I'd rather be a cat than a poodle': what do celebrity politicians say about political communication? In L. Barus (ed.), *Ji-Hoon Park* (pp. 74–94). Newcastle upon Tyne: Cambridge Scholars Publishing.

Ruddock, A. (2011). Cultivation analysis. In V. Nightingale (ed.), *Handbook of Media Audiences* (pp. 340–359). Oxford: Wiley-Blackwell.

Ruddock, A. (2012a). Cultivation analysis and cultural studies. In J. Shanahan, M. Morgan, & N. Signorelli (eds), *Living with Television Now: Advances in Cultivation Theory and Research* (pp. 367–385). New York: Peter Lang.

Ruddock, A. (2012b). Cultivated performances: what cultivation analysis says about media, binge drinking and gender. In H. Bilandzic, G. Patriarche, & P. J. Traudt (eds), *The Social Use of Media: Cultural and Social Scientific Perspectives on Audience Research* (pp. 53–68). Chicago: Intellect.

Ryan, J. (2008). The Finnish country-of-origin effect: the quest to create a distinctive identity in a crowded and competitive international marketplace. *Journal of Brand Management*, 16(1/2), 13–20.

Scharrer, E. (2001). Men, muscles, and machismo: the relationship between television violence exposure and aggression and hostility in the presence of hyper-masculinity. *Media Psychology*, 3(2), 159–188.

Scharrer, E. (2007). Should we be concerned about media violence? In S. Mazzarella (ed.), *20 Questions about Youth and the Media* (pp. 117–134). New York: Peter Lang.

Scharrer, E., Weidman, L., & Bissell, K. (2003). Pointing the finger of blame: news media coverage of popular-culture culpability. *Journalism & Communication Monographs*, 5(2), 49–98.

Schatzman, L., & Strauss, A. (1973). *Field Research: Strategies for a Natural Sociology*. New York: Prentice-Hall.

Schemer, C., Matthes, J., Wirth, W., & Textor, S. (2008). Does 'passing the Courvoisier' always pay off? Positive and negative evaluative conditioning effects of brand placements in music videos. *Psychology & Marketing*, 25(10), 923–943.

Schmidt, T. (2007). Reaching out early for the youth vote. Retrieved 15 November 2011 from www.time.com/time/politics/article/0,8599,1639707,00.html.

Schultz, D. (2006). Challenges to study on alcohol advertising effects on youth drinking. *Archives of Pediatric and Adolescent Medicine*, 160, 857.

Selvanathan, E. (1989). Advertising and alcohol demand in the UK: further results. *International Journal of Advertising*, 8(2), 181–188.

Serazio, M. (2010). Shooting for fame: spectacular youth, Web 2.0 dystopia, and the celebrity anarchy of generation mash-up. *Communication, Culture & Critique*, 3(3), 416–434.

Shabazz, R. (2008). Obamania: media tactics drawing youth to the voting booth. *Youth Media Reporter*, 2(1–6), 237–241.

Shade, L. (2007). Feminizing the mobile: gender scripting of mobiles in North America. *Continuum: Journal of Media & Cultural Studies*, 21(2), 179–189.

Shade, L., Porter, N. & Sanchez, W. (2005). 'You can see anything on the internet, you can do anything on the internet!': young Canadians talk about the Internet. *Canadian Journal of Communication*, 30, 503–526.

Shanahan, J., & Morgan, M. (1999). *Television and Its Viewers: Cultivation Theory and Research*. Cambridge: Cambridge University Press.

Shanahan, J., Morgan, M., & Signorelli, N. (eds) (2012). *Living with Television Now: Advances in Cultivation Theory and Research*. New York: Peter Lang.

Shaughnessy, H. (2012). Stop Kony/Kony 2012 closes on 50 million YouTube views: meanwhile the Guardian investigates. Retrieved 20 July 2012 from www.forbes.com/sites/haydnshaughnessy/2012/03/09/stop-kony-kony-2012-closes-on-50-million-youtube-views-meanwhile-the-guardian-investigates/.

Sköld, D., & Rehn, A. (2007). Makin' it, by keeping it real: street talk, rap music, and the forgotten entrepreneurship from 'the 'Hood'. *Group & Organization Management*, 32(1), 50–78.

Sky News (2003). Beckham move hits Real where it hurts. Retrieved 19 December 2011 from http://news.sky.com/home/business/article/1311624.

Smith, S., & Granados, A. (2009). Content patterns and effects surrounding sex – role stereotyping in television and film. In J. Bryant & M. B. Oliver (eds), *Media Effects: Advances in Theory and Research* (3rd edn, pp. 342–361). New York: Routledge.

Snyder, L., Milici, F., Slater, M., Sun, H., & Strizhakova, Y. (2006). Effects of alcohol advertising exposure on youth drinking. *Archives of Pediatric and Adolescent Medicine*, 160, 18–24.

Sparks, G., Sparks, C., & Sparks, E. (2009). Media violence. In J. Bryant & M. B. Oliver (eds), *Media Effects: Advances in Theory and Research* (3rd edn, pp. 269–286). New York: Routledge.

Sparrow, A. (2005). Quality of life important to the young, says Cameron. Retrieved 8 December 2010 from www.telegraph.co.uk/news/uknews/1497429/Quality-of-life-important-to-the-young-says-Cameron.html.

Squires, C., & Schriner, M. (2009). J-schools, high schools, and youth media: bringing journalism back into the classroom. *Youth Media Reporter*, 3, 153–155.

Stack, G. (2010). Celebrating 10 years of 'color revolutions'. Retrieved 8 April 2011 from http://resistancestudies.org/?p=821.

Stanyer, J. (2012). *Intimate Politics: The Rise of Celebrity Politicians and the Decline of Privacy*. Cambridge: Polity Press.

Stein, H. (1979). American muckrakers and muckraking: the 50-year scholarship. *Journalism Quarterly*, 56(1), 9–17.

Sumiala, J., & Tikka, M. (2010). Web first to death: the media logic of the school shootings in the era of uncertainty. *Nordicom Review*, 31(2), 17–29.

Sundar, S. (2009). Media effects 2.0: social and psychological effects of communication technologies. In R. Nabi & M. B. Oliver (eds), *The SAGE Handbook of Media Processes and Effects* (pp. 545–560). Thousand Oaks, CA: Sage.

Tewksbury, D., & Scheufele, D. (2009). News framing theory and research. In J. Bryant & M. B. Oliver (eds), *Media Effects: Advances in Theory and Research* (3rd edn, pp. 17–33). New York: Routledge.

Thompson, E. P. (1961). The long revolution, Part 1. *New Left Review*, 1(9), 24–33.

Thompson, E. P. (1963). *The Making of the English Working Class*. London: Gollancz.

Thompson, J. (2009). Using social media to reach young readers. *Nieman Reports*, Spring, 27–29.

Thornton, B. (1995). Muckraking journalists and their readers: perceptions of professionalism. *Journalism History*, 21(1), 29.

Thornton, L. (2008). New media and the man. *American Journalism Review*, 30(6), 2.

Thussu, D. (2006). *International Communication: Continuity and Change* (2nd edn). London: Hodder Arnold.

Tolson, A. (2001). 'Being yourself': the pursuit of authentic celebrity. *Discourse Studies*, 3, 443–458.

Turner, G. (2004). *Understanding Celebrity*. London: Sage.

Turner, G. (2010). Approaching celebrity studies. *Celebrity Studies*, 1(1), 11–20.

Turner, G. (2012). *What's Become of Cultural Studies?* London: Sage.

Turner, G., Bonner, F., & Marshall, D. (2000). *Fame Games: The Production of Celebrity in Australia*. Cambridge: Cambridge University Press.

Tyree, T. M. (2009). Lovin' momma and hatin' on baby mama: a comparison of misogynistic and stereotypical representations in songs about rappers' mothers and baby mamas. *Women & Language*, 32(2), 50–58.

UNESCO (1982). *The Grünwald Declaration on Media Education*. Paris: UNESCO Educational Sector.

United Nations (1948). *Universal Declaration of Human Rights*. Available at www.un.org/events/humanrights/2007/hrphotos/declaration%20_eng.pdf.

United Nations Radio (2012). Secretary-General Ban Ki-moon 'hangs out' with Google+. Retrieved 1 July 2012 from www.unmultimedia.org/radio/english/2012/04/secretary-general-ban-ki-moon-hangs-out-with-google/.

Uy-Tioco, C. (2007). Overseas Filipino workers and text messaging: reinventing transnational mothering. *Continuum: Journal of Media & Cultural Studies*, 21(2), 253–265.

van Dijck, J. (2009). Users like you? Theorizing agency in user-generated content. *Media, Culture & Society*, 31(1), 41–58.

Varsity Leisure Group (2008). Carnage UK. Retrieved 10 May 2011 from http://image.guardian.co.uk/sys-files/Education/documents/2008/09/16/carnageresponse.pdf.

von Drehle, D. (2008). Obama's youth vote triumph. Retrieved 18 November 2011 from www.time.com/time/politics/article/0,8599,1700525,00.html.

Wang, L. (2004). http://wangleehom.com/news/archive/2004/12/cecce.htm.

Washington Times (2009). Iran's Twitter revolution. Retrieved 5 May 2010 from www.washingtontimes.com/news/2009/jun/16/irans-twitter-revolution/.

Weber, I. (2003). Successful strategies for selling television programmes to China. *Gazette*, 65(3), 273–290.

Weber, I. (2008). Youth and online morality: negotiating social differentiation and civic engagement in China. In U. Rodrigues & B. Smaill (eds), *Youth, Media and Culture in the Asia Pacific Region* (pp. 45–70). Newcastle: Cambridge Scholars Press.

Webley, K. (2010). Obama girl. Retrieved 21 November 2011 from www.time.com/time/specials/packages/article/0,28804,1974961_1974925_1973099,00.html.

Wells, P., & Bull, P. (2007). From politics to comedy: a comparative analysis of affiliative audience responses. *Journal of Language and Social Psychology*, 26(4), 321–342.

Werbner, P. (2007). Veiled interventions in pure space: honour, shame and embodied struggles among Muslims in Britain and France. *Theory, Culture & Society*, 24(2), 161–186.

Wilcox, G., & Gangadharbatla, H. (2006). What's changed? Does beer advertising affect consumption in the United States? *International Journal of Advertising*, 25(1), 35–50.

Williams, R. (1961). *The Long Revolution*. London: Chatto & Windus.

Williams, R. (1974). *Television*. London: Fontana.

World Health Organization (2006). WHO Expert Committee on Problems Related to Alcohol Consumption Geneva, 10–13 October 2006 , Available from www.who.int/mental_health/expert_committee_recommendations_english.pdf.

World Health Organization (2007). WHO Expert Committee On Problems Related to Alcohol Consumption. *WHO Technical Report Series*. Geneva: World Health Organization.

World Health Organization (2009). Global strategy to reduce harmful use of alcohol. Available from www.searo.who.int/LinkFiles/Meeting_reports_GSRH-Alcohol.pdf.

Wu, J. (2009). An exploratory study of American youth's political engagement during the 2008 presidential election. *American Communication Journal*, 11(1), 1–12.

Xenos, M., & Bennett, W. (2007). The disconnection in online politics: the youth political web sphere and US election sites, 2002–2004. *Information, Communication and Society*, 10(3), 443–464.

Yeo, E. (2004). The boy is the father of the man: moral panic over working-class youth, 1850 to the present. *Labour History Review*, 69(2), 185–199.

Yousman, B. (2003). Blackphilia and blackophobia: white youth, the consumption of rap music and white supremacy. *Communication Theory*, 13(4), 366–391.

YouTube (2011). President Obama on the situation in Egypt. Retrieved 13 October 2012 from www.youtube.com/watch?v=RR1n_7GN2vw.

Yu, H. (2011). Doing Chinese media studies: a reflection on the field's history and methodology. *Media International Australia*, 138, 66–79.

Zaller, J. (1994). Positive constructs of public opinion. *Critical Studies in Mass Communication*, 11(3), 276–286.

Zhong, Y. (2007). Competition is getting real in Chinese TV: a moment of confrontation between CCTV and HSTV. *Media International Australia*, 124, 68–81.

Zhong, Y. (2010). Relations between Chinese television and the capital market: three case studies. *Media, Culture & Society*, 32(4), 649–668.

Zhu, Y. (2008). Transnational circulation of Chinese language television dramas. *Global Media & Communication,* 4(1), 59–80.

INDEX